Praise for *Contextual Pricing*

Contextual Pricing delivers a knock-out punch to complacent and low-return pricing approaches. The authors' creative insights in to company abilities to pro-actively influence pricing dynamics will compel you to reassess the foundations of your current strategy. This book is full of intriguing, fresh insights that will expand your perspective on what is possible in maximizing revenue from your company's products and services.

> —*Mark Greatrex, Chief Marketing Officer, Cox Communications.*
> *Former SVP leading Global Still Beverages, The Coca-Cola Company.*

This book presents a leading-edge approach to pricing in competitive markets. The premise of the book is simple: To effectively price, managers must understand mar-ket context—the frame of reference for buyers. Context is far more important than the usual measures of price variation. Using case studies and other evidence, the authors show how to create pricing strategies and structures which lead to superior revenue results. I strongly recommend this readable and useful book to any busi-ness leader who suspects their company is falling short of achievable revenues.

> —*Dave Calhoun, Chairman and CEO of the Nielsen Company.*
> *Former Vice Chairman of the General Electric Company.*

Contextual Pricing is a ground-breaking work. It develops the dry theories of consumer behavior and pricing policy into a highly interesting look at pricing. The book is fresh, blends in humor and real-life observation, and is a must-read to anyone concerned about monetization strategies.

> —*Professor Raul L. Katz, Columbia Business School, Columbia University;*
> *Director of Business Strategy Research, Columbia Institute for Tele-Information*

In clear and practical language, *Contextual Pricing* reveals the "black box" of the buyer's decision process and has resulted in tremendous win-wins for buyers and sellers in the entertainment industry. The prescriptions in this book have driven hundred-million-dollar revenue uplifts in my industry. The prescriptions outlined in *Contextual Pricing* provide the framework and strategies critical to both routine and on-off pricing negotiations, which have become increasingly important as old business models evolve and new ones emerge.

> —*Lynne Costantini, Executive Vice President,*
> *Scripps Networks Interactive (The Food Network, HGTV, and DIY).*

This book makes clear that you don't have to have expensive systems or masses of data. You just need a firm priority on getting better at pricing using the guidelines provided in the book.

—Catherine Wolfe, CEO, Walters Kluwer UK (CCH, Croner)

The harsh reality today is that if you do not really understand customer's decision-processes then your yields will suffer. Particularly when the internet drives both pricing transparency and commoditization of so many products, the only means for addressing revenue pressures is to address market *contexts* such as differences in customer knowledge, competition, costs and offer terms. *Contextual Pricing* arms management with those insights. Unpleasant surprises result when companies do not really understand the context in which customers will view their offers.

—Hans Gieskes, President and CEO,
Cision A.B. Group, former Chairman of Monster.com

Although ostensibly focused on the narrow topic of price, *Contextual Pricing* is also a comprehensive book about business strategy and business principles in general. While many of *Contextual Pricing*'s examples come from the B2B services area, the message and lessons translate perfectly into the steel and project business. Pricing is the single most important profit driver, but the book's appeal benefits from humor and the author's love and familiarity with The Beatles—which means this business book really *rocks!*

—Hans J. Sack, President and CEO, Berg EuroPipe Holding Company,
and former President of Latrobe Specialty Steel.

To capture value in competitive consumer goods markets such as skin care and personal care means understanding the timing and context of sales on a systematic basis. This book outlines the new realities with compelling examples, broad principles and occasional humor. This book is revolutionary. The book identifies a roadmap to achieve replicable gains from 4% to as high as 30%.

—Robert Urbain, Former CEO,
Boots Healthcare Americas (Clearasil, Boots Hand Cream, etc.)

Contextual Pricing

The Death of List Price and the New Reality

Rob Docters

John Hanson

Cecilia Nguyen

Michael Barzelay

New York   Chicago   San Francisco   Lisbon   London   Madrid   Mexico City
Milan   New Delhi   San Juan   Seoul   Singapore   Sydney   Toronto

1 2 3 4 5 6 7 8 9 0   DOC/DOC   1 6 5 4 3 2 1

ISBN: 978-0-07-177246-4
MHID: 0-07-177246-4

e-ISBN: 978-0-07-171841-9
e-MHID: 0-07-171841-7

This publication is designed to provide accurate and authoritative information in regard to the subject matter covered. It is sold with the understanding that neither the author nor the publisher is engaged in rendering legal, accounting, or other professional service. If legal advice or other expert assistance is required, the services of a competent professional person should be sought.

—*From a Declaration of Principles Jointly Adopted*
by a Committee of the American Bar Association
and a Committee of Publishers and Associations

McGraw-Hill books are available at special quantity discounts to use as premiums and sales promotions, or for use in corporate training programs. To contact a representative, please e-mail us at bulksales@mcgraw-hill.com.

This book is printed on acid-free paper.

Contents

Part 3 Pricing Programs and the Marketing Mix

Part 4 Tools for Management

Acknowledgments

When four authors from very diverse backgrounds join to write a book, they pull from many sources and enjoy the support of many thought leaders.

Rob would like to acknowledge the contributions of his partners at Abbey Road: Dan Aks brought his COO experience as a print and media executive; Bert Schefers brought his CMO experience in consumer products; Christine Durman brought a CEO perspective and insights such as product "depth versus breadth"; Martijn Gieskes brought his skills in meticulous examination of demand curves and market evolution; meta-paleontologist Susan Bednarczyk brought her razor-sharp insights on company agendas, and Tracy Korman brought his CEO strategy skills from leading an online medical services company. Rob would also like to thank Julio Zamora of Morgan Stanley for his financial industry insights, Lisa Tilstone for her insights into fashion marketing, Raul Katz and Marty Hyman for their framework on introductory pricing. Finally, many thanks to Nancy Lothrop, Bob Docters, Ann Docters, Mr. Muffin, Steven Lipton, Patrick Thiede, Linda Sullivan, Phebe Prescott, Ray Wolfe, and Randy Burgess for thoughtful suggestions and many chapter reviews.

John and Cecilia would like to thank Tom Jacobson, who brought both wisdom and valuable insights from the broadest client experience.

Also, they would like to acknowledge Tiago Salvador and Justin Kim for their contributions in shaping the overall framework for contextual pricing.

Michael would like to acknowledge the contributions of his colleagues at the London School of Economics and elsewhere.

Finally, we would like to thank Niki Papadopoulos, our editor at McGraw-Hill, for bringing both the rigor and a strong point of view which made this book an important tool for anyone concerned with pricing and revenues.

Introduction to Contextual Pricing

Everything should be made as simple as possible, but
not any simpler.

—ALBERT EINSTEIN (C. 1933)

We would all like to cultivate better pricing at our companies: pricing models that fit the market, an optimum price tag, strongly supportive systems, and foundational price strategy. We would like pricing coherent with brand, product, and channel, which inspires confidence—and is as simple as possible.

Many smart people have proposed simplifying principles to help explain pricing results. Value, costs, messaging, and customer frames of reference have all afforded insight. Each construct offers a crisp and simple explanation—but appears to fail in some market situations. Those failures are painful when encountered, and they discourage management from giving pricing the attention it deserves—that a company deserves.

This book offers a unifying perspective on pricing. By taking into account buyer psychology, market competition, and organizational politics, it provides a holistic outlook on an important topic. Our approach is *relatively* simple: we describe how the customer decision process and market conditions provide the relevant context for better pricing. Thus the unified perspective is known as "contextual pricing."

Success comes from understanding context. This idea has been leveraged with great results by some leading companies. The Coca-Cola Company, for instance, includes *temperature* at the point of sale in its pricing context. An ice cold cola commands a better price in the middle of summer on a hot beach than during a snowstorm in the Arctic! Being able to adjust prices to the immediate context of the buying occasion is how Coke has moved to monetize contextual insights.

Another example: Plastic packaging manufacturer Paktiv has found that the *time frame* of a customer's needs drives the price paid. Paktiv and other industrial commodity plastics have found they can get sharply higher prices on "rush" orders of plastic containers for supermarkets and other customers. Including the time frame is how Paktiv prospers in a cutthroat commodity business.

The contextual perspective on pricing can be applied directly to pricing initiatives at your company. With a few simple pricing tools, it's possible to achieve a 1 to 7 percent realized price gain, and, with a better set of pricing processes and systems architecture, a 10 to 12 percent improvement should be possible. With better price strategy and structure, *replicable* gains of 30 percent or greater have been achieved in a wide range of industries: software, consumer goods, entertainment, education, transportation, retail, insurance, and others.

> Contextual pricing is the concept that a
> handful of factors, mostly relating to the
> buyer's frame of reference (comparison points),
> will explain most pricing, and will provide
> management with the most powerful levers
> for improving price structure and results.

The focus on context is growing. Leading firms such as Coca-Cola, Amazon, GE, IBM, Google, Hertz, Proctor & Gamble, Standard & Poor's, and AT&T have begun to use context to shape their offers. Some have employed this perspective to refocus attention on the local point of sale rather than national price indices. Many are placing new emphasis on understanding competitive offers. Some have shifted management attention from a single-minded focus on product value to the customer view—asking, "What does the customer *know* about our product and its alternatives?"

Notice how when Amazon alerts you that "people who have bought this book also have bought . . ." it changed your context for buying the book? Notice how when airlines made round-trip tickets much cheaper than one-way tickets, it changed your ideas on vacations by air? What about when cable companies added in telephony services into their service bundles—did they change how you thought about the value being offered? This is the application of contextual pricing.

These approaches to shaping the buying process are an antidote to price pressure. The contextual focus matches prices to major purchase scenarios so that you avoid price level battles you cannot win and book higher margins where the opportunity arises. Examples of purchase scenarios include sales to loyal long-tenured customers, skeptical potential new customers, large bids, rush orders, new products launches, and so forth.

Timing matters too, obviously. For instance, during a major software and services buy, a lot of attention is paid to price level, but, after that, add-ons and modifications often face far less price scrutiny. The same feature sold later (after use of the initial purchase) might command far better margins.

Contextual pricing is the antidote to price pressure.

One other unusual aspect to this book you'll notice is the argument that pricing can be intuitive and will mesh with other components of the marketing mix. Pricing and branding ought to go hand in hand; product development could incorporate insights learned from price study; and pricing must reflect the realities of channel. Most importantly: pricing is marginalized and powerless if it does not actively seek contextual insights directly from customers. And we do mean *directly*: talk to customers and consumers, don't expect context to spring from boilerplate surveys.

For a leading B2B information provider, the single most important context turned out to be the buyer decision process. When the purchase decision was made by committee (drawn from various departments) then the price was 25 percent lower than when the decision was made by a single manager. This context was known to the sales force and actually documented in its CRM, so all that was needed was to develop a price structure which would capitalize on this difference. This, and other aspects of contextual pricing, drove a 30 percent+ increase in realized revenues.

In other aspects of life, context defines how things are evaluated. Music is evaluated according to the social and personal context of the time. Food is valued according to contemporary tastes and dietary concerns. Even what is considered beautiful and desirable in marriage partners varies with social context, according to research in that area.

Management teams who adopt a contextual perspective find it intuitive, and their companies are generally rewarded with materially better pricing. While pricing books do not have a reputation as being enjoyable reads, we hope that this one is more interesting than most,[1] and much more rewarding.

Note

1. A low standard, we admit. But perhaps a major contextual element for your book purchase decision.

PART 1

The Journey from Product to Context

Chapter 1

Context and the Death of List Price

Without a story, I cannot give you a price.
The price of used furniture is a point of view.
—FROM *THE PRICE*, ARTHUR MILLER, 1968

Who killed list price? One of the prime suspects is called "competition." Not a lone killer, however; it was a conspiracy. List price died because one price will never fit different customer comparison points, needs, budgets, timing, and applications. This observation builds upon Economics 101: that the value of one commodity at one time and location is not the same as the same commodity in another time and location.[1] Managers involved in price must insist that it reflect the major factors shaping and framing customer choice. Those factors are best labeled "context."

Context

The link of price to context meshes not only with economics but also with common sense and market experience. Here are three market case studies where attention to the contextual "story" boosted price well in excess of any other lever available to management:

- The Coca-Cola Company, the marketing powerhouse, found that its best realized retail price for a can of soda was not a result of product improvement, nor advertising, nor value strategy. In a recent experiment, Coke was sold at Walmart in two shopping aisles: the traditional beverage aisle for one and a sportswear aisle for the other. Same product, same store, same everything, but in one case next to other beverages and in the other case next to sporty clothing. Much higher prices next to clothing, where Coke was the only soda on display.[2] *This was a less competitive context.*
- Internet (VoIP) telephone providers Vonage and AT&T CallVantage found that they can obtain twice the rates for phone plans from those who also buy high-speed access, compared with those who obtain access for free (e.g., at medical, academic, or business campuses). *A bundle context.*
- Equity analysts Morningstar, Standard & Poor's, and others selling evaluations of company securities to stockbrokers and financial institutions found that they can command a multiple of normal prices when inputs are directly tied to a computerized portfolio management program. The information provided is identical. This price obtained stems from being in one case associated with, say, a $10,000 stock trade, while in the other it is associated with a multimillion-dollar portfolio of many stocks. *A richer context.*

What drove these increases in price? Did the soda, the phone service, and the stock information increase in intrinsic *value* and so get a better *price*?

No: neither the cola, nor the phone service, nor the stock reports changed in any way at all. The common sense observation, and the point of this book, is that the other things *associated with each offer*—the market environment—changed, not the product. Product and value did not change, only the *context*.

For companies focused on profitability, the key justification for focus on context is that almost always the leverageable differences in price among different buying contexts is *far greater* than differences between products and competitors. As an illustration: the price difference among different major brands of gasoline is *nil* and the differences between grades of gasoline run from 5 to 15 cents per gallon, but differences in gasoline prices among geographies, days of the week, and proximity to busy streets run from 50 cents to more than \$1 per gallon.[3] The gasoline price differences by location, for instance, are driven by factors such as the income of surrounding areas, taxes, and proximity to refineries. Now, which *should* get more management attention—the pennies or the dollars? The product or the context?

> Context reveals greater pricing opportunity
> than a narrow focus on product.

The Customer's Mind

The context employed in your customer's mind is important because it allows you to understand how buyers evaluate price as part of the purchase process. Context—competition, decision process, timing, availability, etc.—will explain outcomes. Context allows sellers to focus on the right market research strategies and then to design optimum price structure and set optimum price points.

While it may seem strange to focus more on buying occasion and the customer mind-set than on your particular product, context is what makes for reliable pricing. Product value is only one driver of price. For the best pricing, look to context as much as to your product offer. When you consider the nature of "value" versus "context" in Figure 1-1 below, you may conclude that your pricing decisions today are overly focused on product value, while neglecting the price impacts of context.

The message here is that clinging to the idea that your company's product has an essential value *is wrong.* Value is not a concept compatible to diverse markets and a changing world. This is the new reality.

The idea that management should look at the broader context is similar to the strategy developed by the top-ranked soccer teams. The coach of a perennially top-ranked German team emphasizes that winning comes from "moving well *without* the ball."[4] This idea is similar both in pricing and the world's most popular sport. You will lose if you focus only on the product (the ball).

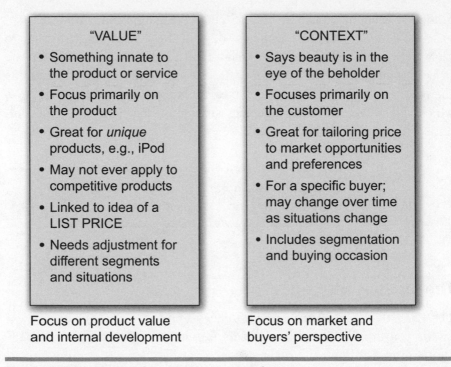

Figure 1-1 Product value versus context focus.

True, most of your competitors are focused on the product, but customers operate in a broader theater. Their purchase is guided by budgets, indirect alternatives, convenience, knowledge, different motivations, and all the variety of life. The seller that incorporates an understanding of context will do better than those who focus narrowly on the product. In similar fashion, the ball gets plenty of attention in soccer, but the team that is controlling the *overall field of play* will dominate their opponent.

As described in the next chapter, this concept requires your management team to become aware of, and become comfortable basing decisions on, some subtleties of the market. Doing so will mean learning to rely on limited test market data, smart customer surveys, or competitive intelligence. This is why GE Patient Care's first action in a recent price initiative was to engage a competitive intelligence vendor to better understand the competitive context for its products. Such a move would not be considered radical for, say, branding or product development, but it is sadly unusual for pricing.[5]

> Context is important because it represents the way
> in which buyers evaluate price. Knowing context—
> competition, decision process, timing, availability,
> etc.—explains why buying decisions are made.
> Knowing context allows sellers to design optimum
> price structure and set optimum price points.

Life without List Price Is Easier

Things we did not think we could live without but now don't miss: paper money, compact discs, fax machines, landline phones, file cabinets, in-house data storage, the U.S. Postal Service, and so on. For business managers, one such missing nonessential, we believe, is the idea of list price.

Consider the contortions involved with keeping a list price. First of all, everyone knows that, generally, list price is a lie. Jokes abound: only fools pay list price. But in pretending that there is a list price, we fail to collect *premium prices above list price* in situations where there is that opportunity,[6] Then we frighten off customers for whom the list price is too high, and we create an endless (and destructive) battle between keepers of list price and those who face market realities (product managers and sales representatives).

Why do businesses engage in meaningless rituals like list price? Perhaps list price is a leftover from when their companies had unique products that allowed easy margins and an enforceable single price target?[7] More important, will pretending to have a meaningful list price keep the good times going? Probably not. In many cases list price is an artifact whose life is prolonged by its broad use in corporations that have not questioned the need for it. Belief dies hard.[8]

Why did we ever come up with the abstraction of list price? Well, in a simpler, less competitive world of tangible stand-alone products, a single list price was the useful price. For instance, when the Model T Ford was the leading car choice, there was only one price, and everyone paid it. More recently, an iPod or an iPhone were unique products, and everyone paid a standard price. However, monopolies tend to have shorter and shorter lifespans these days. The Model T dominated cars for 18 years, Apple saw its market share begin to slip within two years, and Amazon saw its e-reader exclusivity disappear even faster—and with it the power to impose conditions on the market such as one-price-fits-all. Still, if you happen to have a monopoly, you can probably get away with a viable list price for a while.

For companies with competition, the replacement for list price is context-led pricing, which is standard practice in a few industries—not surprisingly, in those industries where pricing is acutely important. These markets have developed contextual pricing tools that set price levels more effectively than a list price. For instance, industries using contextual bases for pricing include:

- Commercial lenders, which vary from benchmark rates (e.g., LIBOR) based on the deal context
- Life and P&C insurers, which use loss history and actuarially based pricing
- Airlines and hotels, which employ demand management (e.g., predictive programs on likely seat utilization)
- Retailers, which use inventory-turnover adjusted pricing

In most of those examples, there is no list price: the prices can change from near zero to infinity.

Yet these successful industries are a minority. In some cases they moved to contextual pricing because there was a convenient posting of context (the public exchanges) or because participants had no choice—it was contextual pricing or exit the business. In contrast, most company pricing is static, anchored on list price, a vestigial marker of value that management is reluctant to modify, no matter the changes in competition, customer behavior, customer wealth, nuances in point of sale, geography, etc.

Sound impossible or impractical to eliminate list price? Well, for much of the service economy, *list price is already gone*. There are very few examples of large successful companies optimizing list price for more than a few of their offers, such as major new products and flagship products. Most product prices were set years ago and then ignored except for an annual (and usually very mechanical) change. Often, broad factors based on cost of living and input cost changes are all the attention list prices ever get. Sometimes list prices become complete abstractions when groups of offers are consolidated into bundles where the list price of an individual product is not known. For instance, a large software security developer stopped determining individual component list prices because almost all transactions were done in bundles, such as entire security suites.

But the focus on context is growing. Proctor & Gamble's chairman, a decorated war veteran, is using price to win share across the world, and he has said, "It does not matter how many men you have in the battlefield . . . if at the point of attack you have more forces, you have the potential to win." Contextual pricing in a nutshell: get the price right for the specific buyer or segment, and it does not matter what some ephemeral global list price might be. To win, P&G is using contextual pricing tactics pertinent to the point of attack, such as increasingly linking new products with the old via coupons and promotions to "guide" sales of new products. Instead of a cold introduction, it is using affinity for existing products to position the new ones. This is a form of "guided sale," and is a very important context.[9]

The Contextual Pricing Program

How can companies operate without a list price? The direct answer is that companies should develop a suite of contextual price bases (or a pricing tool that does the same thing) and exploit those contextual situations. That does not mean having *more* price points. Companies do better when they have a smaller set of *relevant and disciplined* contextual price bases. Better prices, not more prices.

To put that in the context of your company, which half of the following halves of Figure 1-2 looks more familiar, Option 1 or Option 2?

Do Option 1's "1,000+ ad hoc prices" seem like an exaggeration? For most large companies, that number may be an understatement. For online information provider LexisNexis, there were 2,300 core information files sold in five price bands, three media, fifty bundles, and a dozen promotional plans. Almost a half million "list prices," but because the sales force had discounted at will, very few of the list prices represented an actual customer at this billion-dollar company. For network equipment manufacturer Nortel Siemens Networks, a study showed that the full time equivalent (FTE) of people engaged in pricing was 400 highly

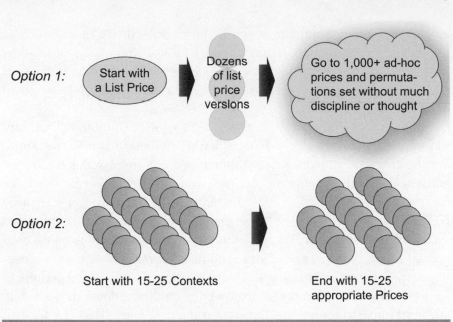

Figure 1-2 Pricing processes compared.

paid professionals. How many actual price points did the 400 FTEs develop? No one knew how many, but a lot!

By beginning with market contexts and skipping the single list price part, not only do revenues improve, life gets easier. Discipline is easier to maintain.

Consider the traditional "start with one list price" approach. No sooner is there a list price than there are scores of subsidiary prices based on the absolute necessity to vary by some high-level context (e.g., channel or size of customer). Then there appear a thousand exceptions and variations to each of the subsidiary prices. This outcome is bad because a thousand variations to list price is burdensome—especially when they are the wrong prices, developed by sales reps and managers who are under fire and lack the training, resources, or time to develop the price for maximum long-term corporate profit.[10]

A solid best practice is to understand the required 20 to 25 market contexts and then turn those contexts into prices that you can stand by. Instead of one useless list price and a thousand ad hoc customer prices, experience has shown that it is simpler to have a score of market-derived prices that management can enforce and sales can believe in.

Context Requires Both a Price Level and a Distinct Structure

Oddly enough, initially when the idea of 20 to 25 baseline prices is proposed, a common objection is that this is too many and too complex, and customers will rebel if they find out that there are different prices in the market. Yet, strangely, 20 or so prices would be a huge *reduction* in number from the myriad of prices usually in play. We suspect that implicit in this fear is the idea that a multiplication of baseline prices (which you can call list prices, if you like) will result in 20 times the number of actual realized end prices.

Not so, if done right. We find that often when managers worry about cannibalization and down-tiering of prices, it is because they neglect to adapt price structure in conjunction with price levels. For instance, at one plastic container manufacturer, smaller consumers of products grew jealous of bulk discounts when phrased as "per-box discounts." When discounts were phrased as "truckload volumes," much of the complaint went away—an example of structure reducing price pressure.

For market success, pricing depends not just on adjusting price level but also on getting the price structure right.[11] Most products should start off life with several price structures aimed at different segments or buying contexts. For instance, typically smaller business customers require smaller quantities of product and often need different quantities for each contract period. For them, a "pay by the drink" (volume-based) purchase might be fitting. For large customers, taking large volumes every contract period, an "all-you-can-eat" fixed price contract might be fitting. In Chapter 6 we discuss price structures, price models, and what fits where in greater detail.

From a seller's point of view, another benefit to drive structural innovation is that you cannot compare prices. An example from retailing: food retailer Trader Joe's offers bananas at 19 cents each, while some supermarkets offer bananas at 69 cents per pound. Which is cheaper? Will anyone ever figure that out?[12] That will depend on context, such as how important these fruits are to your budget, volume of buying, convenience of adding them to a grocery cart, and how good you are at math conversions.

The idea of having more than one structure from the start is just as important as having different price levels from the start. This is because buyers are often more frame-sensitive than price-level-sensitive. Perhaps surprisingly, frequently buyers ignore actual prices and make purchasing decisions based on contextual cues. For instance, experiments in college bookstores and online have shown that used books will sell for more than new ones located next to them. Sometimes used cars lease for more than new cars. Remarkably, even in highly efficient commodity markets, the same commodity will sell for different prices at peak trading times. These examples all show the power of context over product value.[13]

Each price context may deserve its own structure because it is price structure that often helps leverage context and so realize value capture (price level). Therefore, the best practice is that contextual pricing should be part of the "trinity" of pricing. The trinity is derived from the fact that context drives structure, which drives level, which drives context, and so on *ad infinitum*. Focusing merely on product value misses much of the picture—and important drivers of price outcomes.

Think in threes: context, structure, and level.

Developing price structure (as well as contextual pricing baselines) is generally best done upstream in the product management process. Sales and junior management should not be creating new price structures—they don't have the time, systems support, or expertise. Systems make contextual pricing structures easier. Customer relationship management systems can allow multiple parties to reference the key contextual pricing. They can also help instill a new discipline—no longer tolerating needless, random, or destructive price variation.

Better price structure wins share because it gives customers pricing they want. Structure is one of the most important elements of context—if you don't know the structure "story," you cannot know the sale price. Some of the biggest share shifts have happened because a competitor innovated on price. Examples include private-equity-owned Cengage Learning, which is giving students an option to rent their books rather than buy them—a move that scares competitors and "could well become a standard offering," according to major booksellers. Similarly, bond-trading firm Cantor Fitzgerald developed an innovative technology approach for pricing of municipal bonds; as a result, even though a small player, it holds patents that make it a market power in certain trading applications.

> After you understand context, the
> first step is to address the context you
> control—such as price structure.

Summary

Ironically, setting a single list price invites complexity. List price means setting an untenable price and then fighting to defend it, fighting customers, and always fighting sales reps (who are usually faced directly with the market reality). Why not accept the market judgment? It is expensive to fight market forces.

The idea that a good or service has an innate, relatively constant, value carries a certain appeal—companies go to a lot of trouble to infuse value into their offers. But are there any significant market examples where value is a constant? The idea of "value" is old, having been introduced by Adam Smith and carried forward by many advocates. Yet, the fact that "value" is elusive and infinitely changeable, however, has troubled economists right from the start. Depending on the perceived frame of reference, or context, all goods are valuable or worthless.

And that is why context is the better basis for pricing. The belief in value suggests that with just a dash of pricing effort, you can capture the value that is always present. It may be comforting to be told that higher revenues through price are directly and certainly the result of product improvement and other factors under your control, but that is not true.[14] Value does not work well in competitive markets. Better results stem from leveraging the market contexts that you inherit.

> The best practice is for management to accept
> that pricing must be set in accordance with key
> contextual factors—which will include some
> that are not within your control. Unfortunately,
> many managers find it less work to ignore factors
> outside their control instead of adapting to them.

After reading this chapter, you may decide your company may want to rebalance its pricing effort. Among pricing levers such as product, channel, promotion, and context, it is context which probably deserves a lot more attention.

Notes

1. This is a long-lived premise, dating back at least to Henry George (*The Science of Political Economy*, Doubleday & McLure, 1898) and more recently Louis Philips (*The Economics of Price Discrimination*, Cambridge, 1983, p. 6).
2. What makes this experiment meaningful is that the one thing the world knows is that one bottle of Coca-Cola will be identical to the next, so the differentiator in this case *must* have been buying context. *Brandweek*, June 17, 2008.
3. See "The Gasoline Game," *The Wall Street Journal*, June 5, 2007, p. D1. Similar contextual differences drive price differences for most competitive goods studied.
4. "A Fun, Creative Germany—Really," M. Kaminski, *The Wall Street Journal*, July 7, 2010, p. D5. A similar playing strategy also applies to basketball and other team sports.
5. Yes, sometimes questions on pricing get tacked onto those surveys. But unfortunately, often the questions are wrong or invite gaming by respondents. See Chapter 15 for more on pricing and market research.
6. Interestingly, we find that in noncommodity industries, about 2 to 4 percent of customers have bought something at above list price. Too rare for optimal pricing, we would argue. Mostly, list price acts like a cap, either because selling above it would enrage customers, or because ERP (enterprise resource planning) systems cannot accommodate such nonstandard pricing.
7. Some managers cling to the idea of list price with a surprising fervor. One possible reason is that scientists have found that humans are still very much influenced by things associated with past successes ("associative magic"). One example would be that Eric Clapton's old guitar sold for just under $1 million at auction; even exact replicas of that guitar fetch $20,000. Buyers report that that they can play better with guitars imbued with an association with Clapton ("some kind of musical mojo"). "Urge

to Own that Clapton Guitar is Contagious, Scientists Find," *The New York Times*, March 9, 2011.

8. And a desire for conformity inside large bureaucracies can make any broadly accepted practice pass without scrutiny, no matter how absurd. Comedian Mitch Hedberg once reported: "My artificial plants died because I did not pretend to water them."

9. Regarding the view of competition as being local, see "P&G Chief Wages Offensive Against Rivals, Risks Profits," *The Wall Street Journal*, August 19, 2010, p. 1 and p. A14. Also, "P&G Focuses Push on New Products" *The Wall Street Journal*, October 21, 2010. For more on the context of "guided sales," see Chapter 10 of this book.

10. Bob Crandall, the famous former CEO of American Airlines, once commented, "If a flight leaves with 500 passengers, and you tell me they are paying 300 different prices, then I say I am 200 prices short." Note, however, that those are not ad hoc prices: the price a passenger pays is the very deliberate outcome of hundreds of millions of dollars of systems and price development. Robert Cross, *Revenue Management: Hard-Core Tactics for Market Domination*. New York: Broadway Books, 1997.

11. What is structure? It comprises the terms of a transaction, other than the price tag (level). For instance, structure answers the question of who pays, what is the unit of charging, what is the relationship of price elements to each other, etc. See Chapter 6 for a fuller definition. See Chapter 17 for a new definition of pricing.

12. In addition to price-conscious shoppers, one group who will do the math is authors of books on pricing. The supermarket price comes to about 22 cents per banana. This means that if the bananas are of equal quality, the Trader Joe's price is a good deal. Why does Trader Joe do this? See Part 2.

13. Apparently the green "used" tag on books in college book stores trumps actual price tags, in side-by-side selling, at least for students. Also see: "Why Do Some Used Cars Cost More than New Ones?," *The Wall Street Journal*, January 21, 2011, p. B1; "Odd Crop Prices Defy Economics," *The New York Times*, March 28, 2008, p. C1. There are always "odd" prices, and the challenge is how to take advantage of them.

14. The concept has appeal, similar to the medieval idea of alchemy: with the right chemical process, base metals can be converted to gold. The idea of alchemy was pursued for several thousand years before repeated failure finally led to its being rejected during the Enlightenment. Today some say that believing in value pricing can transmute your current revenues into higher revenues. A great selling pitch! Today, incidentally, alchemists go by the name of "consultants."

Chapter 2

Why Value Matters Less with Competition

The single most important decision [you have] is pricing power. If you've got the power to raise prices without losing business to a competitor, you've got a very good business.

—WARREN BUFFETT, CEO OF BERKSHIRE HATHAWAY, INC., 2010

If you could read the thoughts of your competitors, you would frequently find the same concerns present in your management team. Just like you, your competitor is also tasked with revenue, share, and profitability goals—perhaps not the same figures, but often tending in the same direction. The interaction between your company and a competitor's is shaped by how you and your competitor differ, and how you are alike.

Typically there are more similarities than there are differences. The profit objectives are quite similar, the balance between share and profits are not radically different, the ethical standards pretty uniform, etc. The only exception is that if there is a new entrant, either with or without a new technology, they might have quite different profit objectives in the short run, or if there is a distressed player either in or near bankruptcy.

This similarity is, overall, a good thing for the players. It tends to lead to very "civilized" competition. It's unlike Harry Potter versus He-Who-Must-Not-Be-Named: neither has to die. That does not mean that over time there is not a winner who pulls ahead, only that the pricing rarely degrades into a price war.[1]

Understanding Your Competitors

While mutual incentives to avoid annihilation are fortunate for your company, the typical competitor standoff is not foolproof, especially with a combination of unfortunate circumstances. One example of this was a skirmish between two service providers. Because of budget, systems inadequacy, and management inclination, the lower market share service provider had no profitability measures for its "small customer" regional managers. Freed from profitability measures, one of the regional managers (in the Midwest) launched a share campaign involving lower prices. The larger market share service provider, which has very good reporting systems and a strong profit orientation, felt the resulting pain immediately. The larger provider also had a national management structure for its small customers, and so happened to strike back with lower prices on the U.S. West Coast. To the larger company's surprise, doing so did not send a signal to the smaller competitor: the attacks in the Midwest continued. Only after it learned that it had to retaliate inside the same competitor region, to get that attacking manager's attention, did retaliation end the potential price war.

> Any price actions must reflect competitor decision processes. Management must have a view on how competitors make their pricing decisions.

Competitors' costs structures, timing, reporting structures, and objectives must be understood and either accommodated or exploited. Another well-documented example of the consequences of misunderstanding competitor-decision processes took place in New York City, where the alternative data carrier Teleport Communications Group found financing based on its ability to undercut the incumbent telephone company's high rates for service within distances of five miles or less. After Teleport built its network, the incumbent telco lowered its prices for these distances but then raised prices for distances beyond five miles to compensate. This maneuver simply made Teleport revise its business case to include share capture in the next five-mile radius so as to capitalize on the new rates. Eventually, the incumbent reluctantly lowered its overall metropolitan business rates, but by then it was too late: simpleminded and inadequate reaction had allowed a competitor to gain a foothold in the market. The incumbent, now part of Verizon, had ignored the contexts of geography and decision process, and so preventative action had come too late.

Not that we are advocating massive reaction to competitors, just intelligent reaction. For instance, two major airlines with large Chicago hubs found themselves under price attack from a start-up carrier based in Phoenix, Arizona. One of the two major carriers responded by lowering all of its prices to Phoenix. The other major carrier responded by lowering prices to Phoenix only on flights leaving within 25 minutes of the start-up carrier's flights. The first defensive strategy cost that carrier a lot more money than the second, smarter pricing strategy. Timing is a key context for schedule-based industries, and so time must be central to pricing approaches.

Decision Contexts

Contextual pricing dictates that *only* where there is little or no competition can managers take the absolute value of a product and use it for pricing. This is because in competitive markets, only a fraction or even zero percent of the absolute value can be captured. The rationale for this is well known. Typically if a competitor can win business at any price over attributable costs, it is better off. As each company competes on improving the price/value ratio of its offer, each will be incented to lower its price—in some cases to approaching zero incremental margin over costs. Therefore, unless you have a monopoly for a product/market, a value approach to pricing probably won't work in most markets.

That logic is pretty depressing, but it's also limited. A more balanced view is that competition does put downward pressure on prices, but rarely do prices collapse. The reason that prices do not always race for the

bottom lies in context. So better to develop a contextual model that actually answers the questions needed in price management.

Context captures the relevant forces shaping price. These are:

- Relative value, how much more value does one side offer?
- Corporate objectives and management compensation.
- Cost positions: how much room to cut before implicating margins?

These factors are why, in a competitive situation of two or more competitors, the degree of value each will capture will always fall short of full
value capture—sometimes 100 percent short. But outcomes will generally also rise above the cost-based floor—frequently well above.

Consider a classic competitive situation: two companies with fairly
similar offers and shareholder expectations, but some differences in
value proposition, and costs. Each competitor's offer may provide a lot of
value to the buyer, but thanks to the competition, neither one will capture
all that value (absent price fixing). Why? The answer lies in looking at
a typical competitive situation between two companies, imaginatively
named Company A and Company B. As diagrammed in Figure 2-1, there
are some normal differences between these two companies.

In this case, Company A appears to offer greater value than Company
B. Perhaps it's a data processing device that runs 30 percent faster or
an advertising vehicle that reaches viewers whose household income is
higher on average than Company B's vehicles, or perhaps it's a flight
monitor with a larger display and lower power consumption. For whatever
reason, Company A provides greater value.

Typically, such a product should command a premium for its incremental value, and we have generally been able to prove the existence of
such a premium when a thorough competitive comparison is performed
and all elements of competitive offers are included. For instance, at one
software firm, its superior backup capability was said not to be valued
by the market. It turned out that most of the market did not, in fact,
value the incremental capabilities. The one segment that did value the
capability, however, was indeed paying a generous premium. Client
product management had failed to segment and had also not properly
communicated the competitive difference.[2] Differential value should
be recognized by the market because when the two competitors have

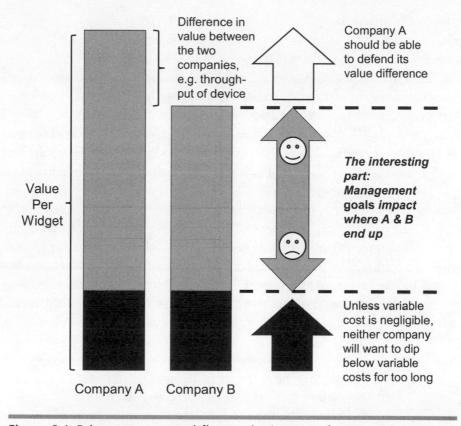

Difference in value between the two companies, e.g. through-put of device

Company A should be able to defend its value difference

The interesting part: Management goals impact where A & B end up

Value Per Widget

Unless variable cost is negligible, neither company will want to dip below variable costs for too long

Company A   Company B

Figure 2-1 Price pressures and floors: the impact of competition on value realization.

whittled away the similar value component, the less valuable competitor (Company B) has nothing to offer the buyer to neutralize the higher value offered by Company A.

In some cases management complains that its quality premium or differential product attribute is being ignored by the market. Assuming that the quality premium is meaningful to the market, there are ways to make sure that the market recognizes it. One way is to tier the product with and without the attribute in question. By pricing the "without" product similar to the competitor's "without" product, you force buyers to value the upgrade. Of course they will want the upgrade for free, but that is part of buyer negotiation. The offer gives your company better leverage and frequently turns the tables, since the burden of justifying the difference has effectively shifted from you to the buyer. Your sales argument can now take on the role of dispassionate expert advice.

Look to context and segmentation to explain why a differential in value does not appear to be valued. As an example, consider the telecom equipment market of a few years ago. During the 1990s the leading manufacturers of PBX (private branch exchange) equipment included Lucent, Nortel, and Siemens. These manufacturers produced reliable, scalable, and durable systems that handled calls within large buildings and companies. Scarcely noticed in the market were "inexpensive" machines, which bordered on the disposable, by Panasonic.

Yet for a period of three years, the Panasonic machines commanded the highest price per user line, representing the utter inversion of product value and price. This was because the "low value" PBX market was subject to the context of relatively lower supply and higher demand per vendor. Product specifications did not drive value because higher value equipment tiers were locked into destructive price battles. Panasonic was not.

> Management needs to clearly communicate value
> differences in price terms. One such method
> is offering the product at the competitor's
> price, minus the value-add component—this
> squarely places the choice with the customer.

Costs play an important role, although in an indirect way. Looking at the cost represented at the bottom of the bars in Figure 2-1, you'll find that there are very few examples where competitors have sold below variable costs. For high-margin industries, that would represent quite a discount: for some information services the prices would have to drop 90 percent or more before incremental (variable) costs are implicated. Similarly, both sides will resist pricing below incremental (or variable) costs of sale because typically neither Company A nor Company B has management that is incented to go cash-negative.

We often see sales below fully allocated costs, but that is less of a source of alarm both because it represents less of a drop and because allocations are usually not situation-specific anyhow. In addition, in extreme cases, there is a somewhat self-regulating aspect of pricing. The lower the price, the fewer buying decisions will be made on price. For instance, as the costs of promotional giveaways (e.g., branded pens and mugs) become small, buyers will simply order such goods from whichever supplier they have a relationship with rather than put the order out to bid. Hence, in addition to the financial pain of going below costs, there is often no market reason for competitors to get down below variable costs.

The middle sections of the chart columns are the most interesting areas for pricing. Either or both competitors could choose to push price down to variable cost, which is why product value can never be a reliable guide for pricing in competitive markets. The absolute value of a product can disappear in smoke. The question any pricing approach must answer is: how much of the value in the middle section of the chart columns can be captured through the adroit use of context?

While the middle part of the column could disappear totally, there are typically strong incentives for competitors not to engage in mutual self-destruction. These are:

- Management incentives include profitability incentives.[3]
- Managers facing powerful competitors are concerned about starting a price war.
- Even when seeking share growth, cash flow is typically a factor.

Together these, and many other factors, comprise the universe of "context" and help keep market price from collapse. Context is a bridge between the value-oriented managerial-cost literature, which typically aspires to capture all or most of the product value, and more academic economic literature, which looks to economic returns and costs. The economic literature is ready to assume that costs and minimum shareholder returns are the only floor for pricing. Not true.

While management-incentive factors have been all but ignored in the classic economic literature, they are absolutely determinative in some pricing situations. The management team making the pricing decisions no doubt has a profit objective, and will hesitate to set prices which imperil that objective. In most cases, management will even insure that there is some cushion between minimum prices to achieve the profit objective and its target prices—many management teams enjoy having that cushion!

Part of context is the disposition of equity holders, which needs to be considered alongside management (although the two groups may be aligned). The equity holders can be a force for price disruption (e.g., private equity, LBO, venture capitalists) who need to show extraordinary profit growth, or they can be forces for profit conservatism (e.g., at one point telephone stocks were considered "bond substitutes for widows and orphans").

Management incentives and equity holder objectives will directly shape market prices.

Cost in Commodity and Near-Commodity Markets

In most markets costs play a role, but they should not single-handedly determine prices. There are some industries in which costs play a very large role: commodity markets and cost-plus markets. In fact, even in these markets, costs do not constitute the entire driver. Special circumstances still clearly impact price. For instance, when one Ontario steel manufacturer experienced a "breakout"[4] that shut down production, it obtained replacement product from a nearby mill to honor its contracts, but at a premium.

There are many reasons to vary price from cost in any industry, and some of the most common occasions for price premia in commodities all link to changes in context. Typical changes are:

- *New product.* Even in the toughest industries, unique new products are an occasion to obtain higher margins. For instance, in the commodity plastic container industry, new hooking mechanisms for clamshells and resealable plastic bags both allowed material price premia for a while.
- *Rush orders.* Every company in existence should have a delivery interval, and if customers want it sooner, then this is the time to apply the rush-order tariff.

- *Special orders.* Whether or not they really incur material incremental costs, special orders are an opportunity to get more money. The premium could take the form of a price lift, or a longer-term volume commitment.

As usual, even if cost is not really the driver, the rationale of higher costs is a very good message to accompany the new higher price. It suggests that you have no choice but to raise price, and says that the price rise is not simply a margin grab. For instance, where dies and forms need to be set up to produce the new product, cost differences can in many circumstances be explicitly referenced as a rationale for a higher price or an accompanying volume commitment on that or another product.

Costs are often considered to be straightforward—a product or transaction has a cost associated with it. In fact, there are many different kinds of costs. There are many ways to measure costs and margins, and they often play a legitimate role in pricing,[5] not in the simplistic way often portrayed, but in influencing the pricing behavior of competitors. The right balance of simple and more insightful costing is part of being a sophisticated pricer.

Different types of costs may be appropriate when considering your company's costs or modeling that of competitors.[6] For instance:

- In utilities, where regulations limit pricing flexibility, knowing overall cost levels may be enough.
- In more competitive industries (e.g., consumer nondurables), costs must be known at the product level.
- In the most competitive industries, costs must be known *by customer and by deal.*

For example, in the commodity plastics business—Styrofoam plates, shopping bags, and wraps—most large orders are priced somewhere between incremental and average costs. In that industry you need to know costs by product, geographically, and by volume, or the bulk of the orders will damage the bottom line. Only pricing well above average cost when context (such as rush orders and competitor oversights) permits makes these businesses profitable.

Noncommodity businesses should also adopt the mind-set of searching for premium pricing opportunities. Messaging the rationale for premium pricing is important because the right message can avoid potential customer anger at higher prices. Having a posted schedule of events (contexts) which will lead to add-on charges is good practice among rental service companies and retailers. Making these charges public can also lead competitors to adopt the same charges to their pricing.

> Many commodity industries earn little profit from the average transaction, but are ready to take advantage of situations where the context is favorable (e.g., rush orders). Context-driven premium pricing is a strategy which noncommodity providers should consider when the opportunity arises.

Summary

Management needs to know what prices a new or ongoing product will command. Basing that price blindly on the product's average utility or value will not serve that purpose unless you have a monopoly in your market.

For all other markets, management needs to look at context to establish the price. The implications of context, put in the starkest possible terms, are almost painful to product developers who have given their blood, sweat, and tears to develop better products. Depending on the perceived frame of reference, or context, all products are valuable or worthless. To take an example isolated from the context of management incentives: a life jacket is worth a lot on board a sinking boat, but it is of negative value at a formal dinner party.

An interesting analogy to "value" comes from the Middle Ages. Then, scientists believed that there was a substance called "phlogiston." This substance made things burn—supported fire. If something did not burn, it lacked phlogiston. Makes sense, right? The only problem was that it ignored a more complex (but useful and more accurate) explanation for fire—fire being the rapid oxidation of materials in an exothermic chemical process of combustion, releasing heat and light. Combustion requires two components: oxygen and fuel. We suggest that the best pricing requires consideration of context, which may include some form of value, or costs, or any number of other factors. Just like combustion, higher revenues do not come from one ingredient (value) alone.

Context is not just about customer perspectives, important as they are, but is also about competitor perspectives. Perception and context shape competitor pricing behaviors, and so the price obtainable in a market.

Notes

1. Robert G. Docters, et al., *Winning the Profit Game*, McGraw-Hill, 2004, pp. 84–85.
2. Another example of premia for unique value is in women's fashions, where "me-too-ness . . ., has plagued retail for years," according to Robert Drbul, an analyst for Barclays Capital. ("To Stand Out, Retailers Flock to Exclusive Lines," *The New York Times*, February 15, 2011).
3. Fortunately. the vast majority of U.S. management is incented to avoid mutually destructive price battles. A survey found 74 percent of companies have profit performance incentives. See "Study of Performance metrics Among S&P 500 Large Stock Companies," James F. Reda & Associates, LLC, March 2009, p. 10. Hence the disincentives to drive prices to cost.
4. Meaning that the molten steel burned through the continuous caster, and in that case 30 tons of liquid steel sloshed through the mill. The molten steel got into the electric motors for forming the steel, and production ceased.
5. R. Docters, "Improving Profitability Through Product Triage," *Business Horizons*, Indiana University, January/February 1996, p. 71. Even cost-plus contracts (price = costs + margin) do not yield similar results, since how companies approach tasks directly impacts outcomes (e.g., overheads such as whether they own or lease office space).
6. Variable, fixed, incremental, fully loaded (saturation), average, and other categories. As Professor Gordon Shillinglaw of Columbia University once commented, "If you ask me 'what is the cost?' I need to ask you 'Why do you wish to know?'"

Chapter 3

Which Contexts Matter to You?

Con'-text, n. Parts that precede or follow . . . and fix its meaning.

Con-tex'-ture, n. Act, mode of weaving together; structure; fabric . . . composition.

—*THE CONCISE OXFORD DICTIONARY* (4TH EDITION)

Which contexts matter to your pricing? That question requires some careful analysis of your product and buyers, frequently resulting in some surprises.

One such surprise came from a supplier to Wall Street trading desks. That supplier's sales team had been working hard to reach the "decision makers" directly and to avoid the buying organization. A survey of the sales force indicated that they ideally would present their offer to the head of trading and would work hard to avoid the vice president of purchasing. As it turned out though, this strategy was not ideal for achieving best price levels.

A look at the numbers showed that consistently when the buying decision was made by the head of trading, the client walked away with both a lower realized price and lower revenues. Why? The answer, as usual, lay in the decision context.

In a typical Wall Street environment, the head of trading is a powerful individual and apparently someone who is very familiar with the needs of the trading desks. Comparatively, the VP of purchasing is a lot less influential and is often removed from the operational needs of the trading desks. This means that when the VP of purchasing considers a price, he cannot afford to take the risk of saying no. Were he to cancel a service vital to the trading desks, without a seamless replacement, the consequences would be dire. Hence, the VP of purchasing could bark, but not bite.

In contrast, the head of trading was typically able to balance cost versus benefit because of his familiarity with the trading operations. Equally important, if he canceled a product or service, the complaints would flow to him and he could address them with less internal political risk. Finally, since he knew the needs more directly, he was more confident in cutting out less necessary service components. All this meant that the client would walk away poorer from the exchange.

The Effect of the Buying Decision on the Pricing Outcome

This is a clear example of context framing the buying decision, which in turn flows down to the pricing outcome. Further, the context also frames the ideal price structure. In the case of Wall Street trading departments, a good pricing structure worked to overcome the formidable defenses that the investment houses had erected so as to keep suppliers from encroaching on their treasure.

Trading organizations such as Goldman Sachs set up cost standards for their traders. A successful trader might bring that institution \$35+ million a year in revenues—a lot of money. But each trader was limited to about a 10 percent expense ratio, from which came his or her base salary (small compared with bonus) and overheads such as floor space and benefits. This left about a \$40,000 a year per trader target for other expenses, including purchases such as turrets, communications, training, data, and support. If you were a vendor who fell into one of the categories capped by this number, your price would be squeezed despite the huge margins enjoyed by Goldman—unless you refused to put your price in terms that allowed ready allocation of costs by a trader. An enterprise license independent of usage and crossing functional boundaries is difficult to allocate to each trader. Allocation can be done arbitrarily, but doing so often presents fairness issues (e.g., not every trader might use all the services and would complain) and is just more effort. So it was easier for the purchasing gatekeepers to allocate enterprise buys against entire departments. Fortunately department budgets did not have the same rigor as per-trader expense caps, hence pricing was less strongly resisted. Thus price structure, in this case the "unit" or measure of the service or product offered, helped liberate price level.

> Thorough understanding of decision processes frequently does not happen in the course of normal sales activity. Yet it may be the only way to overcome contextual barriers to price.

The choice of purchase unit is an opportunity to have an impact on context and price, and it is often ignored. As described later in this book, most services or products can be sold in super-sets (bundles) or in partial sets (or "slices" or "intervals") of ownership rights, and associated financing or warranties. Each of these choices should reflect the buyer decision process and frame of reference.

Frame of reference should include the channel context. For instance, a number of amusement park vendors have begun to charge more for tickets over the Internet than at the door. While this is different from what many consumers expect of the Internet, it makes a lot of sense. Most major amusement parks have found that visitors view their pricing in the context of the entire visit. In the case of a large amusement park, located in a major U.S. city, there is a wide range of visitors: local, in-state, from a long distance, and international. This means that for some visitors the travel costs are small—a trip on the local rapid transit system. For others, it means an expensive airfare, hotel, and incidentals.

This context sets price sensitivity. To someone who has spent over a thousand dollars to travel, for example, to Atlanta, a $39 admission ticket appears small. To someone who has spent $4 on mass transit to get there, the $39 will receive more attention. In fact, distance and travel cost drive price, so an Internet purchase favored by out-of-town visitors should be higher than an in-person purchase.

Context of overall purchase amounts applies to large industrial negotiations also. In the course of a multi-hundred-million-dollar negotiation,
the seller asked the buyer to cover a $100,000 cost item, and the buyer
team (focused on the large-ticket items) casually agreed—a concession
that in any other negotiation would have been inconceivable.

How Customer Concerns Influence the Buying Decision

So many things can represent factors that have an impact on price
outcomes: contexts and drivers may include buyer title, choice of unit,
geography, related expenses such as travel, and the size of the negotiation. The list goes on and on. Furthermore, we find that key drivers in
one market turn out to not matter much in other markets. Bundling of oil
field services and geophysical analysis matter, but bundling of steel types
does not matter at all. Bundling of cable television and telephone service
matters to market segments of modest means, but it actually destroys
value in high income segments. Therefore, an examination of context
and resulting drivers is required—of course, that is ostensibly the job of
product and market management, not to mention sales.

Yet repeatedly many managers resist looking into the black box of the
customer's mind and buyer decision processes. Two examples:

First, the brilliant CEO of Bell Canada Mobility, and before that the
savior of Ford Canada, Bob Ferchat was a seasoned CEO with a sterling
management record. Yet Bob was frustrated by the total organizational
resistance to a very pragmatic suggestion: *learn* about Bell Mobility's best
customers.

Since long-haul truckers were one of the most important segments
served by Bell Mobility, Bob said that any employee who wanted to spend
a few days riding with a trucking fleet was encouraged to do so and would
be compensated for it. Much to Bob's chagrin, none of Mobility's 20,000
employees took up this offer. Not one employee wanted to understand
first-hand the company's best customer groups' needs and how they made
their buying decisions.

In the second example, a manufacturer of narrow body short-haul
airframes noticed that one of their smaller airplanes was not selling well,
and often buyers were going up one size even when they did not need
the extra seat capacity (or expense). Investigation found that the larger
airplane readily qualified for an investment tax credit, while the smaller

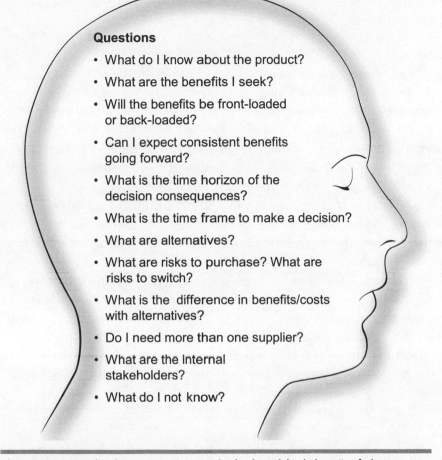

Questions

- What do I know about the product?
- What are the benefits I seek?
- Will the benefits be front-loaded or back-loaded?
- Can I expect consistent benefits going forward?
- What is the time horizon of the decision consequences?
- What is the time frame to make a decision?
- What are alternatives?
- What are risks to purchase? What are risks to switch?
- What is the difference in benefits/costs with alternatives?
- Do I need more than one supplier?
- What are the internal stakeholders?
- What do I not know?

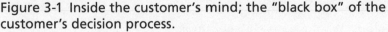

Figure 3-1 Inside the customer's mind; the "black box" of the customer's decision process.

airplane typically did not. When the difference in the buyer's tax obligation was pointed out, product management said that it was "none of our business." From a pricing point of view, it was *exactly* the manufacturer's business.

Thus, one step towards contextual pricing is to encourage your company to look inside the black box of the consumer's mind, or the decision process of a business customer. Many questions important to pricing are not always asked, so the decision process remains dark and obscure.

> As with all change, expect some resistance
> to a customer-centric pricing approach.

You may be wondering, even if your team recognizes that the buyer's economics has an impact on your company's sales success, how do you improve your team's understanding of price context and price drivers? How do we identify potential drivers, and how do we test them? The answer is simple. We find that drivers and context are usually well-known to management, and certainly to customers. Asking management to document and discuss potential drivers is a good first step.[1]

Some degree of impartiality is required for the evaluation of drivers, however. For instance, in sales-oriented organizations, often the factors important to sales are given priority and a sales issue with minimal impact on pricing is given priority over an actual pricing issue that is destroying customer loyalty. At one company, sales management used the inquiry into contextual pricing to club customer service management over the head about some minor service issues, while the real issue provoking customer defections was pricing.

A generic list of potential contextual pricing drivers may be useful as you consider your pricing initiatives. This generic list has been organized by the four *P*s of marketing:

- *Product.* In addition to basing pricing on the familiar measures of performance and quality, spend more time looking at *uses* and competitor offers (including both tangibles and intangibles). Most important, don't assume perfect information—what do potential buyers know? What do they not know? Over time?
- *Promotion.* Sophisticated promotion and branding management is already worried about what the buyer thinks and what the buyer knows. The shortcoming is that often these insights are linked to messaging and ignore pricing. Branding is an effort to communicate and influence buyers, often through context; extend this discipline to pricing.
- *Price structure.* Forms some of the most directly applicable context. A price structure powerfully communicates what context should be used by buyers: for Band-Aids, pricing by the box says, "Compare by the box," and a fixed price often says, "Here it is, whether you use it or not." Make sure the message is right.

- *Channel* ("place"). This is often the core of contextual outcomes. Sales channels differ in effectiveness, ability to communicate, and ability to shape decision criteria. Pricing must weave the story most useful to channel, including the point of sale price strategy.

Graphically, Figure 3-2 shows some of the more frequently encountered contextual factors. Word size represents frequency of occurrence. This diagram may form a starting point for discussion, but sometimes

Channels

Agencies and consortia

MFNs

Sales force compensation

Usage levels

Risk of Customer deflection

Discount discipline

Your brand

Length of relationship

Negotiation skills

Customer objectives

Time spent with product

Ability to price discriminate

Evaluation criteria for buyers

Regulation and legal

Purchase pattern Timeframe of evaluation

Title/function/power of buyer

Financial criteria for organizational success

Percent of budget Committee versus single decision-maker

Penetration of customer work flow

Customer budget cycle

Cumulative purchases

Risks of product

Obvious vs. hidden attributes

Understanding of product

Your price structure

Loyalty Incentives

Terms and financing

Bundles

Chargeback of costs

Tiering of service

Complexity of product

Uniqueness of product

Breadth of product

Cost savings

Reputation of competitors

Switching Cost

Dependency or link to infrastructure

Related costs

Comparative advantage of competitors

Sophistication of competitors

Number of competitors/alternatives

Figure 3-2 Proportional representation of common pricing contexts.

markets march to their own drummer and the usual suspects are not the drivers of price.[2]

If the universe of potential contexts seems large, it is. The business world is big and diverse, and so is the world of contexts. They are not all primary, however, and the good news is that no company division faces more than a few primary contextual drivers.

The academic literature reinforces the many ways in which context matters, and perusing it reveals some proven contextual influences.[3]

- **Time.** Most consumers will not pick the first offer presented, even if it is the best one.
- **Comparison of prices.** Most consumers see price differences as a percentage of the base price and are less motivated by the same absolute dollar-price difference on a large purchase than they are on a smaller purchase.
- **Premium products.** Adding a premium product to a product line enhances consumer perception of the product line, even if buyers choose not to purchase the premium tier.
- **Discounts.** A discount works better when consumers have a clear understanding of the normal price.
- **Bargains.** A higher list price minus a discount will sell better than a lower discount with a surcharge, even if the resulting prices are equal.
- **Nonprice fees.** These can outperform explicit dollar fees in some circumstances, for example, "tokens."

There may be no contextual commonality across your company divisions, but that is okay: focus and relative simplicity is of course why many companies divide their management into different business units.

The Other Side of the Mirror

So now we've seen context from a market perspective. An underpinning of contextual pricing is that unless you have a unique product, your company may need to pay attention to what the market wants. But what about the perspective from *inside* your company? Typically, business units must adapt to a range of customer and selling situations, and they do this by thinking in terms of the tasks to be performed. While there is some loss of fidelity to the market by doing this, such a task-oriented view is okay.

Some common contexts requiring different pricing capabilities (and, likely, different price points) are:

- Large bids, generally involving negotiations
- Standard product sales in moderate dollar contracts
- Small and one-off sales
- Special orders
- Rush orders
- Direct sales via proprietary channels
- Sales to consortia
- Sales through retail
- Sales to competitors and resellers
- Sales via bid
- Sales to loyal and sole-source customers
- Sales for marginal customers
- Highly competitive sales
- Add-on sales
- Up-tiering
- Pilot sales of new offers
- Bundles
- Direct to buyer versus intermediary
- Preemptive (e.g., stock-up strategy) versus reactive
- Complex choices versus clear choices or guided sales
- Intended (by seller) use versus unintended use
- Certain use by buyer versus contingency (e.g., insurance)

A complete list would be quite long. The list here covers a lot of ground, perhaps 70 percent of your company's pricing situations.

Suppose you want to condense the list further. One way to condense contextual pricing factors is to lump them together according to how robust or fragile is your customer relationship. If you have—by reason of product, delivery, branding or pricing—a very strong appeal in a particular context, that should be handled very differently than if your offer is not compelling in a particular context. Therefore, one potential approach is to categorize your selling contexts by market strength.

High Market Power ⟵ ⟶ Low Market Power				
Southeast region

Promotion-oriented retailers

Rush orders | Small outlets

Non-traditional outlets

High-growth outlets | Large bids from secure long-term customers. | Northeast large chains

Add-on orders except where specialized competitor present | Where a third specialized competitor was present

Large bids to at-risk or competitor customers |

Figure 3-3 Contextual price bases: example of five contextual price bases used by a large consumer goods company.

One example of contextual price points, ordered by strength of customer relationships, that served a large consumer goods company selling through retail is illustrated in Figure 3-3 above.

These five categories of contextual price pressure replaced a complex pricing formula and matrix, yet proved implementable across the market. The five explained price variation better than the existing segmentation; so this insight was incorporated into this company's market strategy.

Often you can categorize your contextual baselines by reference to your market power (measurable, in some cases, as customer price sensitivity).

Organizational Acceptance of Contextual Pricing

Management today has an array of tools for identifying and evaluating the contexts for purchase decisions. Each can provide a richness of insight and means for lifting revenues, but often management hesitates to embrace implications. Why?

Outside some industries where pricing is a primary management activity (e.g., finance and travel), the unwillingness to draw conclusions from data seems to be motivated by a combination of fear and inertia.[4] One cable television company delayed making major price decisions because it was waiting to build a multimillion-dollar data warehouse—despite having a rich inventory of customer surveys. Upon completion of the warehouse, the cable company then decided the data warehouse data was imperfect (surprise!) and therefore unsuitable for pricing decisions. After several consulting efforts cobbled together data from various sources, all fairly consistent in direction, the cable television company is still looking for more data to support the various evidence-based (but imperfect) strategy recommendations.

No pricing strategy is risk-free or based on airtight evidence. But neither is any sales strategy, any financial strategy, any product development plan, any branding strategy, and so on. Yet those imperfect plans seem to be implemented more often. Why? One possible answer is that in many industries, top managers have reached that position through sales, finance, or marketing. A former chief marketing officer for Dun & Bradstreet said she found evidence that their pricing was an issue. Forced to undertake a program to shore up revenues, however, she chose the tool that had brought her to the office: branding. Managers do not like to bet their careers on functional programs with which they and others are unfamiliar. This is possibly why there is sometimes tolerance for indefinite delay in addressing pricing.[5]

Context may make pricing principles familiar to company management teams because in many cases contextual logic can make the results intuitive. That is the hope, in any case. Context rejects simple mathematical measures such as elasticity, and rightly so. Instead, contextual logic requires a relentless focus on why and how decisions get made. That is often not known, but is a familiar question to those who address branding and sales issues.

Summary

The potential frames of reference have a striking amount of diversity. Yet when we consider specific cases, the context is relatively simple. In each case the process of ascertaining context is fairly similar: investigate the buyer decision process, through interviews, survey, or other means. The menu of contexts presented here may be a useful starting point.

Notes

1. If you ask, you are more likely to end up with too many potential contextual drivers rather than too few. The trick is that many are closely related, or colinear in statistical terms. For instance, as a B2B example, be aware that the "buying size of the customer" is often related to how long they have been a customer, which is related to how long the company has been in business, which is related to how senior the sales rep is on that account, to many other considerations. In other words, all these factors may be really measuring the same thing. Determining which related factor is primary often requires some statistical testing.

2. Going after the most common drivers of price is not always the most effective method in finding the real sources of pricing difference. When Captain Renault says "Round up the usual suspects" near the end of *Casablanca*, he's letting the real culprit (played by Humphrey Bogart) go free. Do not let teams assume the usual contextual drivers are applicable—you may miss the real culprits.

3. *Warning: on advice of counsel we are obligated to warn you that this may be the world's most boring footnote.* Linking price outcomes to mental processes has been well established in a slew of academic studies. A few examples: Kent B. Monroe and Joseph Chapman, "Framing Effects on Buyers' Subjective Product Evaluations," *Advances in Consumer Research*, vol. 14, 1987, pp. 193–197; Richard Thaler, "Mental Accounting and Consumer Choice," *Marketing Science*, vol. 4, Summer 1985, pp. 199–214; Amos Tversky and Itamar Simonson, "Context-Dependent Preferences," *Management Science*, vol. 39, no. 10, October 1993. But that research is more focused on price level and couponing, so it is a bit narrow for managerial use. A few authors take a broader view, and describe how to link price framing ("contextual") insights to pricing practices. For a nicely writ-

ten look at use of context see Benson P. Shapiro "What the Hell is Market Oriented?" *Harvard Business Review*, March 3, 2009.

4. Oddly, many managers seem to think that price decisions can be avoided and pricing issues addressed through other means. This course of action is similar to comedian Mitch Hedberg's dental strategy: "I was going to get my teeth whitened, but instead I got a tan."

5. In part we suspect that the ambivalence in coming to grips with pricing issues occurs because pricing can be unusually complex. That can be a reason managers refuse to move on pricing initiatives. "Why So Many People Can't Make Decisions," *The Wall Street Journal*, September 28, 2010, p. D1.

Chapter 4

Living in the Digital World

The Cat this time vanished quite slowly, beginning with
the end of the tail, and ending with the grin, which
remained some time after the rest of it had gone.
"Well, I've often seen a cat without a grin," thought
Alice, "but a grin without a cat! It's the most curious
thing I ever saw in all my life!"

—LEWIS CARROLL,
ALICE'S ADVENTURES IN WONDERLAND

Supply and demand represent an effective summary of context. If demand increases or decreases, or if supply increases or decreases, price levels generally shift also. With dramatic shifts, any previous calculation of intrinsic product "value" is rendered completely immaterial.

One of the most dramatic shifts of supply and demand in recent memory occurred as a result of digitization (e.g., the Internet, software applications, modularization of electronics). Many incumbent manufacturers and service providers view digitization as a threat to revenue and profitability. The oft-quoted admonition "not to trade cable dollars for Internet pennies" illustrates this fear.[1] While the evolution of content, services, and software to digital formats can indeed destroy a traditional business's profitability—often it is the poor transition pricing *that ignores context* that is the true culprit.

What are typical concomitants to digitization? There tend to be at least a half-dozen changes, including:

- Easier to embed different content and functionality
- Splitting of content from services, including splitting purchases by vendor and category
- Sort products into categories and rebundle them
- Faster service and greater transaction timeliness
- Disintermediation between users, buyers, seller frontlines, and product management

Often these changes lead to a significantly improved range of consumer and B2B choices. The expectation among product developers is that customers will be gratified with these new choices. However, sometimes customer satisfaction actually suffers due to user unfamiliarity with the digital distribution platform or vehicle (e.g., application software). Also, complaints may also increase, in part because digitally oriented Millennials are more prone to complain.

Digitization often leads to splits in the customer base, between technology-savvy and tech-resistant market segments. Some of this is partly due to user attitudes, but sometimes management forgets that a move toward digitization is often *not* a cure-all or even an improvement that will satisfy all customers. For instance, most readers (of any age) still read about 20 percent to 30 percent faster on paper than on screens, and complex digital systems can underperform physical or analog goods in quality or reliability. For instance, reliability is why Boeing continues to allow pilots to override digital "fly by wire" controls of the aircraft—Airbus design does not, and that has triggered extensive discussion about safety. A final example: most audiophiles feel that vinyl LP records outperform CD recordings—and certainly outperform MP3 files and players.

Digitization has a fairly typical set of concomitants—
e.g., ability to offer parts of a previous unitary offer.
This has specific contextual price prescriptions.

Management and project teams should keep three principles in mind as they develop and tweak pricing strategy to make money in a digital world:

1. Pricing needs to reflect market evolution in a realistic manner. Digitization is usually not a *revolution*; rather, it is an *evolution*. Almost every company overestimates the rate of change and spends insufficient time and attention on the lagging nondigital segment. Ironically, the lagging segments are often the most profitable. In the legal publishing industry, for instance, the legal-book business contributed more margin dollars than the electronic side of the business until the mid-2000s—far longer than expected.

2. For the digital world, the "unit of charging" must change. So instead of dollars per mile/per book title/per movie/device, etc., the units of charging need to shift to dollars per digital event, per application, or per user, per use, or whatever fits the digital market context. For instance, a new manufacturer of retinal eye-scan devices changed the playing field by pricing its start-up digital analytic product on a per-use basis, while traditional film-based eye-scan incumbents continued to focus on selling and pricing entire devices.

3. The cart can come before the horse, just as the smile can exist without the Cheshire Cat. Where there is a multielement (sophisticated) sale, changing the lead element can make all the difference. For instance, a new school textbook entrant successfully entered the market by giving away teaching guides before the textbook adoption contest, which built awareness and teacher loyalty to a new brand. This strategy enabled the new entrant to sew up the school adoption contest by the time buyers started formally reviewing and evaluating at the basal texts. *Free* is more often an option in the digital world because of lower incremental costs, and so add-ons can actually precede the main product.

Changes in the market environment, like digitalization, allow new pricing strategies based on rebundling and restructuring of offers.

Supply and Demand Sum Up Context

Management may have concerns about digital pricing because often pricing has eroded with digitization. Will your digital prices go up or down? The answer depends partly on supply and demand, and partly on management's execution. We often find that management does not consider supply-and-demand factors and market evolution before making investment decisions. When the right factors are considered, the resulting roadmap can provide valuable strategic insights, as in the following example.

A 1996 pricing study considered two dimensions that were likely to affect a cable company's core business: how the advent of digital content creation would have an impact on *content* pricing and how network development would have an impact on *distribution* pricing. The results accurately foretold the client's actual margin results for the next decade. As digital technologies made video content production easier and cheaper, the supply of content expanded. Relatively slower growth of fiber networks and conventional content-distribution mechanisms (e.g., movie theaters) meant that demand grew slowly. The prescription of higher supply and lower demand of content foretold lower video-content value and margins.

This forecast was realized in the fortunes of content producers. Movie studios, networks, and music producers that were minting money in the late 1980s (e.g., Viacom, Paramount, BMG, and EMI) saw declining margins over the next decade. At the same time, content distributors, such as cable companies, saw margins grow throughout the 2000s. Newspapers suffered the most because of increasing competition and decreasing demand as the print medium went into decline.

Although this was the state of play in the 1990s and the early 2000s, the future looks different. Many sectors that have *already* shifted toward digital production of content will no longer experience the same increases in content. Conversely, the number of distribution channels is what is expanding. Most major content providers have established digital footholds and have reallocated resources toward branded online sites, social media, and a mobile presence in addition to their traditional distribution channels.[2]

If the number of digital distribution channels continues to increase, we would expect the *value* of most distribution channels to fall over the next few years. Flat supply and increasing demand (distribution) means that the value of content may rise again.

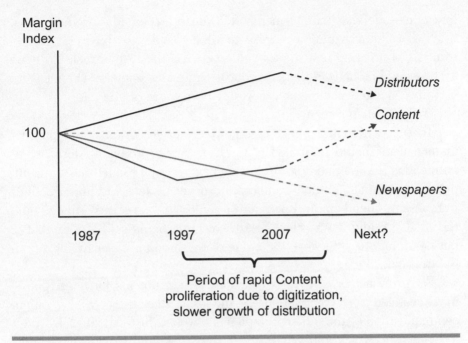

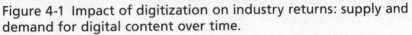

Period of rapid Content
proliferation due to digitization,
slower growth of distribution

Figure 4-1 Impact of digitization on industry returns: supply and demand for digital content over time.

The country of sale is an important contextual variable. In consumer markets, price levels differ by country because of differences in income (demand) and the number of competitors (supply). For a mobile telephony device, we found that prices ranged from an index of 100 in the United States, to 122 in Germany, to 89 in Italy. In less developed countries the index fell to the teens, yet some global vendors fail to vary prices to the optimum of local price. (Of course there are limits to variance due to the danger of reimported "gray goods.") Nor is the problem of price variation limited to global marketing. Within the United States, similar data service price differences are apparent between buyers on college campuses and demographically identical working Millennials—again reinforcing the need to price to context.

Digital Price Structure

How should a digital transition and segmentation be managed? We believe that the *unit of measure* for a digital product is the core pricing question—one that management often glosses over. Management must ask: what changes have occurred to what people are buying? A good example of creating new digital value is when NBC News took old news archives and monetized them as educational video content. The measure of value changed completely, however, from viewers and ratings to per classroom licensing plans.

To succeed in the midst of digital evolution, pricing and product management should be joined at the hip. In the predigital world, communication, interaction, and understanding among product management, pricing specialists, and consumers were never perfect, but imperfections were less frequently fatal. Each player could "kick the tires" (understand the product), and it was clear to all what was being sold. Today that is not possible, often because the value of the product is set by its role in the workflow.

For instance, price drivers of avionics (instruments for an airplane) have changed with digitization. In the past, the altimeter, navigation, communications, and other components would be evaluated by their individual accuracy and reliability. Today, these individual components have been replaced by avionic systems—integrated cockpit information systems—whose components are more similar in accuracy and reliability than ever before. Differences among systems lie in the sophistication of the package and numerous features (e.g., three-dimensional synthetic vision, situation evaluation, and error correction), which are not as easily compared in best-of-breed dimensions. Accuracy, reliability, and functionality are what drove older instrument prices. These measures have given way to new dimensions in differentiation (e.g., screen size, graphic capabilities, and backup).

Similarly, in the B2B digital environment, technical and professional book prices are less and less decided on the basis of the book (hardcover or softcover, length, etc.) but rather on how the information in the book relates to alternative media. In our work we have found that the better way to price, say, a $100 business reference handbook is *to split the value of its content from the physical media* (the printed volume). This suggests that B2B publishers and educational publishers:

- Sell the content separate from the bound book. For example: if you are selling 100 copies of a technical publication at $100 to a large firm for $10,000 ($100 × 100 = $10,000 total), sell the content for $8,500 and the books for $15 each (100 × $15= $1,500.) This initially produces the same total, but we find it sends an important message resulting in additional sales. The message is: "The content is what is valuable, not our printing press." Also, when companies seek electronic versions, they will see fewer advantages to cutting the print copies.

- Charge on the merits of media. If you offer a value-added platform, charge for that value add. Often we find that supposedly "value-added" platforms actually offer little value add (e.g., complex work platforms lose to simple mobile applications), and companies fool themselves where value lies. Hiding content value in an amorphous bundle with media usually destroys value; separating it out often *liberates value*: customers will punish vendors who appear to be "force bundling" elements. A 15 to 40 percent price *penalty* exacted by customers from unwanted bundling is common.

- Don't insist on the same unit of volume! Digitalization liberates you from selling by the book, the integrated software package, the record album, the cockpit instrument, or the TV spot. Clients are often afraid that this unbundling will reduce revenues, but frequently we find the opposite.[3] The prerequisite to revenue gains is, however, a solid understanding of market price drivers and bundle configuration practices.

Thus, whereas books, news feeds, and periodicals were all previously sold in silos, on a stand-alone basis, they should now be viewed increasingly as part of an overall content/media price structure. Content often has the highest value when sold as a pure play and the delivery media are add-on fees. Some types of delivery may command higher prices than others, but we have found that buyers are able to distinguish the content from the delivery media and will penalize vendors who try to double-charge for either component.

Price drivers, of course, must be reflected in any plan to adapt the traditional business to the new world. A key digital pricing question (related to choice of unit) is scaling. In the predigital world, scaling often took care of itself—that is, when information buyers needed 20 tax guides, they bought 20 tax guides. In the digital world, many users can make do with a single electronic feed. Thus, the question is: how can the feed be priced so that you capture the value of many users? Again, this should lead pricers to shift their pricing focus from the product ("How much is a tax guide worth?") to the buyer context (context being: "How many tax professionals are being supported? Are they senior or junior practitioners?") Poor scaling decisions have destroyed value among many service and information providers, including tax software, computer networking, maintenance and repair, and news gathering.

Be careful in retaining the same—or similar sounding—pricing "unit of measure" when the environment changes. For instance, digitally appropriate scaling of users and functions is key to pricing changes and preserving margins.

One source of revenue leakage is digital piracy, an interesting challenge. Some entertainment, business-information, and educational publishers face an 80 percent or more loss of volume to illegal copying and distribution in certain markets and geographies. Such losses are often avoidable. Pricing can often play a role in combating illegal copying. How? To begin with: give users what they want. Several business-to-business information providers (e.g., energy, construction, legal) have found that simply allowing *all* customer employees use of information through enterprise pricing immediately eliminated cheating—and provided the information provider with an immediate *uplift* in revenue.

Bundles and Context to the Rescue

Another mechanism to eliminate illegal use and republication of digital content is to create a price mechanism that offers some elements of the product for free but also links other elements to a more defensible for-pay environment. The strategy is to make it less worthwhile and harder for users to cheat sellers out of revenues on higher-value elements of the product. In the consumer market, an example is the two-level pricing for Microsoft Xbox Live where the silver level of play is free, but to get to the more desirable (and harder to pirate) gold features, payment is the easier option. Microsoft has created the payment boundary where it is easiest to defend: the multiplayer capability. This is a good example of highly coordinated pricing and product design.

In the case of Xbox, the linkages were designed and a result of careful management strategy. Similarly, Microsoft is embedding "sleepers" in business software that can be activated if an application turns out to be of interest. One example is Microsoft SharePoint, which helps with collaboration.

In the more free-flowing ecosystem of iPhone applications, the same thing may happen as stages in evolution. For instance highly addictive Smartphone apps, such as Angie's List and Angry Birds, begin as free applications, and over time move to a for-pay application. In the case of Angry Birds, the attractiveness of the original simple application obviated the need for a sophisticated pricing strategy to move it from free to for-pay—but not all apps will have that advantage.

Another consideration that is crucial to pricing success—or at least a way to avoid a pricing disaster—is to make sure that product management and pricing proceed in parallel, an approach we consider a best practice. Pricing is often a reaction to product plans, therefore if the product management team is overly optimistic about digital adoption, the price will be wrong.

Many companies in setting prices for a new digital offer frequently set the price too low. For companies that link price to cost, a lower price may be appealing because of management's belief in the myth that digital is lower cost. This is frequently wrong: studies have repeatedly shown that in many cases digital is more expensive than the legacy product when you include all costs.

To compound the digital product pricing error, sometimes management handicaps legacy product pricing. Annoyed with the burden of maintaining both digital and traditional products, management either cuts support for the old product and/or raises its price materially to harvest that product (and perhaps to pay for new digital development). The result? Material underperformance of the digital product because of premature release and inadequate support—and fatal harm to the traditional product line.

Unless your company has matured as a digital product developer, the better approach is to let the market decide, and to separate the price and product development on your existing product lines. Mandate that each will exploit context to maximize revenues. Give both digital and nondigital products their best shot. This approach actually requires less effort than reorganizing all the resources to emphasize the new digital product. Typically, established products run on long-standing momentum. You don't need to kill the old to optimize the new—the market will do that when (and if) it wants.

> Unless your company has proven competence in technological change, consider optimizing the prices of both old and new technologies, and let the market decide which wins.

In some sense, digitization has changed none of the fundamental rules of pricing—pricing should always reflect market price drivers. However, the potential penalty for maintaining the incumbent pricing structure has grown with digitization. Price structures developed over decades to fit an older generation of products cannot be relied upon to perform in the new digital world.

Digital price drivers (i.e., factors in the market that shape the structure and level of digital offer pricing demanded by customers) will penalize companies who do not think through the logic.[4] "Price benchmarking" and trying to apply rules from other companies whose strategies and value offerings are different from your own is not usually a substitute for understanding digital product workflows. Sadly, many supposed digital pricing benchmarks face different contexts and so are focused on different and inapplicable price drivers.

Summary

Digital evolution is a perfect case study in the need for contextual pricing. When comparing similar analog and digital products, there will be material differences in their use and context. Don't assume that digitization is bad or good—it can be either. What is likely is that the differences in purchase context (and buyers, in some cases) will require some thinking about the unit of measure by which your company will price and sell. Digital evolution requires understanding of your consumer needs and business customer context.

Notes

1. Generally attributed to Rupert Murdock, chairman of News Corp. While this chapter focuses on digitalization as a driver, often non-digital drivers of change can be just as dramatic. For instance, prices in the contemporary art market have been lifted—sometimes a hundredfold—by a dramatic increase in galleries and promotion—increasing demand. "The Gagosian Effect," *The Wall Street Journal*, wsj.com, April 1, 2011.

2. An interesting question is how much content will be generated by the new social media; is social media a net plus or minus to content versus distribution? The answer may depend on the application and market segment. An example of content from new sources was that 1.8 million people learned of Michael Jackson's death via social networking and Wikipedia within hours of the event—well before traditional media broke the story.

3. Frequently, bundles containing unnecessary and irrelevant components actually increase in value when those components are removed. See Chapter 7 on scientific bundling.

4. This appears to have been the case for other technological evolutions also. For instance, when commercial airliners migrated from piston engines to jet engines, the unit of evaluation changed from cost per hour to cost per passenger mile. This subtle difference completely changed the economic analysis. Those who stuck to the cost per hour said that jet engines would not replace pistons, but they were proved wrong. Future technological changes will likely require similar adjustments.

Chapter 5

Antidotes to Price Pressure

What customers really want is a better product for free.
—POINTY-HEADED LADY IN *DILBERT* CARTOON

Price pressure is typically a story about villains. Typically, the villains are said to be competitors or customers. Sometimes the villain is an aging or inadequate product. Sometimes the villain is a misaligned baseline price level and uninspired structures. No doubt some of this is true some of the time.

Still, the villains are part of a *normal* set of conditions. Customers are supposed to minimize cost; competitors are supposed to try and eat your lunch. Your price structure is not ideal or you would not be reading this book. The question is *how* can your company minimize that pressure?

To begin with, let's review some worst-practices benchmarks. One is after-the-fact recriminations. By the time that unattractive contracts are sent to executive suites for approval, there is little to be done. The company should never have gotten into that position in the first place. Another bad practice is to begin the pricing waterfall with unrealistic and absurd pricing—since all participants know they will fail to obtain that price, departing from it is easy and so managers will drop price. Finally, and most importantly, there is the failure to understand what your company's offer means to the market through a refusal to consider its buying context.

Figuring out how to get out of that position is the focus of this chapter.

Three Strategic Actions for Reducing Price Pressure

The antidote to price pressure is to have worked on building up healthy contextual pricing practices and to deploy them ahead of time. Think of sales effort as the last line of defense in revenue protection—don't let it get down to that last line of defense.[1]

The following three strategies will materially reduce price pressures on your company's revenues:

- Being precise in discounting
- Using killer tactics and offering bundles
- Knowing the level of play

Being Precise in Discounting

The first and most immediate task is to make sure that the discounting process contains the essential logical elements required for optimum pricing. The logic requires three questions:

- Is the account at risk?
- Is price a factor in that risk?
- What is the optimum price?

A common practice is to jump to the third question without considering the first two. Without answers to the first two questions, managers will typically conclude that a big discount is appropriate. As a practice, that is flawed.

Threats to an account (or barriers to gaining an account) may stem from several sources. One is that some event affecting clients is likely to induce buyers to move to another company. For instance, in a B2B setting, the arrival of a new manager can set up such a dynamic. Often, the new manager wishes to demonstrate his or her determination to initiate change, and the subordinates will need to show they are not entrenched in the past. One way to demonstrate this determination is to switch out a supplier. Sometimes the change agent will warn the incumbent vendor, sometimes not.

Another source of risk is a competitor on the warpath. BellSouth (now AT&T) faced this problem when a GE subsidiary, more focused on selling dishwashers and building infrastructure in apartment complexes, also offered telephone services at very low rates. The answer to that threat was a model that predicted which property management companies and real estate investment trusts (REITs) would be approached by GE, and when. It turned out GE's priorities were based on the size of the apartment complex, the income level of the residents and their existing cable/television infrastructure, product fit, usage, and decision-maker title.[2] A model reflecting these factors allowed BellSouth to get to GE prospects first, and lock in that business.

Once the risk has been identified, the next question is "Does price matter?" The answer is clear: not always. Examples of situations where price is not useful either in addressing or limiting risk of loss include major service failures, poor personal chemistry, acquisitions of a business account by another company loyal to another supplier, and your offers being rendered unwanted through new technologies or super-bundles to which your company cannot respond. In many situations, either because price is not the problem or because price is not a cure, it means that price is not the answer.[3] In that case, do *not* drop the price bomb.

Only a minority of your customer base is in any danger of leaving because of price. Don't drop the price bomb when you don't need to.

Level of risk linked to price level. If an account is at risk and price does matter, what is the relevant price point? Interestingly, we have found that price response need not be linear to risk—in other words, more risk does not mean higher discounts. The proposed price level should be linked to the *customer* point of reference, and different reference points will suggest quite different price points.

Four cases are typical:

1. *Low risk.* In cases of low risk, buyer awareness of competitive offers may be quite low. Then the price comparison (context) will center on *your* company's own price. There may be a need to show some responsiveness to price concerns, but the price response must be nominal. To do more will only provoke questions, such as "Why didn't you do this earlier?" and "Maybe it's worth investigating other suppliers—perhaps something has changed so that the other suppliers may be offering even bigger discounts?" This cannot lead to a good result.

2. *Medium risk.* In the case of medium risk, a comparison centers on the difference between your company's offer and that of the competition. This case involves the usual trade-off of different features, functionality, and appeal. Price may not have to move.

3. *High risk.* In high-risk situations, the comparison will center on the *competition's* offer.[4] This means that you must demonstrate your *superior* value to that offer, with switching costs and other adjustment factors in order to win. If you are in this position, the price must communicate strong reasons for customers to decide in your favor.

    High risk is a good time to practice triage. This means that in some cases the better practice is to recognize that winning will be an improbable long shot, and would require an impossibly deep discount. That has other risks: if the market is highly communicative about pricing, it may be that any low price you offer will become known and will be the standard for future sales, even if you do not win the competition.

    In that case, the best approach may be not to compete on price even though it will mean you are certain to lose. In some cases, the customer will effectively tell you that they have mentally switched vendors, such as when B2B customers "go silent" and do not respond to calls by your sales force—this is a very bad sign if it persists.

4. *Opportunity to acquire business.* This is the mirror image of the risk analysis: is there an opportunity to take business away from a competitor, and what price point will suffice?

    The big difference between attack and defend is that you will have less information about prospects than about one of your own customers. Therefore you will have to use "proxies" for risk. For instance, for one software vendor we found that many add-on and custom additions to a competitor's system was a good sign that the buyer might not be finding the competitor's systems a good fit.

So the basis for price level depends on the state of mind of the buyer. When your company's offer is the reference point, you can set price based on your existing offers. When a competitor, or alternative solution, is a potential buyer's reference price, your pricing must accommodate that benchmark. This applies not only to price level but also to price structure.

> The pricing context in buying decisions can be your company's prices, or the context may shift to competitor prices— which would signal higher risk of loss.

To reiterate, a three-step process will help ensure more precise and profitable pricing:

- Isolation and quantification of risks
- Relevance (efficacy) of pricing actions
- Price response according to scenario

While these three steps and scenarios may seem like a lot of work, consider the benefits they offer in pricing:

- Every nuance captured means eliminating an unnecessary discount, or saving a lost customer or segment.
- Stick to the script of different contextual scenarios, and avoid dropping prices where it is unnecessary. Postmortems have shown this can rescue about 2 to 15 percent of revenues.
- Also, once embedded in a CRP tool, the incremental effort by marketing and sales is very small.

Using Killer Tactics and Offering Bundles

Another approach to price pressure is to isolate the cause and exterminate it. Usually, competitive threats are quite specific (e.g., a competitor is hitting your largest customers), or they are using low-cost channels (e.g., insurance via the Internet), or they have a cheap and simple product to replace your expensive and complex product (e.g., medical diagnostic devices). Another common threat is an established competitor under new ownership trying to earn back an acquisition premium. In almost *none* of these cases will there be a universal threat. Even an established competitor will pick its battles because it needs to show return on investment (ROI).

Strike back in a targeted way. Contextual examples of striking back usually involve both price level and messaging, but they should also involve price structure:

- *Message.* Use price transparency selectively. If a competitor is offering outrageously low prices to win your best customers, try informing the *competitor's* best customers of these prices. Chances are this will provoke anger amongst those customers: "Is this my reward for long time loyalty?" This can be done as part of an offer: "To match your supplier's prices, we are now offering $X." Frequently, this causes such a problem for the competitor that it will limit its attack on your customers.
- *Target.* If your industry pricing is driven by costs (e.g., transport), retaliate where the competition is at a disadvantage. Make sure the message tells the competitor's management of the linkage (that it is a retaliation) so that they have the option of ending the problem. Again, message is key to avoiding a price war.
- *Structure.* Often a price attack will take the form of a flat-rate structure. This is effective with customers currently paying under variable plus fixed structures, and with some paying under a variable plan. Structure is key to attack or defend. If an attacker offers a flat-rate price, you probably need to respond with the same basic structure for threatened segments or customers. But don't respond identically. The response structure should be sufficiently similar to say "We do that also," but the differences should be sufficiently complex to require *competitors* to spend some time to refute its attractiveness.
- *Transparency.* You need to control different parts of the price transparency—it does not need to be all transparent or all opaque. For instance, transportation networks and communications networks

can offer simple pricing and complex pricing, depending on circumstances. A leading network-equipment vendor's systems architecture made it the advantaged product on highly meshed intracity communications, while it did poorly in interregional backbone applications. The pricing structure needed to reflect this: very open in advantaged configurations, very opaque and complex for regional backbones. Opacity was accomplished by tying together different components and having multiple discounting factors tied to context.

- *Specific attack.* Consider attacking the specific product set that poses the difficulty. If it's a bundle causing the problem, create an attack bundle. If it's a product within the bundle, drop prices on that one product. For a leading tax software company, creating a suite of "killer bundles" aimed directly at specific competing bundles had the advantage of preserving overall price and rationalizing some bundles with too many components (markets hate stuff they can't use in a bundle).[5] We believe that general corporate competence in designing market-effective bundles is poor, so chances are your attack bundles, if properly constructed, will be very effective in blunting price attack and pressures.

In countering price attacks, do not strike back blindly or broadly. Precision is efficient.

Knowing the Level of Play

Price pressure can also come from a shift in the overall evolution of the industry, and so it needs to be considered a potential cause for alarm. For instance, many industries undergo a pricing evolution of: (1) uniform pricing across all customers (e.g., "national pricing") (2) segment-specific pricing, and then (3) deal-specific pricing.

If your industry is about to undergo such a migration, you must try to be one step ahead. By being more astute in contextual pricing, you will be closer to the ultimate pricing end state (deal specific). Commodity plastics is an industry where pricing is already in the third stage: each

sale is deal specific, depending on the degree of substitutability of the
product, transport, timeframe, availability, input costs, etc. Any player
still working on a segment basis only will find it wins only unprofitable
orders. Specificity is key as deals go down to the warehouse level.

Another element of the level of play is the full competitive suite.
For instance, a firm selling the second-best audit system for accounting firms faced severe price pressure when the competitor repeatedly
updated and improved its product. To counter this pressure, the firm
grew the unit of purchase (bundle) to include not only the audit manual
and procedures but also its document management system linked in
with project management software. This altered the field of play, so
no longer were the superior qualities of the competitor's audit package
determinative. The company's superior document-management system
trumped the audit system, and price pressure was reduced, for the
moment anyhow.

If you can change the level of play, then price pressure can be
reduced. For instance, Bloomberg killed the incumbent financial-
information service Quotron by eschewing bundling of information with
telecommunications or hardware. This spotlighted the core information
functionality—and let Bloomberg win. We find that this sort of de-layer-
ing is common as new industries mature, and former market creators lag
in technology and pricing.

Another tactic is reduced comparability. Buyers are best at comparing like with like, such as comparing product to product, or service to
service. Mixing product and service makes the comparison harder. So if
your company is facing pressure on a product, offering an intangible with
a product can blunt comparisons. For instance, warranties are sometimes
useful in suppressing price pressures. Volvo, Volkswagen, and others
reacted to aftermarket competition for replacement mufflers with a "lifetime" warranty. A close look at the details of these plans shows they have
a large number of exceptions, but the plans have helped keep replacement business at their dealers.

> At what level is the battle happening? Is the
> context the deal, the segment, or a national
> level of play? The product or the bundle?

Summary

The more you look at price pressures, the more it appears that the villains of customer buying power and competitive initiatives thrive mainly because someone left the door open for the thieves to enter the building. Sometimes the more thematic explanation for price pressure is a lack of product understanding and pricing precision. Many times a close look at how buyers make decisions will suggest a way to avoid price pressure and competitive defections.

Notes

1. King Herold Godwinson of England repulsed a major Viking invasion with the cry "Let us kill only wet Vikings!" Meaning that the time to solve the problem was before they were fully ashore. Stephen Lipton, head of a global financial services outsourcing firm, similarly commented that timing was critical to major outsourcing wins. Dialogue with potential clients is most effective when the notion of outsourcing is first considered, and similarly dialogue with existing clients is most useful before a competitive offer is placed before them.

2. A business-to-consumer example of the same idea was employed by Johnson & Johnson in its baby shampoo business. In that case, the competitor offered a specialized application, so J&J offered coupons and promotions in all the places it knew the new entrant would target consumers. Because of superior market knowledge (an incumbent advantage, usually) and deep pockets, however, it preempted the new entrant, who eventually gave up. See Chapter 14 for more on how to construct a risk model.

3. In some cases, antitrust lawsuits or other nonpricing actions may be the answer. As an average across many studies, we find that rarely are there more than 24 percent of accounts or customers at risk because of price. This is a lower number than estimates usually obtained from surveys or sales reps. Why? Surveys are often flawed and respondents game them. It is the same with sales rep opinions.

4. Evidence of this comes from logistical regression of win/loss and price differences, and is confirmed by hundreds of buyer

interviews. Note that you need to flip the price delta in predicting the likelihood of a win to obtain the right logit outcome.

5. While the military is not known for excellent pricing or for producing profits, it is a good role model of how to focus on hurting your competition. During the Cold War, the United States and the Soviet navies developed very focused shadowing tactics. Next to every U.S. aircraft carrier, the Soviets stationed a cruiser to sink the carrier in the event of war. The United States then stationed a couple of destroyers next to the Soviet cruiser, to sink it in the event of war. In some operational theaters, the Soviets then deployed smaller torpedo boats to sink the destroyers. While this was ridiculed by some observers, it does demonstrate a ruthless dedication to specific threats.

PART 2

Pricing for Poets and Profit Maximizers

Chapter 6

Price Structure

My new book is coming out soon. It'll be the usual rubbish, but it won't cost much. That is the bargain we are going to strike with you.

—JOHN LENNON, BEATLES CHRISTMAS MESSAGE, 1965

Price structures, sometimes called price models, are what translate events into a dollar amount. Structure can also be defined as the terms under which you sell your service or good. A simple "flat" price structure is a transfer of ownership with a specific price tag. Other price structures are more complicated, and can be considered the "formula" by which the transaction will command cash flows. More complex sales may have components of a flat sale price, plus components which are variable with usage (by the unit, by the input, by the event, by the action, etc.)

Sellers regularly ignore their market's price structure preferences in the name of internal convenience. Frequently we see evidence that some part of the market wants to pay for goods and services in a particular structure, but since that is not how billing systems are set up, marketing plans are constructed or profitability plans are quantified, and the sellers ignore the buyers.

71

If all the market's suppliers uniformly ignore a particular pricing preference, little of the harm from poor-fitting price structures is readily apparent in standard corporate market tracking. The market may be smaller than it could be, but that can be hard to prove. Certainly, it does not appear in financial reporting.

If a major supplier breaks ranks or there is a substantial new entrant, however, the market will tend to reward that supplier for providing it what it wants. Our experience has been that often large companies scoff at evidence that a market segment desires a particular price structure, but follows slowly when proof surfaces in the form of lower growth or share loss, buttressing the argument for price structure change.[1]

Examples of where managers felt confident about their price structure included telephony (until prepaid cards), music (until iTunes), insurance (until GEICO), and publishing (until e-readers.) Examples encompass both consumer and industrial goods.

As a more in-depth example, consider the mobile telephony (cell phone) market. Conventional wisdom for years was that users wanted flat rate plans, and management considered churn and pressures on rates independent of price structure. When AT&T introduced "rollover minutes," industry pundits derided this as a gimmick, not realizing that it represented a material shift in pricing structure. Rollover minutes effectively converted fixed monthly plans to variable (by-the-minute) plans. All in all, it amounted to a fundamental price change.

To see how this change in terms was fundamental, consider how customer-calling volume, especially among moderate-usage-level subscribers, varies by month. This meant that for many customers, their plans were too small some months and too large other months, as they ran over minute caps or came nowhere near them. Allowing excess minutes as credits for later months countered customer awareness that they were being forced to pay for minutes they would not use in many cases—and paying for unused services is not popular with buyers.

Figure 6-1 illustrates how rollover credits work. Usage in minutes is represented as a fluctuating (jagged) line, and a fixed-minutes pricing plan as a dashed line. Because it appears to preserve minutes during low-usage months and credits those minutes to high-usage months, consumers find that rollover minutes turn a fixed plan into one that accommodates variable usage.

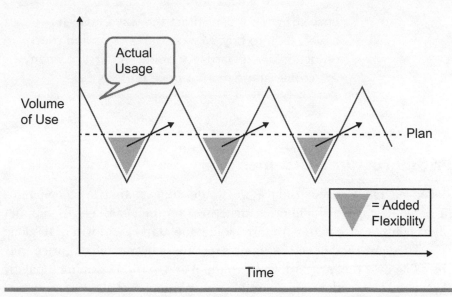

Figure 6-1 Illustration of how "rollover" credits converted a fixed plan to a variable plan.

The benefits of this plan for AT&T were material. Credit Suisse praised the plan in its Great Brands report and attributed a portion of AT&T's subscriber growth to the plan; other analysts saw the plan as a bulwark against customer outchurn.[2] On both counts, it was a price structure innovation that benefited the innovating company.

An industrial example of structure propelling share shift is jet engines. Rolls Royce, behind GE in share, began to sell engines under the "power by the hour" price structure. So, instead of selling a $2 million engine to an airline, and parts and service as needed, the plan sells for example, 100,000 hours of engine operating time, or a number of flights, for a sum of $65 million covering all costs of the engine for those hours.[3]

This program has proven very successful for Rolls Royce and has been rolled out to several families of engines. Customers have also been enthusiastic about the new structure as it fits their needs better than simple sales. Another example of a market where buyers have chosen the variable output over purchase of a device is solar power—one vendor successfully went from selling solar cells to selling kilowatts.

Price structure must reflect the way in which
buyers wish to buy. Market share gains and churn
reduction are rewards for being the first company
to accommodate market price preferences.

Price Structure Fundamentals

Based on many price studies, we would suggest that few companies
are able to impose single price structures on their markets. If supplier
plans conflict with market requirements, the market will win in the long
run. The most fundamental split of structure is between fixed price (pay
the same over time, regardless of volume) and variable pricing ("pay by
the drink"). A seller can also offer a combination of the two. When is
each structure appropriate?

The rule is that high-volume purchasers often want to buy under
a flat price ("all you can eat"); low-volume purchasers often want to
buy under variable ("pay by the drink") plans. Members of each group
are cognizant of being either a high- or a low-volume purchaser and so
believe that they are likely to pay more or less depending on the structure. For instance, high-volume purchasers appear to believe that they
will be denied the benefit of economies of scale if forced to buy under a
variable plan. Low-volume purchasers may fear that if lumped together
with high-volume purchasers (or users) in a fixed price plan, they will
be assigned too high a price relative to their actual consumption.[4]

So one factor in the market is that price structure must often relate
to volume. There is another factor, however: seller profitability. The economic literature shows that where sellers can get a two-part tariff (i.e.,
charge both on a variable *and* a fixed basis), they tend to be able to
extract higher revenues. This is because the second fixed tariff allows
the seller to extract the "gains to trade," or the triangle in the supply
and demand illustrations we all remember from college,[5] as shown in
Figure 6-2.

So sellers should be looking for opportunities to sell under a two-part
tariff so as to maximize profit. Usually sellers with market power can do
so, until that market power fades away:

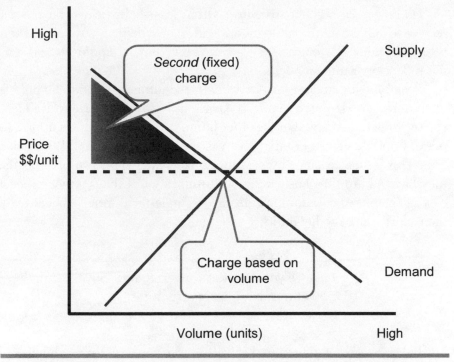

Figure 6-2 Gains from adding second tariff: classical economic demonstration of why two price charges can capture more value.

- Before competition, rental car companies charged by the mile (variable) and by the day (fixed). Now they can charge only by the day, and some minor (and changing) set of add-on fees.
- Before hyper-competition, telephone rates were set by distance and time, now they are only flat rate.
- Before deregulation and competition, banks charged both flat fees (e.g., required balances, yearly fees) and rates linked to volume (wire transfers, amounts borrowed, etc.). Now only one measure is typically applied.

So a happy seller is able to impose a two-part charging mechanism. But the seller desire to maximize profit is sometimes counterbalanced by the desire of most buyers to pay as little as possible.

Do buyers care about structure? Often less sophisticated buyers *say* they care only about the ultimate price level. While that may reflect their conscious point of view, it is not a very savvy buying approach and may not reflect their ultimate behavior.

When buying under a two-part tariff, the ultimate price to be paid is often a mystery. If you're renting a car for a day at $60 per day, it's clear you're going to pay $60. On the other hand, if you're renting a car for $45 per day and 32 cents per mile, it is less clear what the final bill will look like. This is one reason why cost minimizers will shun two-part tariffs: they have a hard time ensuring cost minimization if they cannot forecast costs. Therefore, cost minimizers favor single-tariff prices because of their clarity and predictability.

Balance your market power against buyer power in setting price structures.

Pulling together these market rules, you can visualize a high-level architecture, or roadmap, of price structure linked to how buyer and sellers interact. Somewhat to our surprise, we have found a remarkable consistency across markets, matching the high-level roadmap. The roadmap is based on the two contextual fundamentals: your competitive strength and the volume of purchase contemplated, as illustrated below in Figure 6-3.

Begin reading the road map, left to right, by assessing the price sensitivity of your customers. If you do not have market power (i.e., buyers will defect to other vendors), you must accede to simple fixed *or* simple variable pricing. If, on the other hand, you have market power, you should decide on a two-part pricing structure (left side of map).

Then you must consider the purchase volumes of your customers. Are high-volume customers able to buy under a relatively fixed plan? Are small- or low-volume customers able to buy in a variable way? If not, consider offering price plans under which each customer can buy more in the manner he or she wishes. If your company has little market power, offer a pure fixed plan to volume buyers. If your company has substantial power, with volume buyers, have a two-part tariff but bias the split more towards the fixed-price charge.

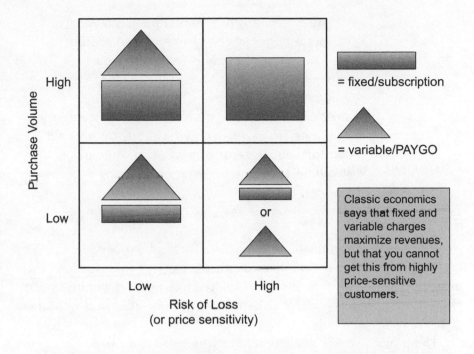

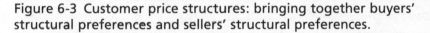

Figure 6-3 Customer price structures: bringing together buyers'
structural preferences and sellers' structural preferences.

For instance, echoing the examples earlier, you might license *commodity* cloud computing software either on a monthly fixed-price plan *or*
a per-use plan. With a little market power, you should be able to add in
a sliver of a monthly fee on top of the per-use plan, and some variable
fees on top of the fixed-price plan. With more market power, the balanced
two-part structures become optimal.

Depending on the diversity of your market, you may be able to sell
under one structure (homogenous market), or you may have to offer all
four versions of fixed/variable pricing structures (diverse market). Where
possible, try to adjust to the buyer's volume and preferred structure—no
benefit comes from needlessly thwarting buyer preferences. If satisfying
customers is a concern at your company and you do not offer the indicated
roadmap price structure to customers, consider testing a price structure
like this in your market.

> Where a company has market power, it will
> impose a two-part charging system. Where it has
> little power, it can only offer a single-part tariff.
> The managerial logic behind this is intuitive:
> where sellers have power, they control price
> structures; where buyers have power (choice), they
> eliminate structures with which they do not feel
> comfortable, in favor of easy price comparison.

Elements of Structure

Now that we have outlined a powerful structural framework, the next question is: just what are the elements that comprise the one or two charging elements? There are literally hundreds of price structure options. However, the main points of departure can be summarized into about eight buckets.

These price structure elements are listed in Figure 6-4. This figure also shows how the different elements are interlinked in the sense that you may need to consider how, for example, chargeback of your costs links to whether you charge on a fixed or variable basis. As another example, tactical structures which draw buyers toward increased purchase quantities can allow for much more aggressive introductory strategies.

Often companies focus on too few elements of structure. Sometimes discounting and promotion are the sole focus of managers. Smarter companies leverage the entire suite of elements of price. For instance, the chairman of GE recently exhorted his managers to pay more attention to postpurchase economics, such as tax credits and government subsidies for wind power and alternative energy.

The rewards to the right structure are twofold: growth and price level. This should not be a surprise, because pricing is about revenue outcomes, and greater market success and optimal transaction price are two of the most common objectives in pricing.

Changes in the "Unit of Purchase"

The "unit of charging" often has unexploited potential for revenue improvement. Let's take a close look at a couple of examples of changes in units of purchase and their results.

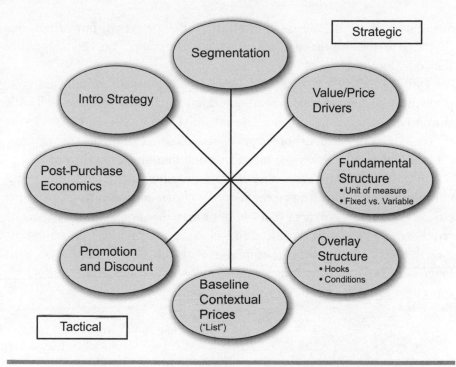

Figure 6-4 Structure "daisy": major categories of price structure and common linkages.

First example: an online B2B service provider changed its structure from a single per-user price to two prices: "regular" and "lite" user counts. The demarcation between the two was based on the user's number of hours online. The two levels allowed the provider to capture revenues from occasional users who otherwise would not have been deemed worth their own user ID, *and* it allowed a somewhat higher price for heavy users who derived a lot more value from the service.

In this example, the context that shaped buyer satisfaction was the *internal* company comparisons of value and average price per user. When you look at it from an internal customer view, one single user price is often a poor match for some users—with a single price (the average price) per light user that is in excess of the value (in this case, measured by hours of use) obtained from the service. The fact that many heavy users obtained excess value compared with the average price does not fully offset that apparent unfairness—excess value is often not as salient in the overall satisfaction as a shortfall. Whether overall fair or not, the shortfalls between price and value get the attention. This relationship is shown in Figure 6-5.

Units of price measure always have implications for how buyers view price but are often taken for granted and left static for long periods. That's okay when the unit of measure works well for your company, otherwise it's something to correct. Not surprisingly, it is often the implicit points of comparison, driven by choice of unit, which matter most to buyers.

In the case of the B2B online-service provider, the benefits of moving to two types of pricing units were reduced churn and capturing some new customers from competitors that did not make this price change in unit of purchase. The long-term result of this change in structure was a five-year growth trend with a compund annual growth rate (CAGR) of 38 percent. Price structure was the single most important driver of the provider's revenue and profit growth over that time period.

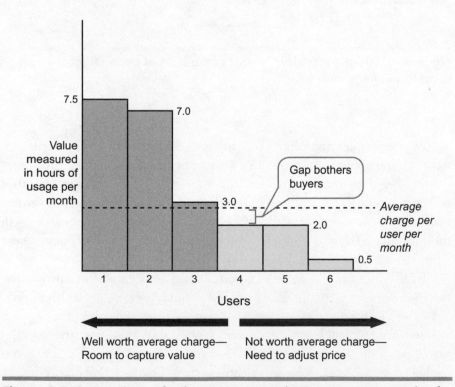

Figure 6-5 Comparison of value to average charge per user: match of unit to internal perception of cost.

Second example: a large industrial specialty chemical company sold its product by the barrel and provided material levels of in-kind support to users, in the forms of containers, technical support, storage, transport, and marketing assistance. Sales were under longer-term contracts based on dollars per barrel. Upon examination, it turned out that one category (segment) of buyer would repeatedly make liberal use of the in-kind support but then fall short on volume estimates. The result was that on a per-barrel basis, net of in-kind support, this segment would underperform price and profit targets.

By separating out the in-kind (fixed) services from the per-barrel (variable) services for the underperforming segment, the provider fixed its pricing problem. Its price negotiations benefited because under the new approach the supplier was relatively indifferent on forecasted volumes described by the buyers. Since the errant segment was easily identified, this practice was soon adopted by most industry participants. The lift in margins was over 4 percent, which is dramatic in that industry.

> Adopting price structures suited to your markets
> can pay material dividends in share and price level.

Price structure helps companies win in the market. But do companies with better price structure always win? No. Better structure is typically measured by the ebbs and flows of market position and comparative discounting.

While better price structure will *help* a company end up with the largest market share, it does not follow that the best price structure is always associated with the best selling product. Why? Why do we have to measure the trend, not the end result?

This is because, much to our chagrin as pricers, there is more to demand than price structure. Things like product and competition do matter. For instance, most purchasers of downloadable movies and audio books would prefer to own them, with full rights to copy them. However this is not how movies and books have been offered to the market, so this is not a choice for buyers, and so price structure does not play a role—yet. Similarly, until the 1980s, IBM primarily leased computers, despite preferences by many parts of the market to purchase. Demand for IBM computers was still very strong, and IBM was the clear market leader. But once IBM offered a choice between leasing and buying, buying computers quickly prevailed over leasing. It's the *comparison* that shows market preference, not absolute volumes.

> Market structure preference and results are best measured by *relative* purchasing patterns and differences in price pressure.

Summary

Structure is the heart of contextual pricing and the formula for long-lived pricing results. Price level changes can give you an instant lift, but such an option is not always open to your company. Price structure improvement is usually an option because many markets are starved for the right structures. Managers looking for a solution to market challenges should always use structure as an improvement lever.

Notes

1. Of course, sometimes the rest of the industry will not follow an innovator's example. That is fine if the innovation is beneficial to you, but not so good when the innovation attempts to do something unpopular—e.g., attempting to discipline the market. AT&T's capping of data usage by subscribers so far has not been emulated and has been called a PR disaster. AT&T might have tried a more graduated strategy, beginning with loose bands and eventually letting users grow into them. Abrupt banding called attention to the change and so formed an unfavorable context.
2. Credit Suisse, "Great Brands of Tomorrow," March 30, 2004. One blogger on the Applease site commented: "The best thing about AT&T is rollover minutes."
3. "'Power by the Hour': Can Paying Only for Performance Redefine How Products Are Sold and Serviced?" See knowledge@ Wharton, February 21, 2007. Other markets where what used to be sold as a product can now be bought as a service include

electrical power. "Pay for the Power, Not the Panels," *The New York Times*, March 26, 2008, p. H1. Transforming what used to be a product into a service is an expanding phenomenon.

4. Note how the variability in demand for small users, and the consistency of demand for large users, is consistent with this split in preferences. Groups of users/buyers tend to have more predictable demand because the "law of large numbers" means individual fluctuations in usage cancel each other out.

5. Well, some of us. If your memory is foggy, please see the great article by Walter Y. Oi: "A Disneyland Dilemma: Two Part Tariffs for a Mickey Mouse Monopoly," *The Quarterly Journal of Economics*, vol. 85, February 1971, pp. 77–96.

Chapter 7

Scientific Bundling and Tiering

A new scientific truth does not triumph by convincing its opponents and making them see the light, but rather because its opponents eventually die, and a new generation grows up that is familiar with it.

—MAX PLANCK, C. 1949

Few pricing and product tasks are more important than combining multiple products and services into a single offer—a practice known as bundling. Technology and cost-cutting are creating a world in which many customers now prefer such integrated solutions, and this demand must be met in order for companies to stay competitive. Also, bundling is a way to rapidly create a unique offer and capture the benefits of differentiation.

Few pricing exercises are more context-sensitive than bundling. This is because bundling in fact poses a direct question to the potential buyer: "Do you want to buy these products *in combination*?" Then buyers ask themselves whether they really need *all* the bundle elements now; if the answer is only "maybe," what *reward* would they need for expanding their purchase?

What Constitutes a Bundle?

While many managers think of their market offer as a single product or service, often it is really a combination of products and services. Every market offer is a bundle. Sometimes a rigorous listing of components may surprise product management. For instance, the product management of a leading implantable contraceptive device said with assurance that no bundling was possible—or legal—because of FDA regulations. Yet, in fact, the offer on the market *was* a bundle of many services, each of which could be tweaked to optimize the bundle for differences among ob-gyn buyer segments.

When considering a product, note that very rarely is the product available without support, without financing or payment terms, without delivery, without packaging, without guarantees, etc. Thus, the birth control device actually comprised many components, both tangible and intangible, as seen in the decomposition of a single "product" shown in Figure 7-1.

The primary advantage in understanding the components is that it expands the discussion and the strategic choices. If you regard a bundle

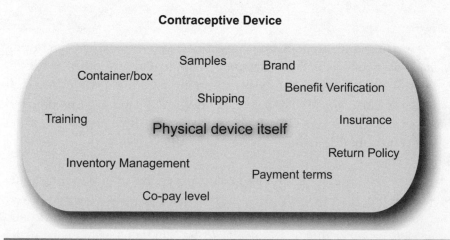

Figure 7-1 Contraceptive device: almost all products and services are bundles and offer management choice.

as inseparable, then it is much more difficult to adapt price to context or segment. So thinking carefully about bundling often moves the discussion from merely a price level question to one which provides sellers with more flexible market tools.

For instance, in the case of the contraceptive there could be many economically important variations. While the device itself could not be varied for different buyer segments, other parts of the bundle could be—like the box. To discriminate between low-volume buyers and high-volume buyers, the manufacturer could make the box very big or small. Big is bad because it fills up storage closets. For high-volume buyers, only the first boxes might be large and the remaining ones could be small—a rationale for the box sizes would be that the first few boxes need voluminous product documentation, while later boxes might have less. It's a perfect excuse to volume price-discriminate. The same approach applies to shipping, samples, benefit verification, copay levels, and other elements of the "bundle." While marketing may think it is selling a unitary good, it's actually a bundle—and that allows much better price targeting.

> **Almost every offer is a bundle when you consider it carefully.**

Pricing *itself* can also lump together previously stand-alone sales into bundles. For instance, a leading supplier of floorboards for residential housing understood it had a range of ways to sell the product to developers. Traditionally, boards were sold individually or by the palette, FOB.[1] They could also be sold by the truckload, by the development (an "all-you-can-eat" contract specific to a project), or even through a requirements contract for a developer for a period of time.

The pricing dynamics change with progressively larger bundles. When buying by the palette, the seller found that specials at the local Home Depot would eat into his sales. Worse yet, the company's reputation was at risk when inferior substitute boards underperformed. When sold on a requirements basis, there was no builder benefit to buying cheap boards anywhere—the incremental cost of boards from the manufacturer was zero!

Bundle Components Should Be Complementary

Bundles are held together by what we call glue.[2] The glue can take the form of price, product integration, promotion, or channel. For instance, travel involving airplanes and hotels can be bundled along all four dimensions through travel agencies: one price, one trip, promoted jointly and sold jointly (a "hard" bundle). On the other hand, the bundle can be much more limited: after you have made your (stand-alone) flight reservation with an airline, you might be asked "Will you need a rental car with that? May we transfer you to a rental car company?" In that case, the only link is channel, so less glue (a "soft" bundle).

In general, bundles using less glue are lower risk. Success rates for hard bundles are surprisingly low. This is because buyers will need to see the benefits to a bundle buy, the bundle needs to be priced right, and the bundle actually needs to work. The latter issue is sometimes underestimated, but remember that the combination of car + car radio was attempted for many years with no success until a small company called Motorola developed a filter for screening out the electronic noise of the car engine from the radio reception.

In that case, the core (primary driver) of the car + radio bundle was certainly the car. Experience has shown that the vast majority of bundles have a structure, or taxonomy, which includes a core (the primary component motivating the purchase) and add-on components. Because buyers know they would have bought the core element anyhow, they tend to look for discounts on the add-on elements.[3] If those elements do not appear to have an adequate discount, then the bundle will fail.

For practical bundling purposes, most bundles can be analyzed based on a core + add-on taxonomy. Figure 7-2 shows such a structure, in this case looking at a cable TV package.

In this illustration, the core is plain old ("linear") video programming. Most of the add-ons, such as premium channels, are commonly seen as complementary to the core, and so they're favored by buyers with only modest discounts.

For pricers, frequently it's the non-complementary bundle elements that are important. In the illustrated figure, a possible non-complement is landline cable telephony. Cable telephony (VoIP) is not seen as a good add-in by some (high-end) buyer segments because they don't

Bundle Taxonomy

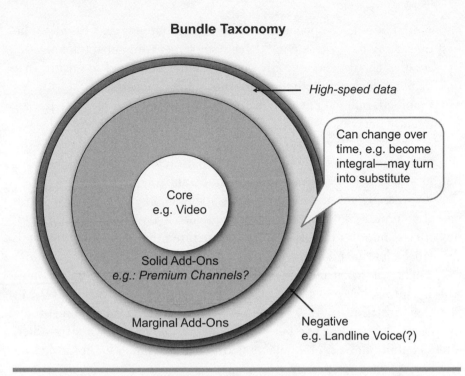

Figure 7-2 Taxonomy of a video + broadband + telephony bundle.

trust telephone service from a cable company—for them it may be an unwanted component. High-speed data today is seen as a complement to video, but that may change if television over the Internet (IPTV), like Netflix or Hulu, becomes a leading choice. Then video and high-speed data may morph from complements to substitutes, as many customers may conclude they need only the data service.

> Almost all bundles have a core component that drives a segment's purchase. To design and price bundles, you must identify that core.

How can prospective bundlers estimate how a buyer will evaluate a bundle? One approach is to examine the stand-alone purchase patterns of potential bundle component candidates for grouping into a bundle. The first question is: are these candidates complements or substitutes?

Bundles should contain only complements. You need to ensure that only bundle elements that go together are offered together. If substitutes are combined, rational buyers will see that they are being asked to pay for redundant components. That kind of offer will either be rejected by the market or severely penalized with a higher bundle discount. This is why successful bundles include pickup trucks + trailer hitches (complements) but not rail tickets + airline tickets (usually substitutes.)

Surprisingly, intuition is not always adequate to evaluate whether two potential bundle components are complements or substitutes. Verizon has offered bundles of optional calling features that have included both the caller identification (CID) and the return call (*69) features. While they might, on the surface, appear to be complements (one lets you know who is calling, the other lets you dial earlier callers by hitting *69), in fact they are used in very similar ways and are viewed as substitutes by potential buyers. This became apparent to Verizon when bundled offers containing both products tended to achieve much lower marketing yields.

How to bundle "like with like" operates from the customer point of view. For instance, usually department stores promote like with like clothing by economic tier. A mannequin will typically have a dress, blouse, and handbag from the same strata of fashion. When a store foolishly put a $500 hat in the same display as $100 hats, the expensive hat rapidly became shop-worn as visitors handled it, but did not buy it. That promotional display mistakenly bundled substitutes, not complements.[4]

The measure that indicates whether different components are complements or substitutes is correlation. Correlation will show whether different bundle candidates tend to sell together, or if one tends to cannibalize the other. When increases of sales of product A are associated with increases of sales of product B, it's a complement. This will manifest itself as a positive correlation.[5]

Note that correlation of sales, not percentage cross-sell, is the more reliable measure of bundle complements: you can have positive cross-sell but no real complements if you have a strong sales program. In other words, at the cost of goodwill and price pressure, a powerful seller can force suboptimum bundles on its customers. This is why frequently the effectiveness of bundles needs to be measured over time. If a bundle is associated with a decrease in market share or an increase in discounting, it's a bad bundle.

Bundles should be comprised only of complements, not substitutes.

What Is the Value of a Bundle?

It's widely known that bundles tend to sell at a discount off the sum of the stand-alone bundle component prices. If you sell a software program + training as a bundle, the combined price is likely to be less than the sum of each sold separately. One reason for this is because not everyone wants a bundle, and in some cases many of the buyers are unsure that they will take advantage of both components. Therefore, buyers must be offered a discount to buy a bundle. This means that through a form of alchemy, the market value of some bundle components instantly change when they go from being stand-alone sales to being part of a bundle—the context has changed.

That discount may be a reasonable cost for sellers. Your company, may welcome exchanging a 20 percent discount in return for channel efficiencies or reach. How do you calculate the bundle discount? In certain circumstances, use of correlation will also allow a measure of the bundled value of a bundle component to the market. Generally, the value of a given bundle component can be calculated based on the formula:

Value of the bundled component = Stand-alone value of the component × Correlation of component to core component of bundle

Thus, for instance, if the correlation between regular cola and diet cola is 0.9, each is priced at \$9 per gallon when sold stand-alone, and regular cola is the "core" of this bundle, then a bundle of the two should be:

Baseline price of the bundle = Regular cola @ \$9 per gallon
(\$9 × 1.0) + Diet cola @ \$9 × 0.9 = \$9 + (\$9× 0.9) =
\$17.10 per bundle (2 gallons)

This logic is the basis for scientific bundle pricing. It will weed out negative contribution additions to a bundle. Adding together all the component values gives you a first cut at a market price for the bundle.

> The market value of some bundle components instantly changes when they go from being stand-alone sales to being part of a bundle. There are scientific ways to estimate the new value of a component after it is included in a bundle offer.

Bundling Mismatches and Mistakes

Finding new ways to bundle your products and services is very worthwhile. Bundles can increase share, reduce loss, and improve efficiency. Yet pitfalls lurk because the more novel the bundle, the greater the danger of bundling missteps. There are two dangers in particular: (1) mismatching the various elements of a bundle and (2) mispricing the offer. If a bundle includes elements no one really wants, customers won't buy the bundle without a deep discount. Similarly, if a company combines products or services without enough thought as to price, the result is often gross overpricing or underpricing.

In helping clients with their bundles, we find there are four marketing mistakes which typically lead to mismatches and mispricing:

- Failing to create bundles for special purposes
- Making bundles too big
- Using tiering instead of bundles
- Failing to innovate on bundle definitions

Sometimes mistakes are obvious, but often, the more successful the core product, the more its supporting bundle components can fall short of the optimum while appearing to be successful (i.e., "a rising tide floats all boats"—even unseaworthy ones).[6] We'll examine each category of mistake, in turn, showing how things can go wrong and what to do about it.

Failing to Create Bundles for Special Purposes

Bundles can have very different objectives. Bundle missions can include reducing customer churn, displacing competitors, rendering competitor pricing irrelevant, increasing channel efficiency, or deterring aggressive price behavior by upstarts. Such differing objectives typically demand different bundle structures; a company may even wish to have a suite of bundles available for specific competitive situations. We'll look at two special purposes in particular: bundles intended for attack and bundles intended for defense.

Attack Bundles. An attack bundle seeks to displace a competitor; to achieve success the bundle must better the incumbent vendor's price/value proposition, typically via a lower price. The price must naturally account for switching costs as well, but still preserve long-term profitability. This can be done by *crafting better and leaner bundles for core users*, while often the incumbent is distracted trying to expand bundles to attract *marginal (additional) users*.

For instance, health insurers have added on a number of features to make their coverage satisfy all requirements. An interesting example is "gastric bypass" surgery for insured people who wish to lose weight and find that they cannot stem their eating. This expensive surgery shortens the intestines and so cuts down on food absorption. While a few of the insured will find this feature useful, to many it will be quite unnecessary. This means that for most market segments, a new insurance offer could drop gastric bypass without much notice. Similarly, a new auto policy might cut towing services or legal support without much notice or a notebook computer system might offer only minimal battery capacity. Each of these measures would lower costs and allow a lower price. A lower price is the opening wedge for competitive entry in many accounts. Giving core users what they want, while the incumbent is addressing marginal (but perhaps vocal) concerns often is a successful entry strategy.

Note that this lower price is not a discount; it is merely offering less. The rationale for this offer approach is twofold:

- Many users may never need the added features, but will appreciate the lower price.
- Those who will need these services can add them back at a later date.

An attack bundle is usually focused on the core component and may strip out low-value "add-on" bundle components.

Defense Bundles. Another type of bundle is defensive in nature and typically employed by market leaders and incumbents. Very often, market leaders must fend off upstarts; in doing so, they have a wider range of options than they typically realize. One such option—which we call the Bear Hug—is especially useful for discouraging upstart entrants from continuing to offer lowball prices to customers.

The objective of the Bear Hug is to devalue competitor offers. For instance, in a corporate governance software infrastructure market where companies typically purchased a dozen or so core services, the incumbent offered all the services. The upstart's strategy involved offering fewer services—only three core offers—at lowball prices.

Where the upstart had made inroads, the incumbent successfully defended itself by offering customers an "all-you-can-eat" bundle. This customized bundle consisted of all services currently being purchased by that account—but at a price equal to the full market rate for the relevant products not overlapping with the competitor's product set, plus a bargain rate on the *overlapping* products offered by the upstart. In other words, if a major customer buys products A, B, C, and D from your company, and purchases product E from a competitor, the new price would include all five (A, B, C, D and E) for the old price of A, B, C and D.

A defense bundle invoice to customers showed below-competitive pricing for overlapping services. That bundle was hard to resist, and revenues steadily increased. Because the offer was sold selectively to complex larger accounts that were already splitting their purchases between the incumbent and the upstart, it was immune to comparisons by other customers; there was no danger of a general price meltdown. The pricing sent a strong message to the upstart challenger not to poach on existing customer relationships. Most important, the upstart could not retaliate because the bundle product scope was wider than its own offers.

Many companies react to low-price competitive offers by tieing a weaker product with *one* stronger product. This is bad practice. Unlike the comprehensive Bear Hugs, such bundles tend to be mispriced because of poor component fit and/or the ratio of weak to strong products is often too high. If the bundle price does not accurately reflect the value of bundle components, then—like a poorly fitting shoe—it will start to chafe. Customers will tire of the forced marriage between strong and weak bundle components, and market share will begin to erode.

One example comes from the high-technology arena, where a producer of optimization software for computers, Server Farms, bundled in high-priced support and maintenance charges as well. This plan worked well for a few years, but as soon as rivals matched the software, cancellations rose because the maintenance was overpriced and customers resented having to buy both. Ironically, the software company knew of the growing problem but held on to the lucrative maintenance in order to reach initial public offering (IPO) revenue targets. Today the company is an also-ran in that market space.

> **Ad hoc bundling to defend a troubled product usually fails.**

Making Bundles Too Big

An example of overbundling comes from an information service that garnered a premium position in the early days of its market, pioneering the conversion of forms and print to electronic. The service constructed its bundles around federal materials and grew by adding such further legal jurisdictional categories as states, international, and arbitration.

The jurisdiction-based growth of the bundle made sense in the short term—each additional element added incremental revenues—yet the increments became smaller and smaller each time, particularly as niche competitors established offers in more categories. Soon the sales force began discounting heavily, unable to sell the value of the incremental components.

The solution to this situation was to break up the legacy bundle to match component values to user needs and reprice accordingly. In fact, when this information service provider split its comprehensive bundle into functional sections, it obtained price uplifts for virtually all customers.

Why did this happen? Because although the individual smaller bundles had lower list prices than the larger bundle, most customers needed multiple new bundles—and the smaller, more relevant bundles carried *much* higher value. The internal consistency of each specialized bundle was much higher than that of the old, fat, flabby bundle. It turned out that almost no customer had needed most of the big bundle, which is why they'd negotiated so fiercely to reduce its price.

Another compelling example of overbundling comes from the cable television industry. Although subscribers welcomed the first few waves of channel expansions, enthusiasm dimmed as packages went far beyond the number of channels they would ever watch. A much better approach would be to sell narrower, specialized packages, each extracting value from particular audiences. However, management is often reluctant to create specialized bundles, citing operational and cost constraints. Also, without the ability to actually calculate component added value, many managers ignore market evidence that "less is more."

Packing too many components into a bundle—overbundling—is the most common mistake made by product management at incumbents.

Sometimes operational bundle development costs can be minimized. In many cases when seeking to narrow a bundle, there's no need to touch the product. Often limiting the breadth of the bundle is less important than narrowing the product's value message and price plans. In many cases, customers won't notice they're getting "more" than advertised—and even if they do, complaints are generally few. In other words, actual changes in the product can be minimal: the work is in the message and price, not the actual product. In B2C software, this is particularly easy—just leave components off the menu; you need not delete actual code.

Using Tiering Instead of Bundles

Hierarchical tiering offers is a popular pricing technique. It's actually a form of bundling, but it differs from most bundling initiatives in this respect: rather than build from the ground up, tiering begins with an existing offer, and then adds or strips out features to achieve the end result. Sadly, such additions or subtractions tend to be done blindly.

The value principles are the same as any bundle: try to build a compelling value price proposition for a particular market segment. The purpose is usually to sell to a new tier of customer, but there is another purpose to tiering. Sometimes the purpose of tiering is *not* to sell all the tiers but to show consumers that one of the tiers is a good deal through a tiered context reinforcing the message that they are getting a good deal.

Tiering works quite well when consumers feel they have discretionary spending ability—that is, they can spend more on the features they find appealing (up-tiering). Tiering works less well with buyers faced with highly constrained budgets, who want the lowest price that meets their essential needs.

When customers are reluctant to spend more, a second contextual technique is worth investigating: *linking* bundles so that the purchase of one bundle *must* lead to the purchase of a second bundle. Up-tiering in this manner is a good way to increase revenues either at the time of the initial purchase or later on. The underlying insights are twofold: first, customers will likely experience moments after the initial purchase when added features or bundle elements seem more appealing; second, customers' price sensitivities will vary over time. What seemed unafford-able one day will not be on another. Linked bundles directly help sellers profit from the happy moment when needs are high or price sensitivities are low.

An example of such contextual linking over time comes from the dental supply industry. Here suppliers have found that entry is easy with disposables, such as sponges and tongue depressors. Once that relation-ship is established, hygienist handpieces can be more easily sold. From there surgical handpieces, cosmetics, and cameras are logical next steps in the growth of purchases from dental offices.

Hooks. For this technique to work, structures that we call "hooks" are necessary to encourage customers to voluntarily upgrade. We have found this to be especially true in tough, mature markets. Here are some examples of hooks:

- In the construction industry, many building contractors price their initial bids low but charge high markups for change orders in the midst of construction—when owners have little choice but to pay higher prices.
- LexisNexis sells legal libraries in packages by tribunal and/or geo-graphic region—yet its search mechanism highlights relevant cases in the total legal database, not just by region. Therefore, even if an attorney steadfastly refuses to buy more than the library of his own

state's decisions, he will keep seeing searches that show all cases, from any tribunal. On the eve of an important trial, if the search engine now shows a case outside his library that appears highly relevant, even a very stubborn buyer may decide at that moment to expand his purchase. This factor has led many users of LexisNexis to buy new libraries or to buy specific cases, last minute and undiscounted, at several times the normal subscription price.

- A great consumer example of a hooking mechanism comes from the car rental business. Recently at Los Angeles International Airport (LAX), a sign at the Hertz rental counter explained the following provisions for gasoline:
  - ❐ Gasoline in the vicinity of LAX: $4.29/gallon
  - ❐ Gasoline from Hertz prepaid: $4.04/gallon
  - ❐ Gasoline from Hertz if you return the car less than full: $9.29/gallon

  So, the hook is very clear: if you don't care about expense or are in a hurry when you return the car, Hertz will collect a premium. If you think that is unfair, you have a chance to avoid the charge since Hertz is offering you a bargain rate to begin with. If you turn the bargain rate down, don't complain later!

- Firestone Tire dealers offer tire warranties that exceed the likely usable mileage of its tires. Why? Because the pro rata warranty rebate is well worth it to get former customers back at the dealership at the moment they need new tires.

Migration paths prompted by customers' key needs—the hooks—can be far more effective than price structures founded only on a hierarchy of good, better, and best.

> Where buyers are reluctant to spend, hooking
> works better than hierarchical tiering.

Failing to Innovate on Bundle Definitions

Back to incumbents: another common problem in the bundles of established players is that the bundle definitions no longer effectively communicate value, especially when compared with competitors' offerings: *everyone* is now claiming the same benefits. Worse yet, the market leader may even find that its definitions are being used against it.

For example, a company in the medical-testing market initially grew to prominence by offering services in more cities than did its competitors. This claim was backed by well-equipped facilities in more than 40 states. When competitors arrived on the scene, however, through reciprocal agreements, they laid claim to all 50 states! Even though the competitors' capabilities and quality were inconsistent, customers found the pitch convincing—after all, they had been trained by the incumbent itself to believe that geographic coverage was an important part of the buying decision.

The solution for the incumbent was to redefine its product and message. Promoting depth of equipment, not merely geography, plus using service bundles and pricing to highlight its superior capabilities began to address the problem. Message underscored the low value of mere geographic presence without appropriate equipment and quality.

Depth versus Breadth. One way of describing this idea is that it focuses on depth rather than breadth. Breadth is how customers assess the initial value of an offer; depth comprises the ineffable attributes that customers discover only after experience with the product. This notion applies to any industry: there are always attributes that can't be easily proven or sold up front but must instead be experienced to be believed.

As an example, one transportation concern buys only high-quality Peterbilt trucks, after having discovered that their drivers treat Peterbilts better, with subsequent lower operating costs. This would be tough to prove and quantify ahead of time, but it is now factored into financial decisions. Similarly, television advertisers generally demand evidence or direct experience to assess the effectiveness of media with above-average advertising rates per thousand (CPM). It is the actual propensity of different audiences to buy that is the best evidence. After trial or observing other's results, advertisers will pay premium CPM rates if warranted.

Depth versus breadth is often key in fights between incumbents and challengers. Challengers are typically more innovative—partly because they need to be creative to succeed and partly because they are unconstrained by contracts, tradition, or older computer systems. The classic example of depth versus breadth was the fight between upstart long-distance telephony carrier MCI and incumbent AT&T during the 1980s. AT&T defined a minute of conversation as 60 seconds of talk time; MCI defined it as setup time (ringing, etc.) *and* talk time. Effectively, this meant that MCI had a 57-second minute—and this helped it quote per-minute rates lower than AT&T's.

For challengers, the joy of redefining depth includes the joy of causing competitor managements to throw temper tantrums—but most important, it places a big burden of explanation on the incumbent. Often this burden is insurmountable: for one thing, customers don't care about long technical explanations. It may be better for the incumbent not to acknowledge the upstart at all.

Summary

Bundles are multipurpose instruments that offer sellers many advantages, including the following benefits:

- A bundle may be "stickier" to buyers, and so it may reduce customer defections and churn. Telephony vendors found that when they tied local service with long distance, their churn rates fell: it was more daunting for subscribers to switch their local service—concerns about repairs and other service issues reduced overall churn.
- There may be economies of product scope, either in selling (channel synergies) or the product. For instance, AOL found that including diagnostic applications with its basic service appealed to subscribers *and* actually reduced overall help-desk service costs.
- Bundling may allow the sale of incremental products to groups with diverse product preferences. Thus, if one group places a high value on pizza and the other places a high value on beer, a beer + pizza bundle may sell incremental pizza and beer. Effectively, the bundle combines the value of each and can extract extra value.[7]

Thus, there are many fundamental reasons for companies to bundle, and it is worth considerable managerial effort to get it right. Actually, your company may have little choice to bundle and to get bundling right. Context is the pillar of any bundle pricing.

But bundles are high-risk undertakings. Particularly when scientific bundling analysis is not used, the failure rates are high. For this reason, try soft bundles with relatively less glue (linkages among components) and use the right bundle design techniques—use of correlation and clear bundle missions.

Notes

1. FOB stands for free off board. In other words, the buyer pays the freight.
2. Not a reference to the binding material in the floorboards! Rather a reference to bundle linkage approaches.
3. This can be demonstrated by the sales success rates of different bundles to different segments at different prices. Where there are segments with different cores and there are big differences in stand-alone bundle component prices, then mathematically you can isolate the discount implied by the market that is on the add-on components. For example, a bundle of video (at $60 per month) + phone (at $30 per month) will sell better to the video segment than to the phone-oriented segment.
4. Comments by Ursula H. Moran, top-rated specialty retail analyst, formerly with Sanford C. Bernstein.
5, J. Adams and J. Yellen, "Commodity Bundling and the Burden of Monopoly," *Quarterly Journal of Economics*, vol. 90, No. 3, August 1976, p. 486. This is a seminal work in this area, but full of numbers. To avoid a long discussion of correlation, we note only that the nice thing about correlation is that it has no preconceptions: it just reports relationships. For instance, it turns out that a slumping economy is correlated to fewer auto fatalities. Who would have expected that, a priori? As the economy slumped in 2005 to 2009, so did car-crash counts. Two researchers at the University of Michigan suggest that during a slump, drivers slow down, and that leads to fewer accidents. "New Puzzle: Why Fewer Are Killed in Car Crashes," *The Wall Street Journal*, December 15, 2010, p. D1 and p. D3. Similarly, the "open-minded" nature of correlation is relevant to bundles because it allows management to test creative new bundles before they get to the market.
6. The penalty for a bad structure is best measured relative to other structures. Similarly, bad bundles will underindex compared with

good ones, and if management has been giving discounts, larger discounts.

7. This concept can be shown to generally increase overall revenues, provided that bundle discounts do not offset the gains to the combination. In simple terms, combining two goods A and B (in a "hard bundle") means that money left on the table because some consumers would have paid more for A can be used to pay for B, and vice versa. See http://en.wikipedia.org/wiki/Pricing_of _Bundles_and_Packages.

Chapter 8

Dangerous Ways to Reduce or Increase Price

Now, now my good man, this is no time for making enemies.

—VOLTAIRE, ON HIS DEATHBED, IN RESPONSE TO A PRIEST
WHO ASKED HIM TO RENOUNCE SATAN

Most managers know there is a right way and a wrong way to change price, and a right time and a wrong time to change it. The difficult part is determining how and when.

Dangerous price moves can destroy your business, either with sharply reduced revenues and/or competitive inroads. Yet many managers have little awareness as to which are the most dangerous price actions. For instance, the most dangerous price move by far is lowering your price, because it can alienate customers.

The Case against Lowering Prices

Many businesses lower their prices, expecting to stave off competition and win new customers; however, rarely is this so. For instance, a B2B company with a leading position in managing incorporations and legal registrations listened to customer complaints that its fees were too high and were an obstacle in using its services. The company lowered its prices by over 30 percent and was chagrined to find that business volume remained absolutely flat—existing customers had no need for incremental incorporations, and noncustomers never heard of this bargain because the whole service was far from top of mind.

Another example of the perils of price reduction was the hosiery manufacturer L'eggs, which had observed a high responsiveness to price drops. Reducing its prices, it saw a big uptick in volume, as existing customers bought ahead at lower prices. Before news of the lower prices was fully communicated to *new* customers, however, competitors followed suit with price drops. No competitor won in that sequence of price drops that destroyed profitability for the year.

The fundamental problem, like many issues in pricing, lies in customer awareness. Whatever the objective value of your company's offers, that value does not matter unless customers know about it. Lowered prices require communicating to the world of noncustomers. Doing so may not be easy, despite the best efforts of your sales force or promotions managers. Lowered prices may induce some existing customers to buy more, but often they may already be saturated—it would take a very low price to push customers to buy an additional car, dentist visit, gasoline, telephone line or more ice cream. In some cases, additional volume has nothing to do with price. In some cases, lower pricing is actually damaging, as it prompts buyers to wonder if they did a poor job of negotiating, and may lead some consumers to wonder about quality.

Not so with a price increase. When you raise price, you are going to initially communicate the higher price to existing customers who know something about the value you offer. Yes, a higher price can be challenging, but at least the change affects those who know something about your value (existing customers) or those being targeted with a value message already. Noncustomers may never know the history of changes in price or value, so they are not bothered by it.

Raising and lowering prices are very different—
not symmetrical in any way. Lowering prices has a
much higher communications burden and risk.

Why do many rational managers believe that lowering prices is safe and useful? It's possible that the root of the problem lies with the idea of price elasticity. Price elasticity contains the seductive notion that a single simple number will explain market buying behavior and its relationship to price.[1] This is almost never so. The idea that elasticity could do this is an insult to segmentation and context.

Elasticities have the appeal of seeming to show, in one neat number, the impact of price on volume. Further, they seem to suggest that the reaction to a price increase should match the reaction to a price decrease. While price elasticities do sometimes accurately predict short-term volume changes (e.g., in highly transparent markets such as consumer goods), they cannot say much about strategic changes or opaque markets.

Much safer than a price decrease is a moderate, unsurprising price increase. Even better: a targeted price increase. Best of all: a price increase disguised as a change in price structures. Why is an unsurprising increase good? Because buyers of all demographics share the delusion that prices are linked to costs, and they expect and can tolerate moderate price increases over time. What is "moderate" varies, which is why targeted price increases are better than across-the-board increases. In every market there are some customers on the brink of reducing their purchases and others who would not notice even a substantial increase. A strategic price increase leaves the at-risk segments alone and extracts the greatest increases from the price-unaware.[2]

An exception to the rule that lowering prices is dangerous is lowering someone else's prices. Examples of this include Apple, Amazon, and others who control channels for music, books, and other entertainment. By demanding lower prices from music companies, publishers, and others, these companies have opened up markets and built a solid position for their products. The results for the victims of this market and technological power have not been as positive: witness the destruction of once-enviable margins at Sony, EMI, trade publishers, and others.

Demand Curve

Before any business considers a strategic price decrease, it should study the demand curve for its markets. Demand curves show volumes at different price points and so capture the inflection points where segments behave differently. If a formal demand curve does not seem exciting or mean much to your management teams (although it should), begin with a simple one and educate management on why this is an invaluable tool. (See Chapter 14 for more on how to build a demand curve.)

Strategic price changes attempt to make *permanent* improvements in seller volumes or market position; demand curves coupled with segmentation are very good tools for supporting the strategy, usually at a segment level. Managers must ask themselves which segments they're attempting to add to their base and which segments they need to protect. Each segment, if it's a good segmentation scheme, should be associated with a particular price range and preferred price structure. For instance, in mobile telephony, demographics and propensity to adopt technology clearly define buyer segments and willingness to spend on mobile devices. This links to a usable demand curve and usable prescriptions.

In the demand curve shown in Figure 8-1, note how each part of it is associated with a particular demographic segment. This curve happens to be visitors to tourist attractions in the Atlanta area. The least price-sensitive are business visitors, next is couples, next is nuclear families; the most price-sensitive is large groups, such as clubs or family reunions. When combined with demographic data, demand curves let managers visualize which shifts will happen as they change asking price. The visual combination of a demand curve and segments makes this tool come alive. Unlike elasticities, segments differ in size and so show asymmetries in size of opportunity when raising or lowering price.

Segment-based demand curves apply equally to B2B situations, where different segments of buyers with different characteristics occupy specific places along the demand curve. Of course if your segmentation does not reflect price sensitivity, this will not work, because it's a bad segmentation—and suggests that managers cannot know the benefits of lowering price with any precision. Every segmentation should reflect price.[3]

Before raising or lowering a price (promotions aside), look at a demand curve meshed with segmentation.

Customer Characteristics

In addition to a demand curve linked to segmentation, there are other management programs to improve pricing. Changes in price structure

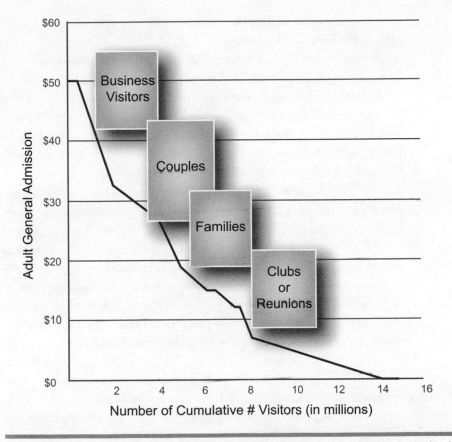

Figure 8-1 Demand curve for Atlanta area attractions: segments linked with demand curves are intuitive and useful management tools.

and level should reflect customer characteristics and your objectives. Three common purposes in shifting price higher or lower, and possible approaches are:

1. *Fixing a "broken" list price.* In many cases companies have let their list prices drift, with automatic price increases and across-the-board increases. This can manifest itself as a large sales discount that has little to do with interaccount differences. By now you are familiar with the shortcomings of the idea of list price, and you may agree that there is no reason to fix the list

price—get rid of it! Replace it with a set of contextually deter-
mined baseline prices instead.

2. *Customer base under pressure.* While some of the customer base
   is under pressure, some longer-term customers might appear to
   be secure against erosion. The answer is to differentiate price
   structure. For instance, often new customers (who are unsure
   of volumes) want variable pricing, while established customers
   insist on fixed prices. Perfect—in most markets neither side will
   bother to do the math to compare per-unit rates.

3. *Maximizing price realization.* Even when overall price level is fine,
   you will want to maximize price realization across accounts. Management intuition, perhaps augmented by impressions of messy
   scatter plots, may be that some accounts are getting a bargain, and
   others are showing signs of curtailing purchases and other signs
   of price pressure. The starting point, assuming management intuition is right, is to understand customer risk of loss. This means
   your company may want a risk tool, which rates the likelihood of
   customer cancellation because of price. (See Chapter 14.).

The benefits of this tool can be enormous. Less than half of customer defections are price driven and therefore should not be addressed
through price. Indeed, lowering price can sometimes destroy trust and set
in motion further purchase reviews.

These three purposes require different approaches because the root
causes of the problem differ. Of course these strategies are assuming that
the market is stable. How can a manager safely shift prices in a downturn?

Pricing Strategies in a Downturn

From time to time, as you have noticed, the economic environment dete-
riorates. What is an optimal reaction to this change in context? Which
pricing strategies address falling demand in an economic downturn?
The pundits generally advise you to "Wake up—pay closer attention to
customers and be more targeted in your pricing."[4] Good ideas certainly,
but what should you do specifically? Which price initiatives do, or do not,
work? Is a downturn the time to lower prices?

There are five key strategies for combating falling revenues. The key to success, in all cases, is not to assume that market-facing management becomes magically smarter. You may need tools to change behaviors. Most of the strategies below focus on understanding the customer buying decision, which is the driver of price sensitivity. Know the decision and you can optimize your pricing. Again, treat price reductions with caution. lowering prices may be unnecessary. That is important to know because in some cases a global price drop will do nothing but hurt results.

Strategy 1: Adjust to the Change in Context

With the downturn, the value of your offer has changed both in aggregate and by component. For many industries, the value of your after-sale service has increased while the value of new widgets has fallen. This is a direct consequence of your customers feeling poorer or having their budgets cut. While such cuts will preclude purchase of new units or services, the old units are now integral to customers' businesses and so must be maintained, recession or not.

Evidence of this sort of shift comes from 2010 IBM earning results. Unlike its more manufacturing-oriented peers that experienced sharp revenue declines, IBM exceeded earnings because it had shifted its business to over 60 percent service and lease revenues—which were less subject to capital expenditure cuts.

The sooner you understand which categories of spending must continue and which categories will be cut, the sooner you can adjust your price structure. We have found this analysis produces the best programs for preserving revenues. Often, a price increase on offer elements less affected by the economy will offset reduced demand for flagship products.

In numeric terms: assuming your "normal" revenue mix is 70 percent new sales, 30 percent maintenance services, and the recession causes new sales to fall by 20 percent, we find that often *you can make up much of that fall* by raising maintenance and spare parts prices (by as much as 50 percent in some cases!). To avoid customer rebellion, naturally, finesse, messaging, and superior bundling techniques are required to pull that off.[5]

Strategy 2: Improve the Value Message

This strategy is linked to the first strategy; in a nutshell, it says that customers do not always realize the value of what you offer. While many sales forces say they sell value, in fact most do not. This is because in good times, in many industries, a sales rep does not do best by selling value. Rather the rep does better by raising awareness and inserting himself into an existing buying process. In a downturn, the value communication role becomes more important.

To have sales sell value, equip and train the sales force with specific messages and evidence of your product's or service's value. For instance, engage third-party evaluators to compare their product with competitors. Credible third-party evaluators are plentiful: often university professors will evaluate your product for little more than the cost of samples. Evaluation organizations such as J.D. Powers and Associates, are very important elements of a value message when customers are parting with their money with increasing care.

Strategy 3: Make a Third Party Pay (e.g., the IRS)

Many companies believe that once the product or service has been delivered, the pricing process is over. Wrong. We find that many buyers are able to obtain reimbursement of their costs and that a majority of buyers can be educated on the tax consequences of their purchase. You as the seller have an impact on both taxes and reimbursements, and you neglect an important element of net realized price if you ignore these impacts.

The means to bringing this about is to understand your customer's tax or reimbursement opportunities. For instance, if you sell to lawyers who can obtain client reimbursement on electronic research but not on books, sell your electronic and print research in bundles; on the invoice allocate most of the price to the electronic. Another example: if you sell bundles of telephone and video services, do not allocate them equally on the invoice; allocate more of the bundle price to the potentially tax deductible second telephone line, and educate customers on why you have done so. A final example: if you are a not-for-profit performing venue selling 10 performance season tickets for $300 (*average price* = $30) and individual performances for $50, then grant season ticket holders who donate back tickets for an individual performance they cannot attend a tax credit of $50, not $30.[6]

Strategy 4: Better Identify Customer Behavior

How will your customer cut costs? Can you get your product out of the scope of your customer's cost reduction program? Given how simple some austerity efforts are, this should not be a difficult question to answer.

Starting with the extreme case: if your erstwhile customer simply decides to spend nothing, you may have to try to arrange to sell based on future payments or future obligations. More likely, your customer will decide to reduce all expenditures over a certain dollar amount. In that case, if you have a $25 subscription price, cut it into two chunks of $12.50 each and see if that flies under the radar.

Often, business customers cut by accounting categories, in which case if capital expenditures are being cut, try to fit more of your purchase into operating expenditure categories. Experience says that this does not happen easily, but it is possible if attempted in conjunction with some symbolic but material change in the offer. For instance, one medical equipment manufacturer offered a limited-time reduction in the cost of its equipment, but only if purchased with a new expanded-scope maintenance program. The substantive change included shifting the initial stock of spares from the equipment to the maintenance program (and making the spares broad classes of parts, not just specific parts, which had the benefit that the spares did not need to be stored at the customer).

Strategy 5: Plan Scenarios and Make Price Adjustments

All downturns are not alike. For pricers, the key scenario question relates to whether they are looking at inflation or deflation. Additional questions would have to do with the costs of inputs, downstream products, duration, and recovery mechanism.

Scenario planning is the tool that has historically performed best for companies planning for downturns. Shell Oil is superb at applying this technique, for example. Comparing two previous downturns highlights differences that should be part of your scenario planning:

- The mid-1970s recession manifested itself with very high inflation, high unemployment, and high commodity prices (particularly oil). That recession ended as oil prices dropped with deregulation of that industry and the collapse of OPEC (Organization of Petroleum Expotting Countries).

- The 2008–2009 recession saw a spike in oil prices and an emerging split between luxury items, low-end goods, and commodities. Inflation split: some goods went up in price (oil) but others fell (real estate and midrange automobiles). Consumer confidence crashed but later recovered, although consumer markets remained split between high unemployment and prosperous segments.

What business environments (i.e., contexts) are ahead?

Let us suppose the future includes a period of declining prices, followed by inflation. This scenario means holding the line on existing list prices but relaxing discounts as a discrimination tool between prosperous customers and those who are languishing.[7] It's a good excuse to move to contextual price bases. For almost anyone who drops prices under pressure, the message to customers must clearly include "We are dropping prices now because our costs are falling, but when inflation starts to rise next year you should budget for increases." For many B2B companies, it means that long-term contracts being negotiated today must have contingencies based on inflation rates (e.g., if inflation tops 7 percent, there is an automatic adjustment incorporated into the agreement).

What about inflation itself—how to handle that? The contextual answer is to avoid large numbers. What does that mean? It means that a 9 percent price rise will get more attention than a 6 percent price rise, and a double digit will get more attention than a single-digit-rise. Further, the power of compound growth mathematics says that the only way to avoid larger increase numbers is to *catch increases early*.

To illustrate this point: if two sellers both are priced at $100 per widget, and because of steady inflation they must both move to $200 in five years, the first two years are critical. If Company A does two years of 7 percent increase, it must do three years of 21 percent price growth to get to $200. Company B, on the other hand, could do 14 percent per year for all five years (ugly, but better than 21 percent). This would mean a gap would open up by the second year between inflation-aware Company B and unaware Company A. That needs to be addressed, but we find that often at the *beginning* of inflationary cycles, customers are not as sensitive to price rises as they are in the middle of them. In the inflationary period of 1972 to 1978, prices rose rapidly, but retailer profits were up initially in 1973.[8]

Any deflation highlights a peculiar management conundrum. Most companies of any size sell to the market at different realized prices. We recommend that while prices are falling you avoid the temptation to simplify or regularize pricing. In other words, do not consolidate rate cards or contracts.

While the initial impression and reaction by senior management to a view of actual rate cards is often "What a complicated mess!" a downturn is not the moment to simplify. There are usually many small customers or distribution partners buying at higher rates because your product or service is not a major expenditure to them. These customers or partners often will not examine price, and the change can only provoke scrutiny—as some software providers have found, let sleeping dogs lie.

> Being proactive in the five ways listed here is foundational for success in periods of inflation and downturns. Recommended prescriptions do not include simplifying your pricing—that will not address a changing environment.

Summary: Cheap Tools for Depressing Times

The best way to manage pricing during a downturn is to understand customer decision processes and market transparency. But that does not mean managers will suddenly grow their pricing skills and understand the customer decision processes any better than before. To help with this, your company should build inexpensive pricing tools and insist on their use. Context and segmentation should be used to understand likely market reactions and demand.

When a downturn or inflation comes, pricing grows in importance because management price actions become less routine and strategy is required. Scenario planning is very useful here. Be cognizant of corporate pricing culture, however: economies change more rapidly than corporate culture.

Notes

1. Especially Arc Elasticity, which is never useful. Point elasticities are more useful managerially for short-term tactics in highly communicative commodity markets. Some software provides estimates of elasticities. But although software prevents scrutiny of elasticity hidden inside systems, it does not actually improve the accuracy of elasticities. For instance over any longer time horizon, elasticity will fail to point out the asymmetry between price increases and decreases.

2. Of course, if you are General Motors and can ensure that every potential buyer knows about your price change, this would be less of a worry. The "employee discount" program of 2008 to 2011 quadrupled its Web traffic and increased sales materially. Acendmarketing.com focuses on tracking of Web traffic.

3. In fact, price sensitivity should be primary in defining a segment. R. Frank, F. Massey, Y. Wind, *Economic Principles of Market Segmentation*, Prentice-Hall, 1972. All too often segmentation seems to be a captive of stock data and channel economics.

4. We suppose that includes the authors of this book, but we claim to be a better class of pundit.

5. Or if you can be fortunate and be solely in the purchase category that thrives. For instance, people turned to painting their houses in the 2008–2009 recession rather than building. "For Sherman-Williams, a Rosy Outlook in Recession," *The Wall Street Journal*, December 24, 2008, p. B7.

6. The idea is that the *market* sets price. While the customer may get the same ticket stub as always, the value and ability to price are different. While the orchestra may be the same, the price of a *single* performance is *not* the same as a series as observed by Gayle Maurin, theater guru. So, if the season pass holder turns back in a single performance ticket, it's worth the single performance price of $50, not $30 ($300 divided by 10 performances). This is the hardnosed contextual value assessment, and shows why markets do not always abide by people's "common sense." Note Einstein's quote: "Common sense is the collection of prejudices acquired by age 18."

7. Compare "Luxury Spending Is Back in Fashion," which reports that jewelry, recreational vehicles, and luxury cars are growing robustly, but "the rising tide isn't lifting all boats." *USA Today*, October 27, 2010, p. 1A. On the other hand, in an article on chain stores like Walmart, management is quoted as saying, "The slow economic recovery will continue to affect our customers, and [we] expect they will remain cautious about spending." "Retailers Are Sold on Frugality," *The Wall Street Journal*, August 18, 2010.

8. Timing matters for price changes provoked by inflation, just like all other changes. It's not linear, however: early is better in many cases. "Higher Prices Looming, Many Companies Say," *The New York Times*, December 2010, p. A17.

PART 3

Pricing Programs and the Marketing Mix

Chapter 9

Segmentation, Context, and Time

Now I am become Time, the destroyer of worlds.

—THE BHAGAVAD GITA

One size fits nobody.

—*THE NEW YORK TIMES*,
ARTICLE ON CLOTHING SIZES, APRIL 24, 2011, PAGE A1

Context and segmentation both stem from the same truth: not every person and every situation is equal. Therefore, both contextual pricing and needs-based segmentation try to base market actions on what is happening in the customer's mind. They both also take into account the question of price structure and price level. So what is the difference between them?

Differences between Context and Segmentation

The main difference is that contextual pricing focuses on the impact of the customer's environment, adding the element of causation and a framework for addressing changes in the market. Another way to phrase it is that segmentation is typically based on the class of person or business; context is based on situation. Needs-based analysis will usually provide an insight like this one: "A single male needs to impress his date, so he buys flowers to give to his date." Context, on the other hand, would go deeper: "A single male who still does not have flowers for his date by 6 p.m. on Saturday is pretty desperate and will pay anything to get some flowers or flower substitutes. On Friday, he will not have given it much thought." Notice the difference?

In many cases, the key contextual element is what has changed—people notice change, and sometimes reduce the weight they give preexisting decision factors. Context may also focus more on whether third-party behavior has influenced the buyer decision framework. For instance, if the potential flower-buyer senses strong competition for the attentions of the lady of his dreams, he may buy a bigger bouquet. The important point is that in comparing demographic bases for competition with different contexts, the contextual differences are more important for pricing. An illustration of how segment and context interact is in Table 9-1.

You may ask: "How the h—l are we going to address a constantly changing set of circumstances? It's enough work to keep up with just demographics change (e.g., an increase in Latino demographics, younger marriage age, income shifts, etc.); it seems like contextual situations would end up shifting even more." Actually, not so.

Contextual events that shift demand and price sensitivity are as predictable as segment or demographic changes; you just have to be aware of them. In fact, much of context is more certain than demographic change: people will *always* be late and require rush orders, committees

Table 9.1 Interaction of Content and Segmentation Provide the Field of Required Prices

		SEGMENTATION			
		Families	Dinks	Prof. Singles	Retirees
CONTEXT	Loyal repeat	$100	$110	$90	$90
	New customers	$50	$60	$60	$60
	Add-on sales	$110	$80	$100	$90
	Proprietary Channels	$120	$120	$120	$90

will *always* be divided, buyers will *always* focus on larger purchases, consumers will *always* compare prices if they can easily do so and make less comparison if that is not easy, people on hot beaches will *always* pay more for soda. Sound reasonable?

An advantage of context is that it explains causality of customer price preferences and in some ways is more constant than segmentation.

Management should take advantage of traditional segment information. To obtain the *best* pricing, however, it must also take advantage of contextual information. Just as some segment information requires work to assemble, so does contextual information. Since segmentation has had a 40-year head start with management, your company probably has assembled more segment information.

Contextual data is also available—it just takes a decision to procure it. You can find it hidden in usage data or coincidentally gathered in market research. One advantage of context over segment data is that context is quite obvious. For instance, you cannot easily tell if a phone user is Latino or Caucasian, but you can tell if she is traveling or at home or at college.[1] You cannot always tell if a shopper is old or young, but you can tell whether he is buying last-minute before a holiday.

A final assurance on context to allay any reader fears of added complexity, which may still be present after many pages: unlike segmentation, which often increases the number of price points, context can reduce the actual number of realized prices by 80 percent or more because it allows enforcement of price points. Welcome news, and easier to administer because actual customer prices are what propel your company's results. Even better news: the modest increase in target prices (contextual baseline prices) can easily be handled by systems. A system lookup table is how your company probably prices now, and this lookup table does not care if it is looking up contextual baseline prices or nominal list prices.

Segmentation and contextual information are not substitutes; they complement each other in decision making. Therefore, you should

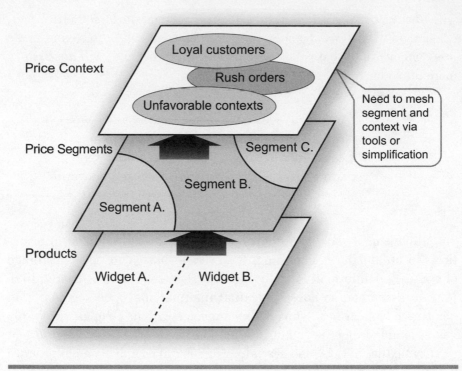

Figure 9-1 Context is the final stage of price setting.

initially consider context as an overlay on segmentation. Since segmentation came first, we show context as the incremental layer on the pyramid of management tasks shown in Figure 9-1.

This is an additional layer, but one (among others not illustrated) that pays for itself, many times over.

How Segment and Context Complement Each Other

Despite having spent some pages distinguishing context from segment, it is important to note that context and segment go well together. Best of all, you can use both to improve pricing. Let us take a look at a case study from a B2B market. This case study involves five steps taken over time, pertaining to the computing and data communications equipment market during the late 1980s to the early 2000s.[2]

During this time, as is well known, the method with which users processed business data evolved from mainframes to distributed processing. This evolution occurred over five distinct phases that companies passed through, each of which represented a context for data communications vendors. Some users passed through a few stages, while others went through all five.

The first phase, which harkened back to the prehistory of the 1970s, was a mainframe-only approach featuring a central information technology (IT) department. This was the *IBM-dominated Hierarchical Proprietary stage.*

Many companies next experienced a radical policy and power shift in information management: the end users of computing decided to buy PCs, minicomputers, and server clusters, bypassing the IT department. Inevitably after buying this equipment, the end users tried to network these devices, leasing lines and setting up networks that were independent of the IT department. Doing so involved major infrastructure buys. For instance, in the early 1990s at United States Trust, the IT department conducted a survey and was surprised to discover that more than 230 networks had been set up by end user departments. This phase was called the *Departmental Computing stage.*

The next phase was an organizational response to the chaos produced by departmental mixing and matching. Companies formed an independent central-purchasing department, or shared service, that tried to regain financial control and reduce costs. This effort economized through the consolidation of purchasing and the physical consolidation of networks. This phase was called the *Telecom/Computing Purchasing Function (Utility) stage.*

In the fourth stage, coming after a period of several years, companies integrated telecommunications and computing purchase, again within the IT department. The new arrangement typically allowed end users greater access to information, which was kept in large corporate databases administered by IT. To access these large databases, high-capacity data networks were created to allow selected ("mission critical") users in remote locations to pull down large files through a corporate network and work on them on-site.

For instance, the pharmaceutical manufacturer Merck & Company allowed mission-critical staff, like researchers, to pull huge molecular models out of data repositories and download the material to their workstations. This architectural phase was called *Mission Internet*.

The last stage is either an alternative or a successor to the fourth stage. Instead of giving over the corporate databases back to the IT department to place in a few large repositories oriented to the most important end users, some companies adopted an architecture to allow *all* end users to access any data they need. Doing so meant throwing out a lot of obsolete equipment and introducing a homogeneous infrastructure in which all the components could connect with one another. This was expensive and, for the time, technologically quite complex.

To pay for the new equipment and endorse the technological risk of this new architecture, non-IT business leaders had to be intimately involved and convinced of the need for the expenditure. Thus, the new power structure was a close partnership between IT and functional departments. This stage saw departmental computer specialists stripped of some of their autonomy as a cohesive new approach to purchasing and technology took hold. This final stage was called *Integrated Computing*.

The Contextual Logic Chain

The initial shift from the monolithic architecture of the first stage set in motion forces that inevitably propelled a company up the evolutionary chain, link by link. This is illustrated in Figure 9-2.

The relative inflexibility and slow response times of the first stage set in motion the contextual evolution. Powerful division and functional heads decided they could do better than the IT department in building needed computing capabilities and funded that effort. They brought in new technologically savvy managers and told them to do what was needed to improve speed and capacity. The new departmental managers did exactly that, but with little regard to expense. This was because the new computers did not seem like a big budget increase when compared with their overall operational budget.

After a while, however, the poorly managed multiplicity of computers and networks in the second (Departmental Computing) stage became expensive—sometimes growing to account for more than 10 percent of a company's total cost base. This expense provoked top management to reduce costs. Thus, many companies ceded departmental control back to IT or, more commonly, to the newly created Computing and Utility

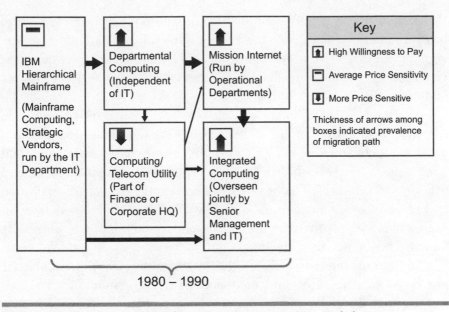

Figure 9-2 The evolution of context as computing and data communications architecture evolved

Purchasing function. Which route they chose depended on whether or not IT had become more flexible and responsive.

Because the Utility phase had a strong focus on minimizing costs, there was usually little attention paid to innovation. This resistance to new technologies, many of which would benefit line operations, caused line managers to look for alternatives to the "penny-pinching" purchase function. This pushed a company to move on to the next evolutionary change in which dissatisfied end users were wooed by a new, more enlightened IT department. Business managers looking for new capabilities, and IT managers looking for greater architectural consistency, drove department heads to accept a return of central IT and seek more forward-looking approaches. This pushed them into the subsequent phases.

The choice of the next step, whether to move to Mission Internet or Integrated Computing, depended on a company's business economics, in particular the contexts of budgets and mission needs.

If a company's overall return on investment was high, it would most likely choose elegant and uniform database architectures (Integrated Computing). This was the case at Morgan Stanley and at Federal

Paperboard, the specialty manufacturer, which both had ample cash to invest in internal information technology. Typically, this architecture was administered by IT, but oversight was by IT and senior line managers, vice president and above, who got intimately involved in funding choices and alternatives.

Alternatively, many larger enterprises with lower rates of return on investments could not afford to replace the existing hodgepodge with a clean new data architecture, which usually required all new software and often a major makeover in hardware. In that case, line managers handed over the problem to IT. That is what happened at the Chrysler Corporation and other large manufacturers. The buying context of Mission Internet was more price sensitive than the Integrated Computing phase, especially for less "mission-critical" functions.

The strong internal logic of the evolution formed the context for purchases of computing and data networks. Understanding this context allowed understanding of buying behavior. In the move from the Hierarchical Proprietary stage, departmental computer specialists sought immediate solutions to interconnection requirements. Thus the performance of equipment and ease of use were key factors. In the move to the Utility phase, cost and centralized control played the central role. In the shift to Integrated Computing, the focus shifted to the ability of equipment and vendors to perform smoothly in conjunction with software packages and to innovate to meet end user needs.

To highlight how different these requirements were, note that a low-cost price tag is needed to win *only* in selling to the Utility phase. Thus, it would be foolish to deeply discount pricing in bidding in the other environments. On a more subtle level, Mission Internet will be price sensitive in buying for nonmission-critical users but not price sensitive for critical users. Pricing was evaluated in terms of individual component buys with limited global procurements.

In an Integrated Computing context, price pressures were low if you could meet the technical requirements. This fueled explosive growth and the success of Sun Microsystems, Cisco, and others. Price structures favored global sourcing and sometimes enterprise pricing, not component buys. Successful vendors had to understand this logic (low cost versus high capabilities, special user groups versus enterprise, etc.) in order to price optimally. This required an appreciation for the differences in context and—even better—an overall road map of potential migration paths.

Although most industries appear to evolve in coherent fashion as managers adapt to the same technological, social, financial, and regulatory changes, suppliers rarely exploit this fact fully. Planners routinely identify key industry trends on an annual basis, but they do not always tie these trends to pricing segments, strategies, and targets when analyzing market opportunities. For analysis, planners often revert to more limited but safe and convenient segmentation categories such as Standard Industry Classification (SIC) codes or customer size. Low effort, but lower utility.

> Most industries appear to evolve in coherent fashion, allowing sellers the opportunity to anticipate changes in buying criteria and decision makers.

Context, as we have seen, involves more than simply purchasing prepackaged groups of sociological/psychographic/demographic classes. These prepackaged collections will rarely bear any resemblance to situations created by fundamental forces changing a company's market. Superior pricing is based on understanding the underlying reasons for the creation of new forms of demand.

Context is also different because industries do not ever repeat a "cycle" in that predictable sense. Market contexts seem to change with broad industrial and social changes, which have the effect of constantly shuffling the deck for all the players at the table. For instance, software companies today are subject to greater economic, competitive, and quality pressures than they were 10 years ago, forcing them to respond in different ways as well.

Benefits

There are three benefits to contextual understanding highlighted in the computing case study: reaching customers when they are ready to buy, understanding how to appeal to them, and setting price structures and contextual price levels. Most important of these is that context helps companies recognize opportunities before competitors do.

Being slightly ahead of the competition is a huge price and service advantage. By utilizing evolutionary understanding, a company can deploy products and pricing in the right way at the right time. Examples of "early is best" include Best Buy. Originally an also-ran electronics superstore, Best Buy boldly innovated to address the increasingly sophisticated customers who desire a friendlier, less-pressured purchasing environment. That context changed during the 1990s in that electronics became more standard and consumers were no longer intimidated by electronics purchases, so they no longer needed the guys in ties to help them select a product. By being the first specialty retailer to understand this new context (which, initially, also happened to mirror an age demographic), Best Buy outperformed its traditional competitors. Best Buy's decade-long compound sales growth rate was more than 75 percent per year.

An understanding of evolutionary contextual paths can turn to gold for a vendor's sales force. That is because every step taken on the contextual journey changes what matters inside a potential customer's organization: decision makers, buying criteria, and budgets. The sales force that can anticipate these changes can get to a new decision maker before competitors do. Arriving first, they can begin shaping the decision maker's time frames and criteria. When the laggards finally arrive at the new decision maker's door, they may find that it has already been closed.

Summary

Context and segmentation are both vital to companies that seek to maximize value capture and profitability. These two concepts work well together, but management might wish to emphasize context because it is the new kid on the block and can be the more powerful lever of pricing results.

Context will help identify times and situations where price can be taken. Time is particularly important because the same buyer (person) will behave quite differently at different times, because context has changed.

Understanding context makes the difference between servicing a growing willingness to pay for a company's special attributes versus responding to a heterogeneous collection of needs with one solution that fits nobody well.

Vendors that understand and categorize context can reap huge rewards. By rigorously isolating different contexts, observing how customers' buying behaviors change in different contexts, and perhaps categorizing customer evolutionary stages and predicting potential next steps, vendors can understand customers' future decisions earlier than the customers themselves—and far sooner than the competition. This can result in superior sales growth.

Notes

1. Actually, with sharp and creative IT, today many companies know a lot more about their customers than what makes it into their pricing. For example, when AT&T was looking for ways to commercialize its calling pattern information, some remarkable inferences emerged. One was an analysis of calling patterns that could show dual road-warrior couples and when there might be a need for flowers. A particular pattern of call frequency spikes and locations showed stressful episodes. Correctly, this kind of inference was treated with caution, but the point is that it is possible. It may be even easier on the Web. See also "A Web Pioneer Profiles Users by Name," *The Wall Street Journal*, October 27, 2010, p. A3.

2. This section is built, in part, from an early article before the concept of context was recognized as distinct from segmentation. At that time we called it "evolutionary segmentation," which was imprecise but still useful. Rob Docters, John Grim, and John McGady, "Segments in Time," *Strategy & Business*, first quarter 1997, pp. 42–51.

Chapter 10

The Hinge of Fate: Pricing Strategy

History will be kind to me, for I intend to write it.

—WINSTON S. CHURCHILL

Many writings on price strategy focus exclusively on relative market power among competitors. While immediate market power is indeed very important, there are a few other factors that can strongly influence results. One of them is time: if you lack market power, you are likely to need some time to accomplish your goals. Time and power are the primary commodities required to construct a pricing strategy.

Why time? The primary reason is that market power changes over time, and the strategy rule is to take price at a time and in a market when and where your customer or competitor is least ready to fight you on it. When we say market power changes, we are not talking about glacial erosion of entrenched competitors but rather rapid changes in customer needs and how you can take advantage of those changes.

For instance, in the college textbook market, major textbook adoptions in higher education last for a period of two to three years and are often decided by committees of relevant faculty. Apparently, these meetings are not much fun: various champions endorsing their particular favorite book or educational materials. Often, few people have read or studied all the alternatives, so the discussion is impressionistic, heated, and endless. Because there is no consistent decision criteria and little systematic comparison, often price is one of the few objective comparisons. As a result, books priced significantly above average will be eliminated from consideration—regardless of their merits.

The price strategy best suited to win such an adoption is to set the price close to average for year one. Then, to achieve superior returns in years two and three, prices should be raised sharply. These raises can be made secure in the knowledge that no one wants to reconvene the adoption committee and reconsider the adoption. Of course the students won't like the price rises, but the decision makers—the professors—don't have to pay for the books themselves. Not until the next adoption cycle must prices come down again.

The same sort of decision-cycle-based pricing applies in countless industries. For instance, when selling a computer cluster, hardware manufacturers know that the initial bid is very price-sensitive, but a year later additional memory or power supplies can be sold at a premium. Leveraging changes in time is central to pricing strategy. That is not to say that the sequence is always identical. For instance, when selling some categories of services, such as entertainment, the time pattern of value capture works in reverse order. Let's take a closer look.

A major entertainment park located in Atlanta had spent tens of millions of dollars on a new exhibit. The new exhibit initially had the excitement and value of novelty. Therefore, the optimal strategy was to charge a premium until the local visitor pool was exhausted. After the local customer segment was exhausted, the second-stage strategy was to merge the exhibit into the entrance fee, *except* for special occasions and events with a high proportion of out-of-town visitors. Then it was optimal to continue to charge extra. The idea is that while the Atlanta pool of visitors is finite, the pool of out-of-town visitors is virtually infinite.

This example illustrates the need for time-based contextual pricing strategy. In some cases, sellers will even *create* a time-based context such as a "limited time offer," for example, selling fashion items for a short time only. Many fashion items are deliberately rationed so as to create scarcity and so a lack of price resistance. A more subtle version of this use of context is expansion, for example, taking products from a microbrewery with a reputation for superior beer to national distribution. The previous scarcity can translate to a bounce in current price.[1]

> **Take price when and where your customer and competitor is least ready to fight you on it.**

Strategy Homework

Successful strategy requires some homework before beginning. One task is to define where you hold a stronger position and where you hold a weaker one. If you know that, then the actions and price structures supporting strategy will flow quite logically. To know weakness or strength, context is key.[2]

Determining Strengths and Weaknesses

While management will generally have some intuition on this, there are often material rewards for doing a better job in evaluating and quantifying differences in strengths and weaknesses. For instance, in 2008 the Food Network felt it was time to dramatically increase the prices paid by cable television companies to broadcast its content. The Food Network CFO announced that the company was seeking a big jump in rates based on its audience ratings success. This helped set the contextual basis for pricing—showing that price should relate to ratings.

To achieve the increase, the Food Network had to negotiate with a half dozen cable and satellite operators. The key negotiation context was that while each negotiation was separate, results from one influenced others.[3]

The Food Network's first step was to quantify exactly what the financial pain would be of losing different cable companies carrying the Food Network if they refused the new rates. Because of its small size, and smaller footprint, Cablevision was the obvious weak point. When Cablevision rejected the Food Network's demands, it dropped the channel at the end of the contract term while other cable companies continued on a provisional basis.

But three weeks later Cablevision recanted and accepted the Food Network's new rates. As one blogger commented, "Sounds like Cablevision needs Scripps [Food Network] more than Scripps needs Cablevision. I wonder how many subscribers Cablevision lost?"[4] Apparently a material number, since eventually Cablevision agreed to the new, higher, rates. More important, after this precedent, the other cable companies then fell into line and accepted the new rates.

As another example of identifying strengths, in the search engine market there are several hundred players, plus many metasearch engines that aggregate other search engines' results. Search engines are specialized in many ways (e.g., medical, legal, semantic, social, visual, etc.). These differences matter depending on the context. For instance, having intraenterprise search abilities (i.e., a search scans your company's databases as well as outside ones) is important for research departments at larger pharmaceutical companies, but less important to smaller ones. Visual capabilities are important for trademarks, motion pictures, and engineering, but less important for blog search engines such as Technorati.

Interestingly, in many markets, differences in capabilities are not clear to many of the users. Yet they do exist upon close inspection. Further, the differences matter to users once they are made aware of the differences. For instance, search tracking matters to medical researchers who are required to show their due diligence in examining the existing literature. This matters less to financial search-engine users, but they in turn care more about differences in security and privacy capabilities.

As with any sophisticated set of products, the list of differences among search engines is long—yet sometimes the lists do not make it out of R&D into marketing or sales. Further, the right message may not make it to buyers and influencers. This failure to leverage differences represents a failure to set the basis for, or engage in, contextual pricing. With a blank slate, pricing cannot be contextual and so cannot really capture the pricing it might with better-defined context.

Often there is the delusion that sales staff will have the time to figure out the differences and will point out the advantages of a product, or the unreliable hope that a buyer (such as an information professional, like a librarian) will understand those differences and then be able to support a higher price. That is very optimistic; make up the list or there can be no effective pricing!

> Often imprecise and sloppy pricing is the result of a failure to carefully distinguish market factors such as product differences. Developing a list of differences is the prerequisite, and communicating that list downstream is essential.

Strategic Pricing by Category

Once you have the list, the next step is to build a map of where your offer is strong, average, or weak. We tend to call these Homeland, Battleground, and Entrants/Opportunistic Raiding market sectors.

Note that there should be a lot more than mere product focus on this map. Limits to channel reach and other offers within the portfolio and customer decision-making process will have an impact on the map. For instance, if your features are not immediately obvious to casual users, the existence of expert buyers such as librarians or in-house experts may shape the classification. Where it takes time to learn of your offer's differential benefits, the map must show where buyers will invest that time and where they will not. This is the contextual dimension to strategy.

Homeland. These secure customers are where you should be extracting value. Usually such a customer believes your product to be very valuable to them, and in B2B situations these customers may have made your product or service integral to their work flow.

The value capture strategy for Homeland customers is to create price structures that are better at extracting value (e.g., employing two-part charging schemes, as described in Chapter 6). For instance, warehouse clubs such as Sam's charge membership fees in addition to the item price. And, of course, in some cases simply raising price is an option.

The more important question is how to do this without exposing your Homeland customers to raids from competitors. Remember that the high margins of this customer category will make them subject to competitor attention.[5] There are three pricing strategies that can help defend these customers:

- Neutralize the attacker's strong points. This means to rebalance pricing so that the likely points of attack are priced competitively. For instance, if a competitor offers a low flat rate on some part of the service bundle, you must meet that price. Any value-added features or higher tiers of service can still command a premium, but your company must make it easy for loyal buyers to say to their bosses, "We did not take the new entrant's low-priced offer. Both our incumbent supplier and the challenger offered the same basic price. But because on closer inspection we needed additional functionality, we stayed with the incumbent and his higher tier offer."
- Message and signal that any competitor price attack will provoke price or nonprice retaliation. There must always be some retaliation, and the retaliation must have an impact on the same chain of command at the competitor as those who are launching the attacks. Counterattacks need not involve lower prices, for instance: making known to the *competitor's* best customers that any low prices offered by them to *your* customers can be a form of retaliation. Sponsoring a study that examines shortcomings in the attacking products (like the floating decimal research used by IBM against Intel) is another potential response; again, it was not linked to a price level.
- Employ retention tactics. These may include price opacity (keeping discounts separate, perhaps in the form of rebates to different influencers), increasing administrative burden of departure (separate renewal cycles for different component parts, making notice of cancellation difficult or limit opportunity) and, finally, offering cumulative discounts over time lost if the customer leaves—similar to the loss of American Express reward points if the customer closes his or her account.

Battleground. For the Battleground sector, the full capabilities of the organization come into play. That means highlighting your product differences (such as the speed, durability, ease of maintenance or reliability of product, timeliness of delivery, scope of reach, unique content, and lowest price) and what it means in different buyer or user contexts.

For instance, in the data processing market there are dozens of buyer segments. One server manufacturer has split its marketing efforts by vertical industry segments. This certainly has some validity: needs differed materially among customer segments. Most important, these segments paid up to 20 percent more or less for the same product.

But on closer inspection, the industry segment price varied more because of differences in user missions than anything intrinsic to the industry vertical. In some cases, their mission was to reduce costs, so they were very sensitive to price tags. In other cases, their mission was to improve computer support to business units, so they were less focused on the price and more on the operational capabilities being created.

Each mission represents a context. The best pricing strategy was to address pricing structure (e.g., timing and apportioning of component costs) differently for these segments. This produces a coherent price approach much more prone to success than simple industry segmentation.

Notice how in Table 10-1 below, the front-loaded pricing and back-loaded pricing won in different contexts. In this case, if your company product offered more MIPs but would be junked with little resale value

Table 10-1 Differences in Evaluation by Objectives

| Context | Goal | DEVICES | | Segment Winner |
		A	B	
Performance maximizers, e.g., departmental users	Most MIPs for initial purpose	Initially $1/MIP Lifetime $20/MIP		Device A
Lifetime NPV maximizers, e.g., IT	Best $/MIP over lifetime, including support, training, and software		Initially $2/MIP Lifetime $10/MIP	Device B

Comparison of devices under two different criteria, linked to organization due to a lack of standards compatibility, you would certainly target the departmental user buyers looking to maximize immediate performance.

To *defend* customers in the Battleground, timing is key because customer understanding of the product changes over time. Here is an illustration of how price plus the right information helped turn a loss to a win back: a leading software provider for small business was facing a slew of low-priced competitors offering subscriptions to back-office applications at prices that were half the levels of the leading vendor. Attrition of small firm customers was material. The market leader had a superior product; competitive research had shown that there were many operational issues with the competitors' applications, but this did not seem to matter to customers.

Looking closely at the decision process at the small firms showed a typical pattern: within a three- to five-person management team, one manager was typically responsible for back-office applications, such as billing or payroll. Other members of the management team were more focused on sales, operations, and other functions. The management team member responsible for back-office applications was usually quite loyal to the market leader and its products. Major expenditures such as a billing system upgrade and other big-ticket items, however, were decided jointly by the entire team.

The result was that when approached with a supposedly equivalent product offered at half the price, the majority of the management team would vote to switch to a low-priced alternative, and the back-office head would be outvoted. After the switch, the defeated back-office head would unhappily adjust to the new provider and gradually drift out of touch with the market leader—losing sight of its advantages and product improvements.

A pricing strategy to retain the firm prevented this drift out of touch. Instead of stopping service upon cancellation notice, the market leader would continue it free for one year. In the course of that year, the loyal manager would check both services against each other and often find fault in the new service. In some cases the fault was major: the billing results were wrong or accounts receivable failed to point out issues. This armed that manager with specific examples where serious harm could have resulted from the use of the new supplier. Against a specific example, often the nonloyal managers would agree to return to the market leader since getting customer invoices wrong can be a *big* problem.

So, as often happens, the situation changed with time. The power shifted among the sides, and what appeared to be a lost cause was won.

> Time is critical to pricing strategy. Take price at a time when your customers and competitors are not ready to fight you on it.

Entrants/Opportunistic Raiding. In addition to entrants, companies raiding competitor's Homeland markets face the problem of changing customer buying habits. Entrants typically will set a superior price/performance offer before potential customers (depending on the quality of the product or service, this price may be above or below that of the incumbent). The idea is to make it worthwhile for customers to change. With multiple competitors in a market, companies are likely to resort repeatedly to lowering pricing as a way of gaining market share. This is why, to no one's surprise, more competitors generally means lower prices.

To send the message of lower price, entrants tend to favor a relatively simple "transparent" price. Underpricing the incumbent works best when customers can compare product or service prices easily; it becomes less effective as the purchase grows more complex. Complexity and hidden price elements are usually not the best tactics for an entrant, because they force customers to work to understand the entrant's price advantage—something customers may not be willing to do.[6]

Understanding underdog strategies is important because every company sometimes plays the role of underdog or challenger or entrant somewhere in its markets. That role applies to start-ups, such as mail-order florist Calyx & Corolla entering the retail flower market. It applies to large established firms in new areas, for example, P&G's entry into the premium pet food market. It can apply to overseas expansion, such as major automobile manufacturers muscling their way into the Chinese market.

An example of "Simpler is better for entrants" is the long-distance telephone service market. Large corporate users' contracts run hundreds of pages and depend on dozens of elements such as usage, geography, installations, and features. Consequently, direct "apples to apples" price comparison is difficult. This is one reason why price is a less effective tool for capturing large business customers than for winning smaller business and consumer accounts. That is why voice over Internet Protocol (VoIP) entrants such as Skype and Pioneer offer simple tariffs to new accounts, either flat rate or a penny or two per minute.

In contrast, customer inertia and conservatism help incumbents. To avoid the effort and perceived risk in changing suppliers, customers will often allow incumbent suppliers a material price premium. For example, as part of its quality programs at one point, Xerox had a policy that allowed incumbent suppliers up to a 15 percent price premium over potential suppliers before it would switch providers.

When customers are not willing to grant incumbent vendors a price premium explicitly, the real price level can often be masked through a complex price structure. Unless they have a monopoly, incumbents have a strong incentive to make it difficult for customers to compare prices directly. For instance, consumer electronics manufacturers such as Sony vary their model numbers among retailers so that consumers cannot be sure they are comparing the same model. Similarly, in the commodity chemicals business, buyers are highly sensitive to price. As a result, sellers make sure that actual prices can be pieced together only from many contracts and deals throughout the distribution chain (e.g., some at the factory, some deals by warehouse, etc.).

The less market power a company has, the less it can obstruct the process of price comparisons—and so must typically offer simpler pricing. That is why new-entrant stockbrokers such as Scottrade offer simple $7-per-trade pricing, while incumbents such as Merrill Lynch, Schwab, and others have more complicated structures linked to volumes, stock prices, and annual fees.

Differences in market power and context mean a uniform price is frequently not feasible. Even the strongest companies are weak in some contexts and in some markets. No company is uniformly strong in all regions in which it operates. Differences in market share and power across geographics is an obstacle to a uniform global pricing strategy. Additionally, there are other contexts that favor or disfavor an incumbent even in its core markets. Therefore, the price structure should vary to reflect these differences: in some cases, an incumbent strategy is appropriate; in other cases, the context favors weaker competitors or entrants, even against strong incumbents.

As an example, in commercial jet engine procurements there is a need for multiple sourcing on spare parts and supplies—a requirement driven by the fear of an airline being held hostage over the price of replacement parts.[7] This sort of requirement can be a nice entrée for a weaker player.

While both primary supplier and second-source suppliers must of course show that their products and service are reliable, many of the other success factors are different for the second-source player than for primary provider. The incumbent will be looking to make up the low initial bid price through sales of higher margin spare parts. The second sourcer is often looking to show its attractiveness through low spare parts costs and compatibility with the primary provider. Hence the context and the messaging can be exact opposites: one is "We are best, we are unique," which suits the contenders for the primary position; the other is "We are just the same and a cheap second-source candidate."

Third Parties, Alliances, and Eco Systems

Leveraging additional parties, beyond your company and your customers, can add pricing strength. In the same way that "third parties" called competitors can destroy value, third parties called coventurers can help create value. They do this by joining with you to create bundles consisting of their products and your products (or services). For instance, Smartphone manufacturers and software developers offer just such a bundle, sometimes purchased together (preloaded) or sometimes a soft bundle, whereby both can be purchased via the same channel. Third parties can also help your company legitimize and monetize the value of your offers.

This role, when applied to multiple linked parties, can be very powerful both in adjusting the context but also in helping with reach. Here are a few examples:

Entertainment. Management at some amusement parks has been gratified that they have many admirers in their communities. These supporters, or "ambassadors," are a major source of visitors and income, and an important context. When out-of-town relatives and friends show up, the ambassadors are likely to urge the visitors to go to the amusement park. In many cases, however, the frequency of visitors is greater than the desire or budget of the ambassador to see the park again.

The answer in one case was to create a membership program that allowed unlimited visits and even to give the out-of-town guest visitors a 10 percent discount by virtue of association with the ambassador. Given the leverage, a huge return followed. For the sake of heavy discounts for a small number of ambassadors, there was a large uptick in related visitors at close-to-full prices. In many markets, the context includes advocates—such as enthusiastic users or influential observers, bloggers, or family members.

Construction. In the construction industry, there is a flow of influence and money beginning with the master developer or owner, going to the architect or the development company, then to the general contractor, then to the subcontractors, and so on. Some vendors have linked up with the next level in the chain, and this has helped everyone's pricing to have that link. For instance, developers such as Trump have a core group of contractors that they use repeatedly, and so they do not have to be educated about the Trump organization's preferences and standards.

Similarly, general contractors have set up links with skilled subcontractors, such as roofers or concrete formulators for foundations. This helps reduce general contractor uncertainty as to quality and has helped higher skilled but higher hourly cost subcontractors benefit from repeat work because both general and subcontractors know what to expect from each other—it takes the uncertainty out. Also, the relationship gives both sides more opportunity to discuss requirements and costs, which can prevent problems. This can mean higher hourly rates, but, more important, overall lower costs due to fewer problems and less risks as the buying unit is redefined. For instance, not all building foundations are equally easy to pour. A dialogue between foundation subcontractors and general contractors can be very productive, and this is more likely as part of an ongoing relationship.

Financing. A lucrative example of an "ecosystem" operates on Wall Street. The start-up financing to IPO lifecycle relies heavily on context to set value. For instance in the case of Facebook, Goldman Sachs played a major role in lining up investors in the start-up. These investors did well. Microsoft invested $240 million in 2007, which by 2011 grew to be valued at $15 billion. Goldman Sachs also created a special vehicle that allowed some of its best clients to invest in Facebook: the vehicle combined hundreds of investors so they were treated as one investor, thus skirting the SEC rule that firms with more than 499 shareholders must report quarterly earnings and audited financial information to the public.

In return for legitimizing the prepublic value of Facebook, Goldman Sachs collects stiff fees: 4 percent placement amounts and a 5 percent share of the investment's profits. It is also likely to handle the Facebook IPO. So far its "friend" investors have enjoyed more than 60 times return on investment, if you believe the valuations. Goldman Sachs may pocket over $2 billion as Facebook and its investor friends cross the IPO finish line. Overall, this arrangement represents a very successful ecosystem context.[8]

The lesson from these examples is that your company can bundle resources or capture legitimizing context from outside of your company. In many cases, such third-party allies are more effective because they help complete a broad picture context, which your company cannot do by itself. For instance, for educational products, marshaling a panel of Ph.D.s is more effective than doing your own product evaluations.

Another nice feature of third parties is that frequently they can ally themselves with you for their own purposes, so they require no support—just an invitation. For instance when Cablevision went dark on Food Network in 2009, vocal critics of Cablevision's decision included food-stuff advertisers like Pillsbury and their agencies, who were deprived of an effective advertising vehicle. No money flows from the Food Network to these ad hoc allies, actually the opposite: these allies actually buy from the network, so the third party actually paid for being a supporter.

> Third parties can influence context, and since context influences price, this can be a useful tool in price negotiations.

Costs

Costs, often maligned as the basis for pricing, can also be inspirational in suggesting a price strategy. While costs have an impact on pricing only indirectly, they do highlight opportunities for better pricing. For instance, the U.S. Postal Service offers its popular flat-rate box service, which has pricing independent of weight (some restrictions, but not material in most cases) because it found that its airfreight charters filled up the airplane in volume before it ever reached the airplane's weight limit. Hence, because the weight was not a constraining factor, the postal tariff could ignore it.

A smaller-scale example comes from a car wash named Car Spa, in New Canaan, Connecticut, where all cleaning is guaranteed for three days following the service. The benefit advertised is that if it rains, owners can come back with their cars and get a free wash. The logic of this offer is powerful: induce car drivers to have their cars washed even if bad weather threatens. Since car washes have very low variable cost (some soap, some power), the incremental revenues are not offset by material costs.

How costs are treated managerially can make a material difference in outcomes and how competitors price. Often the attention to such differences seems to focus on accounting differences (e.g., differences between GAAP accounting and non-GAAP accounting such as between U.S. and overseas firms). Yet that is not the largest difference we have seen. The managerial cost approach can make a much bigger difference in pricing outcomes and the competitive context.

For instance, in the early 1980s Mobil Oil Europe enjoyed considerably better management than most of its competitors and did very well employing marginal costing to its markets. The idea, simply, is that the company applied the highest cost fuel source to the lowest price (marginal) market. This is in contrast to mechanically applying the actual cost of whatever fuel happened to be closest to a particular market. The results, in the illustration here, were material (30 percent difference in total margins), as shown in Table 10-2.

In the table, the marginalist costing, by applying marginal (highest cost) supply against marginal distribution (lowest price) regions, obtains a higher total margin and on lower assets. This worked out even after adjusting for the transport cost differences, although it was "incredibly complex" to do, according to management.

The benefits of marginalist costing go beyond short-term profits. This approach allowed Mobil to buy assets from Texaco and BP to consolidate its position in profitable market regions. Although not needed in that case, it might also have given Mobil more pricing options in matching price competition.

Table 10-2 Marginalist Costing and Profit

COST BY SOURCE			MARGINAL COST		
Revenue	Costs by Source	Net Result	Revenue	Costs (Marginal)	Net Result
Region I: €2.5/ltr.	Region I: €2.1/ltr.	Region I: €0.4/ltr.	Region I: €2.5/ltr.	Region I: €1.9/ltr.	Region I: €0.6/ltr.
Region II: €2.3/ltr.	Region II: €2.2/ltr.	Region II: €0.1/ltr.	Region II: €2.3/ltr.	Region II: €2.1/ltr.	Region II: €0.2/ltr.
Region III: €2.0/ltr.	Region III: €1.9/ltr.	Region III: €0.1/ltr.	Region III: €2.0/ltr.	Region III: €2.2/ltr.	Region III: Exit
		Total €0.6			Total €0.8

Risk as Part of Strategy

Interestingly, in the same way that courage plays a role in military strategy, it also appears to play a major role in pricing strategy. Fear is a common reaction by managers not familiar with pricing. At one level, who can blame them?

Bold strategy does require courage. Don Regan, CEO of Merrill Lynch when they invented the CMA Account (integrated money management account), bet his job on what was then a huge investment in systems to support the product. In that case it was a huge success. Similarly, Dell Computer repeatedly bet on volume price economies to aggressively price its personal computers. Likewise, winemaker Jess Jackson bet on marketing a new type of semisweet wine called Vintner's Reserve at a new price point of $4.50 per bottle. The first year sales volume of 20,000 bottles fell well below the breakeven of 50,000, but Jackson persevered. Eventually sales grew to five million cases annually. This established Kendall-Jackson as a major winery, despite fierce competition from E&J Gallo, the world's largest winemaker.[9]

So why is courage important? Courage appears to be important to pricing success because it takes courage to accept the facts. For instance, in 1991 IBM, which invented the router, was the dominant vendor. A small competitor, called Cisco Systems, had however been effective in integrating more data protocols into its router, so a clear value gap had emerged.

In retrospect it is clear that IBM should have done all it could to regain the protocol lead from Cisco. Failing that, it should have used pricing and bundling to blunt Cisco's inroads. True, offering a lower price would have been dissonant with the concept of the famous "IBM premium," but it would have given IBM time to catch up. Sadly for IBM Communications, its then-chief Ellen Hancock refused to consider the option, so IBM ceded the router market to Cisco. Her refusal to look at reality cost IBM billions.

There is, to be fair, great pressure to go with "normal" pricing in most companies. A similar refusal to accept abnormal numbers was experienced by one of the authors of this book while in finance at Bell Atlantic. Strong advocates urged the purchase of paging companies, which were hot in the 1980s. Application of the capital asset pricing model (CAPM), however, suggested a more than 80 percent hurdle rate was applicable. This killed the deal, but only because finance stood united in the correctness of this analysis. To the nonfinancial mind, an 80 percent discount rate was clearly to be ignored even if correct.[10]

> Successful strategy probably requires courage—in most cases, at least courage in sticking with the numbers.

The Impact of Price Variation

Similarly, in many pricing decisions, there are numbers that do not have the benefit of hard bases and so tend to be replaced with innocuous numbers that result in mistaken pricing. Repeatedly the most difficult number to assess is what a change in price for one customer will do to the prices for other customers. If you hold firm with one customer, will that improve your company's pricing with another customer? If you drop a price, how does that affect your ability to hold price with another customer or customer segment?

A normal practice is for companies to assume zero impact. This can be correct, or it can be quite mistaken. However, solid strategy requires more than a default answer or ignoring the issue. As Warren Buffett commented: "Risk comes from not knowing what you are doing."

The right approach is to assess the interaction of different pricing decisions on one another. This would include understanding if and how customers communicate with one another on purchase prices. It should also include an assessment of how your own sales force or market management will react to a low-priced sale. One study of the consumer cellular market found that the vast majority of subscriber down-tiers to less expensive plans were the result of unintentional communication by their own wireless provider. In B2B markets, often company's own sales force is a primary driver of destructive interaccount communication about price.

> The most important price estimate is also the toughest: estimating what moving one customer's price will do to other customers' prices. The default assumption of no impact can be dangerous.

In addition to assessing the impact of price variation, there are a number of things companies can do to reduce the impact of customer communication on pricing. The first is to adopt the contextual pricing approach advocated in this book. When sales and markets are presented with the right price to begin with, there is less need for damage control afterwards. The perpetual battle over discounts loses much of its meaning.

Another means for controlling interaccount communication is to use price structure. As described earlier, each pricing context often should get its own price structure, partly because the customers probably want it, but also to reduce interaccount communication. Ask yourself: will the customer who gets capped variable pricing easily compare prices with the customer who gets a flat price with rollover pricing? Structure differences render different price points far less comparable, or at least require some math before customers can decide if someone else got a bargain.

Estimating the Risk of Loss

A common problem among market leaders is the desire to never lose a competitor. This policy effectively strips the market leader of much of its negotiation power—and courage. While there are many negotiation tactics you might employ, broadly "If you have no choice, you cannot negotiate." [11] Over time this tends to lead to the reduction of any value premium your company enjoys.

The financial math required to disentangle this situation is not obvious, and it's even tougher without some courageous estimates. In a nutshell, the question is: *which is greater? The risk-adjusted expected lifetime value of the account being priced or the reduction in lifetime value of the other accounts potentially affected by this price outcome?*

The same question can also apply to consumer markets, with the calculation being performed at a segment level. For example, if we lower our price to supermarkets in suburbia, will we have to give that same reduction to Sam's Club?

In both cases the core calculation rests on the signaling impact of holding firm to a price. Since nothing is certain, this is a probabilistic (expected value) number. Through customer interviews and modeling, however, the risk of loss or gain can be quantified. For instance, one group health insurance company found that if it increased its prices to midsized companies with high levels of stress-related illness, their initial share loss was made up in the longer term by other midsized companies, because other group insurers followed suit and employers in this segment had no cheaper options.

Estimating risk of loss is tougher the smaller your number of customers. For relatively numerous customers (e.g., BlackBerry users), a set of statistical tests, perhaps combined with some models of customer utility and alternatives, will provide a clear answer. In the case of monopsony or very concentrated buyers, it requires extensive research into the buyer decision process and some subtle probing and dialogue with decision makers. The good news is also that with few buyers, communication can be much more direct, and there is often a highly compensated account team who should be able to influence outcomes.

Reducing Risk

A final point on risk: it can be reduced. One way to reduce risk is to offer customers a choice—perhaps not the choices they would want ideally, nor the status quo, but a choice. This way if you turn out to be wrong on your price (or other) changes, they can choose the least-offensive option. For instance, if you need to cap data use to preserve network economics, don't just legislate a cap—offer a range of alternatives that amounts to a very large surcharge on usage that causes network congestion.[12]

Another way to reduce risk is to offer "insurance" to buyers who are wary of a price structure change. That insurance can be as simple as a price-paid guarantee: that next year the customer's price-paid total will not go up. We have found that such a guarantee can defer any problems with conversion, yet lays the groundwork for later revenue gains.

Another form of insurance is for your company to *guarantee the value* of its product or service. For instance, in 2008 a major cable network was raising its licensing fees to affiliates such as cable companies. Since the overall economy was slipping into deep recession at the time, many of the network affiliates (buyers) worried about paying for an increase in a faltering economy. They worried viewership would shrink, and with a slip in viewership, advertising would suffer; the affiliates worried that they risked over-paying.

To address this concern, the network offered to compensate affiliates in the event that viewership fell. Pricing this guarantee similarly to selling a put option (according to the well-known Black-Scholes option-pricing model), the network established the price for a guarantee on viewership and offered it to the buyers. The offer silenced the buyers' negotiation lever, even though none of the buyers took up the option.

Most businesses should consider offering a similar guarantee of value, if needed. We find that often the calculated value is quite reasonable, and adding it to the negotiation context usually takes away the opponent's bargaining lever. One reason such a tool is effective is that studies repeatedly show that fear of loss is valued higher by buyers than the benefits of gain—even if the two are objectively equal. Thus, a standard strategic move should be to reduce or eliminate fears of potential loss.

Give customers options, guarantees, or insurance to reduce your market risk from price changes.

Executional Capabilities

Managers with pricing responsibility in increasingly competitive markets need to consider whether they have in place the analysis and the corporate capabilities required to price effectively in the face of new competition. If not, now is the time to develop a pricing strategy and hone your pricing weapons.

Of course, some elements of pricing strategy must be unique to each company and its capabilities, but there are some fairly typical pricing behaviors. Incumbents and entrants classically choose different pricing levels and structures.

Managers with pricing responsibility in competitive markets need to consider whether they have in place the wide analytical and corporate capabilities required to face new competition and preserve shareholder

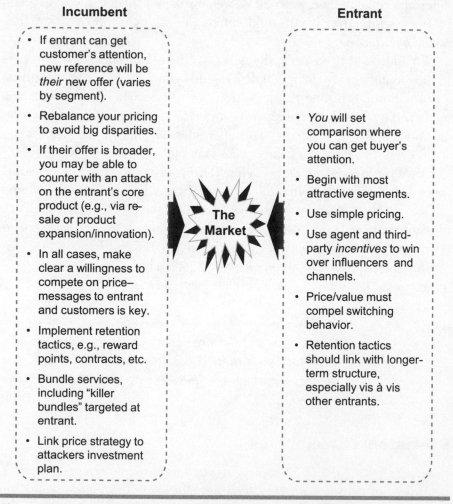

Incumbent

- If entrant can get customer's attention, new reference will be *their* new offer (varies by segment).
- Rebalance your pricing to avoid big disparities.
- If their offer is broader, you may be able to counter with an attack on the entrant's core product (e.g., via re-sale or product expansion/innovation).
- In all cases, make clear a willingness to compete on price—messages to entrant and customers is key.
- Implement retention tactics, e.g., reward points, contracts, etc.
- Bundle services, including "killer bundles" targeted at entrant.
- Link price strategy to attackers investment plan.

The Market

Entrant

- *You* will set comparison where you can get buyer's attention.
- Begin with most attractive segments.
- Use simple pricing.
- Use agent and third-party *incentives* to win over influencers and channels.
- Price/value must compel switching behavior.
- Retention tactics should link with longer-term structure, especially vis à vis other entrants.

Figure 10-1 Competitor levers on reference point: differences between incumbent (defender) strategies and entrant (attacker) strategies.

value. Additionally, managers must understand the *operational risks* of various pricing tools. For instance, discounts can carry operational risks. A few years ago, a major cigarette manufacturer offered a significant price break to its wholesalers. But it failed to structure the new price to pass savings to end users. As a result, the wholesalers got a one-time windfall, end users saw no change in price, and the manufacturer failed to win any new market share.

Information technology capabilities are crucial in some markets. The right IT capabilities can not only help improve the quality of customer service that supports premium pricing but also help support segmentation and price changes. For a company to push its pricing strategy beyond its IT limits, however, can be counterproductive. For instance, a leading telco unintentionally sent almost one million checks, designed to induce users to change vendors, to its *own* customers—needlessly costing it $30 million. We happened to arrive at the client's office that day, and by the look in peoples' eyes you might have thought a bomb had gone off. But the real lesson is that this telecom company had pushed its ancient systems beyond what they could do safely.[13]

Strategizing for Duopolies and Oligopolies

Two major industry players engaged in duopolistic pricing represent a special case of price competition. Often the word *comfortable* appears in front of the word *duopoly*. This phrase nicely describes the optimal pricing strategy for duopolies and oligopolies. No party will benefit from a price war, *but incremental gains* are acceptable. As an illustration, United Airlines fought ferociously and successfully to keep Frontier and other airlines out of its O'Hare Chicago fortress hub, but it had to allow American Airlines to expand its existing operations since it had operated there since the 1930s. That is a fairly neat example of the tiered rules of duopoly competition.

So what does this mean? It suggests that competition needs to take the form of improvements in pricing capabilities and changes in price levels that cannot be construed as directed at the competition. As long as there is credible denial that no direct price attack is intended, the duopoly equilibrium tends to survive. Continuing with airline examples, when in 1982 Continental Airlines was struck by unions and 12,000 employees walked off the job, management rolled out a low $49 fare for any direct route flown by the airline. This price had the ostensible purpose of breaking the strike and retaining customers. While many new passengers flocked to this price, because it was not aimed at any competitor, this low fare did not provoke a price war.

So what are the tactics that allow duopolists and oligopolists to compete on price? There are three common practices:

1. *Improved pricing sophistication.* More sophisticated pricing tools have included better demand-management systems like Sabre for airlines, better cost-based pricing by integrated oil companies that have concentrated their service stations around refineries, better bundling of improved product features (which can backfire if done badly), and price signaling among leading players.
2. *Improved price-related terms.* These are especially terms that secure customer loyalty. An example includes the AT&T cellular rollover minutes plan and other retention tactics described in the Structure chapter.
3. *Product innovation.* While not strictly a price strategy, the nice thing about new products is that there is no direct comparison to the duopolist competitor, plus often the product innovation is a way to undercut existing competitor products. For instance, many "digital" products are actually little different in functionality to preexisting products; however, the changes in underlying technology, cost basis, and (some) differences in functionality have made these effective tools for attack.[14]

The end of the duopoly dance comes either when new entrants succeed in establishing themselves in the market of one of the duopolists or one of the duopolists falls behind in market power. An example of a new entrant succeeding in establishing itself—through clever pricing—happened in 1973 when top-12 airline Braniff International began facing competition from start-up Southwest Airlines on the Houston–Dallas route. To kill the upstart, Braniff attacked with a $13 fare, half of the previous $26 fare. Southwest Airlines, financially stretched, offered passengers a choice of the $13 fare *or* the $26 fare plus a bottle of Chivas Regal. Some 75 percent of travelers chose the higher fare and bottle. Southwest had survived.

Then it was time for Braniff to be eaten by its fellow sharks. By 1975 Braniff withdrew from the Houston–Dallas route, and in a few more years it went out of business because of very smart competition from American

Airlines. Other examples of sharks circling a wounded prey include the dismemberment of publisher Harcourt in the 2000s and veteran financial player Lehman Brothers being gobbled up in the 2008 financial crisis.

The nature of competition between duopolists varies with the level of responsibility inside each company. Outside top management, competition is fierce and lethal, and encouraged. Given sales compensation plans or division management objectives, a win or a loss means a lot to an account manager, a product manager, or a divisional VP.

At the top, however, another game is being played. This could be called Grand Strategy. The difference between battlefield strategy and Grand Strategy is that the former is focused on winning and killing enemies. Not so with Grand Strategy, which is focused on using "war to achieve a better peace—if only from one point of view."[15] This means that top management focus includes how to avoid ruinous price war and to ensure ongoing corporate well-being. Unless presented with an absolutely certain kill of a competitor, top management will avoid risk of mutual destruction. As former Coke Chairman Neville Isdell once told his senior managers, "Be mindful of the consequences of the consequences."

Summary

In summary, when handled correctly, price strategy will help to combat new competitors and preserve margins, or to invade new markets. But price strategy must reflect the relative position of the product or service being priced—a key distinction being that between new entrants and incumbents. Prices will vary dramatically by context and segment; if not, you will work harder than you need to accomplish your company's objectives. Price structure must reflect your objectives and capability to execute a price strategy. Most important, price strategy is the integrated set of management actions over time, designed to create lasting price advantage.

Notes

1. Some of the best contextual pricing lies in happenstance. "After 181 Years, Local Beer Stops Playing Hard to Get," *The Wall Street Journal*, October 21, 2010, p. B1. Note how the volume multiplier makes later price level improvement desirable.

2. Just as military strategists have found strategy requires taking advantage of the unique features of a battlefield (e.g., the "topology"), pricers should take advantage of the unusual aspects of the market—what we are calling context. General Carl von Clausewitz also commented that "No topology is ever the same," and his book *On War* (1873) has chapters discussing defense and offense in relation to mountains, forests, rivers, swamps, and other factors that frame how armies should attack and defend. More recently B. H. Liddell Hart pointed out the importance of factors that may obscure the other side's vision during the "fog of war." That is highly applicable to pricing, except that instead of mountains and swamps we face customer preferences and budget limits. Liddell Hart, incidentally, is the inventor of modern tank warfare and his admirers included General George Patton, Field Marshall Rommel, and others. B. H. Liddell Hart, *Strategy* (Second Edition), Praeger, N.Y., 1967, pp. 335–346.

3. Mike Farrell, Multichannel News, December 9, 2009, 5:00:51 p.m. The jump in rates was large: from 8 cents per subscriber to 25 cents per subscriber, according to the *New York Times*, January 21, 2010, p. B3.

4. Thread on foodnetworkfans.com.

5. In one professional services market, a smart incumbent had figured out what was the pricing threshold for competitive inroads. A strong CEO kept prices just below that level. After that company was acquired, the new corporate owner wanted to improve returns and therefore raised prices. Within three years the company had lost enough market share that it showed a negative revenue trend.

6. See Chapter 6 for a longer discussion of structure. Besides avoiding price transparency, market leaders have strong economic incentives to favor more complex, two-part pricing. The economist Walter Oi pointed this out in his classic analysis of pricing at Disneyland, which charges both a significant entrance fee *and* a small charge for rides once inside. Oi demonstrated that by charging marginal costs for rides and a material entrance fee, Disney (or any entity with substantial market share) ends up with greater profitability than charging only the usage fees for rides.

7. A legitimate concern beyond jet engines. Henry Ford once commented, "I would give away my cars for free, if I could be

guaranteed the sale of their replacement parts." A recognition of context, perhaps.

8. "Goldman's Buddy System," *The New York Times*, January 4, 2011, p. B1 and p. B6. This ecosystem reflects the dictum by Phebe Prescott, a senior transportation strategist, who noted that in noncommodity purchasing "relationships only work if both sides are getting something from the relationship."

9. E&J Gallo employed the right tactics: it developed duplicate products and sold them for competitive prices, but Kendall-Jackson apparently just out-innovated them. "Jess Jackson Dies at 81," *The New York Times*, April 22, 2011, p. B11.

10. Subsequent performance of paging companies fell into line with this hurdle estimate. Often analysts have also been cast out for correct analysis. "The Loneliest Analyst," *The New York Times*, Sunday Business, September 12, 2011, p. 1, tells the story of a Wall Street analyst who was right but paid a high price for speaking the truth.

11. Former President of Mobil Oil Corporation William Tavoulareas. With products of any sophistication, there are components of the offer that can be withheld. For instance, your company can substitute a lower-tier service for higher levels of service.

12. See H. Raiffa, *The Art and Science of Negotiation*, Harvard University Press (1982). Also "FCC Chief Backs Metered Broadband," *Wall Street Journal*, December 2, 2010, p. B3. Another important concept is avoiding overreaching and being rebuffed by buyers, as this destroys what master negotiator Barbara Meili calls "negotiation capital." Just this happened in 2008 to a large chemical company that broke off negotiations with a supplier, only to discover that supplier was its best choice. That chemical company is now paying 40 percent more for the supplier product—substantially more than the 15 percent increase initially on the table.

13. We understand the idea that with urgency, and competitive pressure, you must push elements beyond what they are capable of. Just not too far. To return to military analogies, for the famous World War II battle in the Denmark Strait between the *Schlachtschiffes Bismarck* and the British ships HMS *Hood* and HMS *Prince of Wales*. The *Prince of Wales* was put to sea while it

was still under construction: there were technicians and carpenters still onboard working as she sailed to intercept the German squadron. While it was a risky decision by the admiralty, it was necessary. The *Prince of Wales* scored some hits on *Bismarck*, which forced the German ship to curtail its proposed cruise.

14. Price wars can result from accidents and confused signals, but more systematically they can result when one competitor dramatically improves the price/value ratio of its offers. This forces competitors that cannot increase the value of their offers to drop their prices in order to remain competitive—and ironically results in a decrease in industry pricing. An example of a gradual end to duopoly is the entrance into the 100-seat passenger jet market by Brazil, China, Canada, and Russia. See "Airbus and Boeing Call End to Duopoly," *Financial Times*, June 21, 2011, p. 14.

15. Liddell Hart, supra, pp. 366–372. This is why we have found that often when top management does a negotiation, the immediate price outcomes tend to be less favorable.

Chapter 11

Higher Return: Introductory Pricing Strategies

Let us always meet each other with a smile, for the smile is the beginning of love.

—MOTHER TERESA

Now that your company has a product or service ready for market, how can you use price to attract the attention of buyers and propel them to buy your product?

Two factors determine the success of an introductory pricing plan: knowledge and timing. By its nature, a new product is unfamiliar to potential buyers, and the burden of familiarization is on the seller. Precisely how your company should shape its introductory price will vary with each product, but while the application varies, the framework for success does not.

The good news is that the seller begins with an advantage. Sellers should know more about the product (or service) and its use than first-time buyers, so the seller should be able to shape the introductory pricing to the seller's advantage. Yet many persist in using introductory price schemes that ignore the advantage. Too many companies use the two-step "discounted trial followed by full price" approach. That begins to reflect the evolution of product knowledge and power, but it is a *very crude approximation*. What is a better fit?

Three Phases in Customer Product Adoption

Every market exhibits the same uptake pattern for new products, and this pattern must be the framework for introductory pricing strategy. The three-part pattern is:

1. Learn
2. Use and Enjoy
3. Reassess

Learn

The customer product adoption pattern is driven by customer knowledge. For instance, before a customer uses a product, he must learn about the product. Before she knows what benefits the new service provides, it would be pointless to wonder about alternatives. This pattern can be discerned in many ways, e.g., from customer focus groups at different stages in their usage and familiarity with a service or products, or by observable real-world customer behavior.

Stages in familiarity with a new product or service is the key question for new-product development teams considering pricing.

In addition to surveys of new customers, a good barometer of customer mind-set is the use of call-ins. Very typically a new product, particularly a groundbreaking new product, will require explanation and assistance in the beginning, prompting calls. An example of such a pattern of calls for a software as a service (SaaS) product showed that assistance queries dropped off after about 12 days. So, in that case, managers can infer that the learning phase basically ended within two weeks.

Note that there is a big difference between the customer familiarizing himself with the product and the seller's educating the customer about a product's full value. The latter task can take much longer and be Herculean in scope. The latter involves much more than introductory pricing. Familiarity is the essential purpose of trial.

Use and Enjoy

If the product suits the market, familiarity will lead to usage. Where usage or enjoyment of the product and service can be measured, usage measures often ramp up toward the end of the learning phase. This is because purchasers have learned how to use the product—and with that ability comes higher utility and satisfaction. Again, this can be measured. Satisfaction, measured directly or by proxy such as usage, is the key to determine when to end a trial and press for commitment. If the product offers real value, the customers will exploit the value with a palpable enthusiasm.

A look at the usage data will frequently show how things are going. At several online information service providers, for instance, customer cancellations were directly inverse to usage. Regression showed an adequate goodness of fit between usage and cancellation during trial—and high confidence levels (more than 90 percent).[1]

After some period of high usage and satisfaction, most customers will begin to wonder whether they can obtain the same value for less money. This is a dangerous phase of new-product introduction. The trial may have built understanding, but now the value of that understanding may migrate to a competitor or substitute! In some companies, where calls are categorized by type, an early warning of increasing price focus might become apparent by the number of calls inquiring or complaining about price. From the SaaS example, the surge of calls, and with it the reassessment phase, began about four weeks after initial commitment. Ironically, if the product never gets to the phase where price is a concern, that may be a bad sign also: it may suggest that the product is not priced high enough.

Awareness of the three phases has been incorporated into pricing some of the most successful product introductions in history. For instance, AT&T's consumer data service obtained over 800,000 customers during its initial months of launch. The pricing for this service was carefully tailored to the three phases: low price (actually, five hours free) during the introductory learning phase, a higher-than-market price during the middle high-enjoyment phase, and a competitive market price during the comparison phase. This is diagrammed in Figure 11-1.

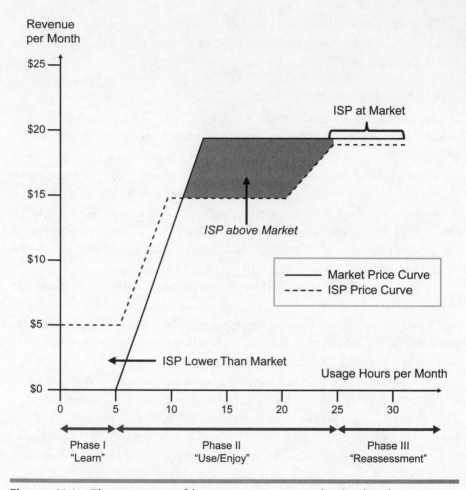

Figure 11.1   Three stages of buyer awareness and price level.

A key message in this example is that introductory pricing does not need to mean a loss in revenues. AT&T actually obtained incremental margins during the trial, which of course means that it could afford a larger-scale trial.

Just as a careful analysis of the product and customer can show that trial need not always mean negative margins, we have found that often an introductory pricing strategy need not involve lower prices. When a company has an innovative, unique, and compelling product but may face competition soon, there may be no reason to begin pricing lower than normal. In fact, intro pricing may be higher.

An example of this comes from the early days of America Online. While AOL was famous for its up-front discounts, this was not always appropriate. When preloaded onto a computer, AOL actually faced less competition than after a user was connected to the Web. Thus, rather than discount up-front, AOL tried an alternative approach: full price up-front, then various discounts *after* getting the contract. This made complete sense because it matched discounting to the reassessment (third) phase when users could learn to search for lower-priced alternatives.

> Introductory pricing strategies must reflect what the customer knows—and what they do not know.

The three-phase framework provided an incisive means for understanding customers and their decision logic. When a computer buyer initially opened the computer box, his immediate goal was to begin to use the Web. In that instant, AOL faced few competitive comparisons and enjoyed unrivaled awareness. Management knew this, but it was the framework that facilitated the pricing conclusion: no need to discount in phases one and two. Only after extended usage, in phase three, would users consider moving to a lower-priced alternative.

Reassess

The third phase, reassess, posed a problem for AOL. While it offered a rich array of services, the $23.99 monthly price was well above competitors', which were as low as $5 a month. Therefore, the third phase was the focus of pricing. AOL designed a pricing scheme that reflected this danger:

- First phase: full price, but option to cancel to reflect customer uncertainty
- Second phase: full price and contractual commitment
- Third phase: full price, but with a *random* month *free*

The power of promising an unspecified month free was that it reduced pricing transparency. It was designed to make users ask: would the next month be free? In which case, would switching providers squander a free month? As it turned out, this was an effective way of preventing new-subscriber drop-off.

The reassessment phase should always include an appraisal of switching costs. Switching costs can include new learning, contact cancellation penalties, and switching end-customer interface. Switching costs should play a major role in designing introductory prices. Where switching costs are high, companies should look for ways to induce customers to "buy into" several contract elements that would require switching should they choose to leave.

Be careful of cost factors that offset switching cost barriers. For instance, customers may buy more than one class of service, such as simultaneously using both Microsoft Windows and Apple OS in a corporate department. This is known as multi-homing. Multi-homing can be very burdensome, and individual purchase switching costs may be ignored as customers rush to shed the burdens of multi-homing.

Breadth versus Depth

We find that introductory pricing should only rarely involve a discount, particularly when facing an incumbent service vendor. Here is why:

- Inevitably, incumbents have spent considerable time and effort developing their product so that it covers a range of customer needs, frequently adding additional applications (e.g., video game players that add in online gaming, online movies, video editing capabilities, or cross-platform mobility; their objective is to capture incremental audiences).
- While the rich product functionality and integration typical of incumbent offers may benefit some customers, often it comes at added cost or added complexity—so that ease-of-use suffers. Such complexity has repeatedly caused products to under-index in some segments (e.g., often women refuse to buy complex technological consumer services such as satellite television, so Dish and other satellite vendors markedly under-index among women).
- This means that overextended products provide an opening for competitors. Such products are ripe for the possibility of an effective introductory pricing attack.

- Therefore, overextended products can be attacked by a narrow and segmented product. Why? Because customers hate paying for features they don't use (even if, as in software, it adds little to cost).

An interesting example of this kind of introductory pricing involved a market for desktop computing support, which is characterized by high switching costs (relative to margins). In this case, switching costs ran about 15 to 25 percent of the annual operating costs because of installation and training of users to move from one company's service to another's. The case involved finding an attack offer that funded switching costs without cutting too deeply into vendor margins to be viable.

The solution lay in the data provider making an offer that included a flat charge service warranty for two years. The scope of the bid was only basic services setup and maintenance, with all other services (e.g., training) as extras. This dramatically undercut the incumbent price, which included many add-on services, for which they had negotiated high-margin surcharges.

In contrast, the entrant's terms meant that after-sales support calls (within limits) would add no charges for the buyer, allowing the challenger to amortize switchover costs. The narrower scope reduced costs further. The result was a price offer almost half that of the incumbents. The incumbents thought that the new price was a loss-leader, but in fact it was the more lucrative service contract.

The reason the economics worked was that the seller was risking only its costs per hour (about $45 per hour) while the buyer was avoiding full price charges (about $110 per hour). It was a mutual win owing to differences in cost context.

Calls to Action and Lifetime Value

A call to action (purchase) is particularly important if the benefits of using a product are slow to accrue and there are switching costs to consumers. Frequently this is the case with "me too" products. Examples of commodity products with some switching costs include financial services such as brokerage and banking accounts, or cell phone accounts (especially before number portability). Even worse, some products may never actually offer any benefit (e.g., most insurance products don't pay out unless there is a loss).

If a new product falls into this category, a call to action may be indispensible. There are many potential calls to action, but they usually cost money if the call to action is not trivial. To see how much can be invested in a call to action, a manager must know the lifetime value of the customer. Lifetime value is dependent on expected churn and spending. One factor in boosting both inputs to lifetime value, often overlooked, is the *permanent* price structure. If the permanent structure is very ordinary, then the lifetime churn will be ordinary.

> Introductory pricing should mesh with the permanent price structure since price structure should reflect market price drivers.

Because price structure is a major driver of churn and lifetime value, a better structure can improve the "budget" for the call to action. So a better permanent price structure allows better introductory offers. There are many ways to determine the best price structure (see Chapter 6), but frequently new products are tougher to give an exact price architecture. An effective way to address this uncertainty is to offer customers a choice of structures and prices. If you are unsure whether they want to buy flat rate "all-you-can-eat" or "by-the-drink," give them a choice. With self-selection, customers will generally take the best option for their needs—and can switch to a better structure if their perceptions change.

> Allowing buyers a choice of price structures and levels will reduce your market acceptance risks.

Retention Tactics

Retention tactics need to be considered in any product launch. For instance, offering discounts in arrears, rather than up-front, naturally has the effect of discouraging churn. An example of this is reward points which accrue with usage, not purchase. While it is usage that builds up airline miles or credit card reward points, it takes some time for points to cumulate to something worthwhile. Until customers redeem them, such points are an effective means to discourage defection because generally the points are cancelled upon closing the account (e.g., if a customer cancels her American Express card, all points are lost).

Structural retention tactics apply to industrial situations also, where contingent volume discounts are paid at the end of a contract term. For instance, industrial plastic packaging contracts producers use volume discounts in a very tactical way, adjusting discounts to gain share and placement for new products. "Tactical" means that discounts might be specific to geographies or even warehouses. An added advantage to many layers of product discounts is that where discounts are geared to future orders, it is very difficult for buyers to disengage. This is one reason that packaging manufacturers did not suffer as badly as other sectors in the recent downturn.

Free

A quick word about "free." This is a powerful word, but sadly it appears to be accepted by consumers without a lot of thought. When applied with less than a concern for honest communication by sellers, the stage can be set for damage to the brand.

What is free? In some cases the appeal for free is really for pricing simplicity combined with the usual desire for lower prices. For instance, when L.L. Bean, the venerable mail-order house, decided to offer "free" shipping, customers understood that the cost of shipping would have an impact on the product costs. But while L.L. Bean says that their customers find this approach less annoying, it is likely that what the customers really like is a simplified understanding of the price.[2]

Another use for free applies when there is some question in the customer's mind about the value of the product or service. In some cases, this value must be demonstrated through direct experience (e.g., a sample or trial offer). The rule here is:

The utility of free = (Experiential value/Apparent value) ×
(Perceived risk − Guidance on sale) × (1/Cost of free)

Therefore, the more unknown the good and the more its purchase represents a risk (because of price or other factor), the more useful free will be. This is why there are food samples in grocery stores: a new taste is conveyed in only a limited way via advertisement. For some categories of goods, interestingly, the cost of free samples has come down sharply, as in the case of simulator software for fashion goods and configurators for cars. In some cases, sampling means using the actual product, such as long trial periods for SaaS services like salesforce.com.

Guided Sales

One reason for the existence of a sales force is that buyers often want advice on a prospective purchase. Again, understanding customer knowledge is key for determining if your product requires a guided sale. Therefore, guidance on sales goes hand in hand with more complex goods (e.g., automobiles, houses, medical procedures, etc.).

In general, the more guidance, the less need for free samples, notwithstanding the risks or need for experiential value. This is why airliners are purchased (or, at least, options for purchase are taken) before the first one rolls off the production floor. Yes, it's important to know how an airplane will fly; yes, it's risky to buy a new generation of an airliner—but there is a lot of guidance by Boeing and Airbus on the airplane. Plus free samples would be expensive.

Guidance is an underrated element to introductory pricing. Every product can benefit from some advice from the maker, but in many cases the product's margin or distribution does not allow it. With the advent of the online purchase, the ability to offer inexpensive guidance has increased. Most online selling could benefit from more guidance to help outline options and set context. For instance, even simple guidance like the Amazon.com advice that "People who bought this book also bought . . . " is a superb source of guidance. Reviews by purchasers can also serve this purpose.

Guidance can also help simplify a long list of product options. For instance, if there are 25 options for adding to data security, a single question ("On a scale of 0 to 5, how concerned are you with data security?") can replace a longer list. When seeking "simple pricing," often buyers are really asking for short and clear menus of choices.

Negative Usage Pricing

If your company is faced with potential customers who are stubbornly resistant to trial and adoption, try a tactic called negative pricing. Applied typically to measurable services (e.g., SaaS applications), this approach provides a strong incentive to users to frequently utilize the service. The idea is to offer a reduction to fixed monthly price every time that a customer use or event occurs.

An example of this is a disaster-recovery service located in Oregon. This service charges a fixed fee of thousands of dollars per month to provide emergency backup computing capabilities and work facilities. Every time one of its clients refreshes the data being backed up, however, there is an offset to the charge. For instance, every time a client tests its backup systems, it gets a $50 credit.

In this case, everyone gains by this structure. The more frequently data is backed up, the less trouble it will be to recover data after a disaster or other computer problem. This reduces the provider's costs. It also ingrains the habit of backing up among customers, often driven by office managers who harass computer users into doing what they otherwise would be uninterested in: using the service.

There is also a subtle upside to the structure. Note how more price-sensitive customers will be very meticulous in backing up—to save money. Less price-sensitive customers will be more haphazard. They won't care about the savings. Thus, this structure is a self-regulating way of price discriminating among customers who vary by concern for costs.

> An innovative introductory pricing approach, when customers refuse free trial, is negative-use pricing. It can provide incentive to potential users and build support for purchase.

How to Analyze a Nonexistent Product

All the requirements for effective price structures for existing products apply to products under development also, but the obvious problem is that the proposed products do not have available proven customer behavior under different contexts—or do they?

Routinely managers charged with new product development will use customer research (e.g., focus groups, surveys, etc.) to gather insights on how customers will view and value the proposed new product. This makes sense, but in many cases it is not enough. Many products are hard to envision or understand by focus group participants and survey respondents. Also, we still face the gaming of answers described earlier.

A very useful technique for exploring new product development is to create a "synthetic product" that matches the one under development. In essence, the synthetic product is a sophisticated analogy drawing upon like characteristics of existing products. The synthetic analogy allows quantitative analysis of behavior to supplement qualitative investigation.

A leading soft drink company that was considering offering flavored ice cubes at fast food restaurants went through something similar. In test groups, qualitative feedback was favorable: the flavored ice cubes (in a range of flavors such as raspberry, cherry, and lime) were found to be fun and even exciting complements to standard soft drinks. The question was how to examine potential pricing.

By considering the different components of the proposed offer, analogies were found. For instance, the beverage company already offered bottled flavors for use in drinks and related foods. The company had experimented with different insulated containers and ice options. Other elements of the proposed offers all had some analog in history. Together they formed a complete synthetic model that provided the means for testing price against actual market behaviors.

Very few products, no matter how revolutionary, have no analog or precedent. Through the use of these analogies, managers can build very accurate models of likely buyer behavior. For instance, the beverage company knew that previous purchases of (liquid) flavors had been driven by specific segments and contexts—and close examination suggested the same would be true of the ice. In this manner the volumes, types of buyers, drivers of purchase and price, and the impact of context were all captured and even proved statistically.

More important, even if the product does not exist, typically the context does already exist. Consider that when a rigorous test of price is performed for existing products often the product characteristics (throughput, accuracy, durability) are not the primary drivers of price.

Instead, context (buyer decision process, organizational mission, brand, etc.) are often the primary drivers of price. Since these more important factors are already known, there is no reason not to do most of the pricing work ahead of actual prototype creation. Don't wait until the last minute to do the pricing, as important product charter lessons can often come from pricing analysis.

Synthetic models of proposed products, based on analogies, are helpful in many new-product development aspects, not merely pricing. Product feature and configuration choices can be addressed simultaneously with price questions. Finally, synthetics allow much more detailed rollout and channel planning.

For nonexistent products (still under development), there is usually plenty of evidence on potential price drivers. Don't forget, even if the product does not exist, typically the context already does.

Capabilities

Beyond the actual strategy, tactics, and price levels, superior introductory pricing requires building solid capabilities to determine price and rollout strategies. If your company lacks pricing capabilities, it cannot develop a strategy to develop pricing or leverage insights based on product knowledge and timing.

To understand value, managers must understand what *customers know* about their company's good or service, and how customers propose to use it. It sounds obvious, but we find that often observers at focus groups, or designers of surveys, do not focus on what the customer knows and at when in the adoption process the customer reaches a judgment on value. This is because generally marketing is fixated on the product and perhaps secondarily on channel and promotion. Price often seems to be a distant afterthought, which is often why introductory pricing strategies are threadbare and haphazard.

In some sense, the ability to develop a powerful introductory pricing strategy is a microcosm of overall pricing capabilities. Management must know the customer, must know the product, and must know the competition and your company's economics. This understanding may be meshed with overall objectives—or may shape overall objectives. It will not happen by itself; it needs to be part of the organizational design.

In some cases, a market launch is not the end of new-product pricing. In some industries, offers are fluid; there are many offers with only slight differences introduced to the market, so the *introductory pricing is iterative* (or should be). That pattern may be best practice: in many cases we find that companies fail to experiment with prices and launch price trials (e.g., launch a product with more than one price structure or price point). The benefits can be material, as in the consumer packaged goods industry, where trial is common. Procter &Gamble and others have well-developed test market procedures and measures, and the consequences of skipping that process are dire: one Colgate-Palmolive CEO lost his job (in part) due to market disasters from skipping test markets.

"Gettin' the Hogs off the Truck"

After management has defined the ideal introductory strategy, various thorny issues always remain. The farming expression just mentioned characterizes these last obstacles very well. For instance, how to account for introductory pricing? How to compensate the sales force? Sometimes most dire: how to bill according to your introductory strategy? Billing is often a limitation because at established large companies, where billing systems have been built and optimized for existing products. At many companies capabilities are often limited, and the IT department believes it will have enough trouble implementing the permanent price structure, let alone a distinct introductory pricing structure.

Some introductory pricing decisions will probably alienate influential functional groups within your company. Your sales, marketing, and IT functions must be willing to support needed introductory pricing programs. To ensure this support, top management must take a role in this. Fortunately, top management is increasingly becoming involved in new-product development and pricing because, in many cases, this represents the future of the company. This involvement prevents crippled product launches through poor cooperation. Equally important, with direct involvement, top management can shoulder the burden of taking risks on new approaches that are difficult to justify without hard evidence. It is well known that some leading technology companies such as Apple often have new-product pricing specified by top management, (e.g., the price structure of iTunes was directly controlled by Steve Jobs).

Of course, creativity is helpful in launching a new-product introductory price strategy when infrastructure might not be ready. There are work-arounds to most problems. For instance, there are highly adaptable off-the-shelf billing systems—such as FTS—that can be configured by events, usage, and other factors that play a role in introductory pricing. These systems do not scale to millions of customers, but they do increasingly scale beyond 300,000 invoices and more. In many cases, this is more than adequate! If your introductory pricing strategy generates too many customers, this is the kind of problem you want to have.

> Creativity in building infrastructure to support new pricing (e.g., billing) is often necessary.

Summary

Introductory pricing is the smile that can propel customers to trial and to buy new products and services. Introductory pricing is more effective when it mirrors buyers' stages of understanding and product experience.

The three stages of introduction—learn, use and enjoy, and reassess—suggest the framework for new-product introductory price structures. Applying this framework requires understanding what customers know about your product or service, and when they are ready to move to the next phase.

Introductory pricing often bumps into constraints on billing, sales compensation and rollout support. This will require creativity in working around constraints, and this often calls for senior management support. Strong leadership and application of the three-part framework will lead away from low-return conventional introductory pricing and to superior results.

Notes

1. While confidence levels on usage were very strong, the goodness of fit (R^2) suggested that there is often more to the story. Further statistical regression analysis often tells an interesting story, linking back to channel issues and product issues, but for pricing purposes looking at usage is often a good start. Incidentally, often you may wish to ignore customers/cohorts with zero usage because they have forgotten all about buying the service and so are not evaluating their usage or utility from the purchase— hence quite stable.

2. "Will Free Shipping Spread?" *The New York Times*, April 2, 2011, p. B4. See Chapter 6 for a discussion of customer preferences for simple pricing and when it must be heeded. In this case, apparently L.L. Bean decided it was subject to customer defections.

Chapter 12

Brand, Messaging, and Competition

Every book is a children's book if the child can read.
—MITCH HEDBERG

Contextual pricing relies heavily on what customers know, or worry they do not know, about a product. This makes pricing exercises a lot like branding exercises, since branding managers spend a lot of time evaluating what customers, and potential customers, know and don't know. Branding managers have the fun job, however, working at multiple levels to increase the propensity to buy. While complex, it tends to focus on the positive: matching customer affinities to company strengths. Customers like being made aware of products and solutions to their needs, and everyone in a company is delighted to see their company's strengths communicated to the world. There is relatively little internal dislocation.

That is not the case with pricing in most companies today. Pricing does not wear quite the "white hat" of branding. But it could.

Suppose pricing did what it is supposed to, which is pay *more attention to context and structure than to price level*? Wouldn't it be effective and enjoyable if you enabled high-usage customers to buy on a fixed basis, when previously all that was available was a variable plan—such as Spotify, allowing digital music lovers huge catalogues for a flat rate rather than pay-per-track? Or suppose you offered a warranty that let customers pick exactly what they wanted to have covered? Or suppose your company cut unnecessary components out of its bundles, so that buyers felt that they were not buying components they did not need?

A focus on context and structure would help turn pricing into a (marginally) more popular and enjoyable function, with only a few impediments to success. Sadly, those impediments are not trivial. Pricing may never be as popular with management, but the evidence is that it could be a larger contributor to revenue and profit than is branding.[1]

One issue with pricing is that it tends to be more interventionist and demanding of internal company processes. For a price structure change, there are often billing system requirements, changes in sales training and practices, new financial and compensation plans, and even changes in branding plans. Change will be resisted, and if pricing management spends all its time fighting internal battles, managers will have little time to look outside the enterprise at the market.

Another issue with pricing is that it does not always end with a win-win at the customer level. Often the best outcome for your shareholders is that your prices go up—not necessarily the preferred outcome for your customers. In contrast, except for relatively infrequent branding missteps, branding can be a win-win most of the time—if buyers feel great about what they know about a product and feel good about what they have bought, then the benefit is mutual.

But both contextual pricing and branding are an inquiry into the nature of the decision process. Figuratively speaking, a good branding market research effort is within 15 percent of being a good pricing market research effort. The inquiry will typically address what buyers know and do not know about their purchase alternatives. Familiarity with potential purchases varies dramatically across industries and markets.[2]

Branding and contextual pricing
should have a very similar focus.

Buyers' knowledge of what they know, or want to know, matters a lot to pricing. For instance, if buyers are convinced that there is no difference among vendors within a category, they will refuse to pay a price differential—this is the definition of a commodity. Effectively, the commodity classification is a judgment by the buyer that he knows all he needs to know. Thus, while there are demonstrable differences among sources of wheat of a specific grade, or a category of steel, there is simple agreement that the differences will be ignored.[3]

The Four Dimensions of Brand

Applying four dimensions of brand, nicely outlined in Hamel and Prahalad's *Competing for the Future*, we see linkage between brand and price.[4] The four dimensions are as follows:

- Affinity
- Domain
- Recognition
- Reputation

Let's take a closer look at each of these.

Affinity

High-affinity brands—such as Apple, the American Museum of Natural History, Volkswagen, and the Food Network—have opportunities based on their customer affinity. They can induce trial and acceptance of new price structures, and they enjoy other advantages. What is not clear is whether they enjoy a material boost in price level. Yes, in many cases high-affinity brands happen to command leading prices, but in many cases they deserve that premium on purely objective grounds (e.g., speed, engineering, scope of offer, ratings, etc.). Oddly enough, while you might expect affinity to have the highest impact on price, there is little evidence that it does. As an example from an industry where branding is central, a comparison of preferences for the two leading cola companies shows significant brand affinity differences by demographic. But despite these differences, there are no demographic patterns in syrup price: the pricing differences fall along other lines.

Domain

This term applies to whether the product or market is within the brand's scope, i.e., whether a brand is plausible in a specific context. This is as applicable to pricing as it is to branding. Is the footprint of a brand domain similar to the footprint of price differences? Not quite. Brand is largely a relationship between customer and product. Price may exhibit very different patterns; for example, the soft handoff between airlines and rental car companies is not a function of airline brand domain, it's a channel strategy that has an impact on price. Other influences on price, such as regulation, also may not match the brand domain.

Recognition

This is the level of product awareness, and it may vary from nil to acute. A particularly apt comparison for illustrating the differences in levels of product awareness is Scotch Tape versus BMW.

Example of Low Awareness. 3M's branding decisions for its lines of clear adhesive tapes are based on how much attention consumers give adhesive tape (very little, it appears). According to 3M product management, the Scotch and Highland brands are kept separate because they offer distinctly different levels of quality. For example, Scotch, the premium brand, can be removed from paper without tearing the surface of the paper. Lower-priced Highland will tear the paper, and it appears less transparent. Since 3M knows that few, if any, consumers will take the time to read the specifications of its adhesive tape, the only way to maintain clarity as to quality is to separately brand the two tapes. Each has a different market focus: Scotch appeals to customers who are price-insensitive, while Highland competes with discount brands of adhesive tape.

Example of High Awareness. Car manufacturers, unlike 3M, have the luxury of knowing that most purchasers view a car as a major purchase decision and will therefore invest a fair chunk of time in investigating purchase options. Thus car manufacturers can support multiple levels of quality under the general umbrella of the total company brand. BMW wants potential purchasers to believe that it produces "the Ultimate

Driving Experience" for different price levels. Although its low-end 3 Series may underperform its other cars, BMW believes consumers will have the sophistication to understand that *for its class*, the 3 Series offers superior handling compared with competitors' cars.

Reputation

This dimension is the confidence of potential buyers that the offer will live up to a producer's claims. Reputation is critical to pricing, just as it is to branding. For instance, bundling of consumer products and service tends to intensify the importance of brand to price. Customers expect, and generally believe, there is a bargain in the bundle.[5] Given the many permutations of bundled offers, consumers can't generally make direct comparisons to competing bundled offers; even if they could, they probably wouldn't take the time required to do it right. Given this disinclination on the part of consumers to investigate the actual economics, brand plays a key role. A good brand may convince the consumer that a bundle is likely to represent a bargain and a well-integrated set of service components, while a poor brand will lead consumers to avoid a buying decision. This is why bundling is a tool that generally favors market incumbents.[6]

Where there is lack of clarity on the relative merits of different products, the "halo" effect of a brand can be vital. For instance, in the case of Web commerce, branding is a vital factor both in choice and price, in part because there is often little assurance on the trustworthiness of the online vendor.[7]

A great example of Web pricing power is Amazon.com. This Web titan enjoys strong customer trust, and so it has been able to sustain prices 7 to 12 percent higher than smaller online competitors'. A study further found that despite beating Amazon's prices 99 percent of the time, smaller competitors' share of online book traffic remained very small.

The Convergence of Pricing and Branding

The situation where brand appears to have the highest impact on price is where there is a convergence of recognition, reputation, and *lack* of information or clarity as to product quality:

- There is high attention due to importance of the purchase and concern that there may be large differences among alternatives.
- The brand value of one competitor or alternative, within the brand domain, is highly differentiated from others.
- There is little opportunity for the potential buyer to easily or objectively confirm differences in product quality or value.

Convergence Examples

Some examples of when this convergence occurs:

Direct-mail advertisers must decide to buy either first-class or bulk-mail stamps for their letters. Their decision-making process illustrates the need to understand customer decision criteria: many mailers pay for first-class mail although, functionally, bulk mail ("Standard A" mail) gets the letter there within an acceptable length of time. Why pay more? The reason is that in some markets, mail recipients are three times more likely to open a first-class envelope than a bulk-mail envelope. Over time, mail recipients have learned that envelopes with first-class stamps tend to contain more important messages—a bill, a legal notice, or business correspondence. Bulk mail tends to be a waste of their time, so they don't open it. Since the business of bulk mailers relies on how many people open their envelopes, many pay for first-class stamps.

Another example is automotive spare parts. A Mercedes diesel camshaft purchased from a Mercedes-Benz dealer costs $500. The same camshaft, in the same box with the same manufacturer's logo stamped on it, can be had for $150 from an independent parts supplier. Other automotive parts also show threefold price differences.

Still another example is sunglasses. Surveys show that many sunglass purchasers pay for a better brand because they believe those glasses offer superior UV protection. In fact, an independent study recently showed that there are no discernable differences in UV protection in sunglasses that cost more than $5.

In each case, buyers make choices based on a lack of information. If mail recipients could somehow know what was in an envelope, they wouldn't rely on the type of stamp when deciding whether to trash a letter or open it. Likewise, if car owners knew they were buying exactly the same part, they would opt for the lower-priced component. Finally, if sunglass purchasers knew that lower-cost sunglasses can offer identical UV protection, many would spend less.

> A key pricing and branding context is:
> what do the customers *not* know?

The Power of Brand

Channel influences the importance of brand. On the Internet, the ability of brands to provide information is even more critical. Faced with an inability to touch, smell, and inspect food and grocery items, for example, patrons of online groceries tend to be more brand-oriented and less price-sensitive than shoppers in conventional grocery stores. Brand is used as a proxy for quality when quality cannot be ascertained easily, cheaply, or directly.[8]

While in some markets brand plays a pivotal role, in other markets brand has no impact upon price. In the 1960s, oil companies were heavy advertisers, and many consumers believed there were significant differences among major brands of petroleum. Since then, most of us have become aware that the differences are minimal. We've become correspondingly less brand oriented and more price sensitive—and as a result there is no longer an oil company on the *Advertising Age* list of top 100 advertisers.

Where product quality is simple and immediately discernable, the power of brand is limited. For example, one Ontario brick manufacturer decided to brand its products, and it invested in advertising and other tools to do so. While consumers eventually learned to recognize this brand, it had no impact on brick prices or market share, so the experiment was dropped. In a commodity business, brand usually isn't worth the effort. Hence, in his book on brand equity, Professor David Aaker values brand equity in the stone, glass, and clay industry as zero.[9]

> Brand can drive price level, but only
> under certain circumstances.

Management Tools to Maximize Brand Pricing Power

If your company happens to be a significant player in a market where brand does play a role, no doubt you have brand management in place.

While normally, brand teams are measured on sales, awareness, and even buying disposition, often the team measures do not include price.

In some cases, that might be a complementary objective. In a time of scarce resources, it may make sense for these two functions to be tied together more closely. This also happens to close the loop: branders create opportunities for value capture and pricing ensures that opportunity is realized.

Some examples of brand actions that elevated price:

- No surprise—one management action is good old-fashioned product advertising and branding. For instance, Clorox, the laundry bleach, spends over $500 million per year on advertising. Perhaps as a result, Clorox routinely commands a gross margin of 58 percent versus less than half that for competitors. It's probably not the product quality that drives the price difference: the U.S. Supreme Court found, as part of an antitrust action, that chlorine laundry bleaches are identical in function and performance. At a minimum, the judicial finding suggests that differences are not easily observable. Consumers apparently agree that brand matters because they pay more for this leading brand.

- Cost plays an interesting role in supporting branding and pricing. Persistently, a belief remains that price should be related to costs. Sometimes it does relate: showing consumers the costs involved in the making of a product will influence their perception of the product. On the other hand, cost is often not a driver of price in most B2B situations.

- Some managers find the variation in the role of costs hard to accept. Recently, statistical proof was required for the sophisticated management of a leading programming network that the monies spent in producing a program had no impact on the price obtained from distributors. All that mattered was the productivity of the show: ratings and advertising carried.

- Solid segmentation can also play a role. One cable company offered a bundle of a premium video service combined with its best telephony package. The trouble was that its VoIP-based telephony had a mixed reputation and, indeed, some minor technical limitations. That bundle did not do well until its positioning was changed to premium video plus cheap add-on phone lines. A strange result?

No, actually—this made complete contextual sense. The core of this bundle, fitting for a cable company, was focused on video users. The premium video package was expensive: over $120 a month. That appealed primarily to higher-income families—who were not going to entrust their safety to a cable VoIP telephone service. When the telephony components were repositioned as an inexpensive add-on (e.g., kid's phone, guest-cottage phone, etc.), however, the brand, context, and bundle were coherent, and sales improved.

These examples all fall at the convergence of the three price and brand factors of attention, value, and lack of easy comparison described above—three factors that come under the umbrella of context. The degree to which brand impact varies with the context supports the comment by advertising veteran Roger Kenrick: "Companies don't own brands—customers do."

> **Management should strategically employ branding for pricing purposes.**

Summary

Companies should consider that it is consumers who determine when and how brand affects their purchase choice and price. Children will determine what is a children's book, not the publishers. It is the context that determines whether brand will give your product's pricing a lift—recognizing that your company's reputation may not be the dominant part of the context. As described, both 3M and BMW are large, prestigious companies. Yet the brand dynamics for the two companies are very different: 3M's Scotch Tape brand cannot support two levels of product quality, while BMW has several levels of automobile size and quality.

The question is: which of your company's offers fall in the leverageable convergence of attention, brand value, and lack of buyer opportunity to determine differences in quality? If your company's brand stacks up well in the relevant domain, it may be possible to leverage the brand for a material price lift in this part of the market.

Many managers view the value of brand as the overall impression that a company wants to create, or else equate brand only with customer awareness—but in fact, brand may be most powerful when tailored to the right context. Brand is an excellent tool for swaying customers and potential customers who will not fully investigate all aspects of their purchase decision.

Notes

1. Various pricing innovations have resulted in revenue lifts ranging from 7 percent at the low end for improved tactical tools; to 11 percent lifts because of improved pricing process, information flows, and controls; to 35 percent compound growth rates over five years and more due to better price structures. On a theoretical note, playing with Compustat will show you that a 1 percent improvement in price is, on average, worth a 7.1 percent increase in profit across the S&P 500. The variation in industries shows a 1 percent increase in price means 6.8 percent in profit in consumer products, 10 percent for insurance, 13.5 percent for transportation and 22 percent for heavy industry. In contrast, brand today is linked primarily with revenues rather than price, and a 1 percent increase in revenues has less than half the profit impact of a 1 percent price increase. That is not a criticism of branding efforts, as branding still comes in way ahead of, for example, cost reduction in impact on profits.
2. Self-reported consumer knowledge varies both by product and market, and over time. See David Aaker, *Managing Brand Equity*, Free Press, 1991.
3. As described in *Winning the Profit Game*, Chapter 2, there can be material differences in quality among commodity products such as cold-rolled steel. Differences in quality in commodity products are manifested in nonimmediate price behaviors. For instance, when one steel mill (DOFASCO) produced cold-rolled steel with better stamping properties, the benefit to the mill was not price per ton but that automobile manufacturers placed that mill in a better position on the "drop" list in case of a demand turndown.

4. Gary Hamel and C. K. Prahalad, *Competing for the Future*, Boston. Harvard Business School Press, 1992, pp. 258–230.

5. Based on focus groups in five major cities, on the topic of medical service bundles.

6. Market leaders can often wait a year before following important bundle trends. Companies with less than a 40 percent market share have been shut out if they waited this period of time. "The New Wholesalers," *Telephony*, January 26, 1998, pp, 26–34.

7. Byung-Kwan Lee, Ji-Young Hong, and Wei-Na Lee, "How Attitude Toward the Web Site Influences Consumer Brand Choice and Confidence While Shopping Online," *JCMC*, Indiana University, January 2004. A cartoon showing two dogs cruising the Internet on a computer described it more succinctly: one comments: "On the web, no one knows you are a dog."

8. In fact, even when it can be ascertained easily and unambiguously, cost of trial may prevent sales. For instance, a new generation of men's blade razors encountered resistance at $16.99 for a four-pack of cartridges. Gillette complained that many potential customers did not believe the claims about shaving. "Razor Burn: A Flood of Fancy Shavers Leaves Some Men Feeling Nicked," *The Wall Street Journal*, July 12, 2010, p. A1. One potential answer to this problem might the two-part charging strategy (how appropriately) called the "razor and razor blade strategy."

9. Aaker, Ibid. The patterns tend to link with common sense, for once.

PART 4

Tools for Management

Chapter 13

First Steps and Missteps

Time is a great teacher, but unfortunately it kills all its pupils.

—LOUIS-HECTOR BERLIOZ

If you have made it to this point in the book, let's assume that you have conceptually bought into the idea that contextual pricing is worth a try. The question now becomes: how to implement these ideas?

There are two parts to conducting a trial of the framework prescribed in this book: (1) Deciding where, when and how, and (2) Strategizing how to overcome opposition. Let's deal with the second point first, since it is more interesting.

Overcoming Opposition

There is always opposition to pricing changes. Pricing is inherently political—someone will feel threatened if there is a change. Why? Because, for instance, change may upset long-standing relationships with customers who have become friends, it may undercut the importance of a manager's role, it may seem to intrude into their customary modus operandi, or it may go against their belief system.[1] Better pricing can gather adherents quickly, but rarely is there universal support.

Some of the opposition is a function of understanding. If all management were more familiar with pricing, there would be less fear, and less opposition. It is the lack of understanding that makes many organizations fear change because they cannot precisely see the consequences of it. By way of analogy: if a group of finance managers were told that henceforth debits would inhabit the right-hand ledger column and credits the left hand, contrary to past practice, they might grumble, but there would be little fear that it would bring disaster. Say the same thing to nonfinancially savvy managers and there might be cries that this was illegal and Enron-esque. Similarly, if a group of market communications managers were told that all e-mails to the company website had to be answered honestly and fully, they might also grumble, but they would be confident they could handle it. Say the same thing to inward-facing operational staff and there would be fear of fatal disclosure of secrets and embarrassment.

Opponents of pricing programs usually don't understand—and often don't want to understand—pricing logic. When they don't understand the logic, and it seems to differ from their vague impressions of what pricing should look like, and since pricing has the potential to have an impact on their livelihoods, then they will feel high anxiety. For example, it will feel safer to try yet another branding campaign or another sales force reorganization or another product tweak than to open Pandora's pricing box. As Mark Nevins, Ph.D., a well-known organizational behavior expert, once observed: "When people don't know what to do, they do what they know."

You could try to educate the skeptics, but that takes time. If you have the clout, you could mandate it, but there are always opportunities to sabotage an implementation: the systems won't support it, the sales force won't implement it, the legal staff won't approve it. The way to overcome the opposition is to find champions who will try it on their turf.

With the right advocate, a good idea becomes possible. Case in point: a CMO at a search engine company had a task force use the principles outlined in Chapter 7 (on scientific bundling) to rebuild a key new service bundle about to be launched. As often happens, the science suggested fewer components to the bundle and a higher price—about twice the old offering.

This did not play well with the sales force. Their understanding of price was that more stuff meant more value (wrong) and lower price meant higher volume (often wrong). A rebellion broke out at bundle launch time. The sales force wanted an earlier iteration of the new bundle, which had more components, and was tagged for a lower price.

Not good, but fortunately the VP of marketing (now CEO) and the VP of sales were very smart. They asked, "Do *any* of the sales managers want to try selling the new bundle?" As it turned out, yes, a few sales managers did like the new bundle, and they were given it to sell. The rest were given the original bundle.

Six months later, the group selling the new bundle had outsold the broader group twofold (in unit terms, not merely dollars). Now the rest of the sales force wanted to sell the new bundle, which the CMO was more than happy to allow. The side-by-side trial had proven useful, indeed.

Had the former rebels learned that in a bundle context too many components actually destroyed value? That a coherent and focused bundle could command more than a big flabby bundle? We suspect not. Contextual pricing had won in the market, but resistance to change and distain for pricing theory die hard.

The Importance of Champions

"It worked, we want it" is an attitude that has broad sales applicability. Therefore we recommend starting with champions. You may be a champion, but you need other champions all along the delivery chain: in IT, in sales, in product development, in product management, in customer service. Even if all these functions report to you, the need to pick effective advocates remains key to success, so choose the right champion even if he or she is not in the ideal product or market group.

Champions, as you know, are smart, driven, open to new ideas, respected within the organization, may have knife scars on their backs, and must have some authority. They must also be equipped with an appealing price reform message for key stakeholders. This can be the promise to cure an ongoing sales "pain point," better pricing for an innovative new product, or anything that requires change and there is no entrenched denial.[2]

Examples of pain points include a pricing structure customers hate, repeat price level complaints in certain types of contexts and lack of organizational incentives to perform due to lack of ability to charge. For instance, at Johnson & Johnson the pain point was pressure from competitors offering dental floss at a lower price. J&J responded by reducing the yards of floss inside each box and then matched the price per box of the competition. Since apparently customers buy by the box, this was a sufficient price structure response to the competition.

Depending on resources available, you also need to think about the scope of early efforts. If you are trying to cure a pain point, consider why your pricing is frequently under pressure. Is the problem specific (like the dental floss), which pricing can address narrowly, or does it require a comprehensive revamp of all pricing? If the problem is discounting, the initial effort may cure it completely.

Understanding the different contexts for selling and ensuring that sales and other functions are equipped with a suite of robust contextual prices will go a long way. But not all problems can be solved by price alone. If the problem is an obsolete product offer, pricing will only make the best of a bad situation. Pricing would not have saved the candy concession stand sales on the *Titanic* as the ship slid beneath the waves.[3]

The Front-End Choice

Contextual pricing has been successful both with a "strategy" front end and with a "systems" front end. Each has its advantages and a different risk profile. Which is better for your company will depend on the state of its pricing practices, degree of buy-in to pricing improvement, objectives, and budget constraints.

A Strategy Approach

A strategy front end is the better choice when your company has reasonable pricing practices, indifferent but not rebellious market-facing management, only a little money to invest, and adequate systems capabilities. The opening thrust of a strategy approach will run through a set of eight steps, as follows:

1. Find champions, socialize them and strategize the obstacles.
2. Pick a target: new products, or a product or segment experiencing pain points related to price. Check that this is actually narrow enough for trial.
3. Understand the market (market contexts, drivers).

4. Develop the necessary 20 or so contextual base prices, or develop a tool that produces these prices. Develop the accompanying price structures (remember the pricing trinity of context, structure, and level).
5. Don't let the trial be sabotaged. Stick with the baseline prices, otherwise the discipline necessary to focus pricing will evaporate.
6. Evaluate results, go/no-go, and expand rollout.
7. Create replicable processes; make sure there are supporting
   a. Contextual information sources
   b. Systems
   c. Culture
8. Make process improvements as needed.

The big advantage of this program is that it should pay for itself as you move along the path. If the initial area chosen produces the likely 7 to 15 percent or more revenue increase, then the program will probably have paid for itself, and more. Subsequently rolling it out to other products or markets will leverage that initial investment for even better returns.

The risks of a strategy front end may also lower. The strategy front end will look the problem straight in the eyes, give you an answer, and allow an assessment of whether your management team and systems infrastructure can support the answer. That is why systems competence must be at least adequate to support the answer, and there must be some budget to support a deep-dive market look.

A Systems Approach

A systems-led approach shows a very different profile than a strategy-led one. This approach tends to be better when pricing practices are in disarray, pricing appears to be materially suboptimal, operational management is stubborn and rebellious, and there is top management determination and budget. In some ways it says, "I assume we can handle the market, but first I need to train my troops."

A systems-led effort is appropriate because a set of pricing analytic tools, CRM functionality, and price-administration tools will be needed to get the job done. You still need to analyze the market to understand contexts and price drivers—it's just that the biggest obstacles will lie internally in your company, and they must be addressed.

Whereas a company with relatively disciplined management can make do with stand-alone tools and informal communication systems, companies with sales and marketing cowboys need strong systems integrity. Sales management in some cases needs to be blocked from persisting in old pricing practices, and product management may play games with informal systems (e.g., fulfilling the form, but not the substance, of the program so that contextual relationships are thwarted, or making up results). There may also be a need to tie compensation systems and pricing systems together at some level.

The other benefit of a systems-led approach is that more formalized price administration can show benefits regardless of the underlying pricing strategy. Simply requiring CRM inputs of relevant contextual account information can help reign in salespeople and makes the threat of them leaving less of an issue. Finally, the system itself is a strong symbol of corporate determination: Managers will understand that after investing $20 million in the new system, as part of a project led by a former business unit head, that management is determined. Change may be a condition of employment.

The Program Details

Having considered two major options for change, some detail on program steps is appropriate. Here is a healthy dose of warnings that should assist you in deciding which avenue to pursue.

Information Sources

Developing the price structures and tools, which can drive contextual pricing, require information. As described in Chapter 15, your company may have less of the required information than you might expect.

Information sources must include *all the factors that drive price*. Not just the impoverished scraps of knowledge currently feeding the price decisions, but radically taking into consideration *how customers actually buy*. What goes on mentally, or organizationally, as consumers and companies decide to purchase. That may sound like old news, but in fact companies commonly ignore these factors and so fall short of actually incorporating context in pricing.

Sources of information may take many forms:

- Interviews, either one on one, in panels, or in focus groups
- A detailed model of your customer's economics or their business, showing how they make financial and purchase decisions
- Conjoint or other analysis of customer views, or
- Best of all, a rigorous analysis of customer behavior and testing of purchase/price behavior through regression or similar techniques
- Market tests, such as those employed by large consumer products companies (and underutilized by most industries)

Note how we did not list surveys among this set of tools. Surveys are excellent means for adding precision to market questions where the broad parameters of the answer are already known, and questions to which a respondent can give a rapid answer: Who influences the buying decision? Which brand do you trust most? What are the alternatives? Surveys are not ideal for identifying new contextual parameters of decision making.

Beware of relying on some of the established providers of market research. While they often claim to have expertise in pricing, they tend to be focused on research on price *level*; this misses critical questions regarding price structure and drivers of price. We find that often focus on price level misses opportunities to address pricing opportunities through structure or messaging.

One time we were called in to comment on pricing at a leading textbook publisher. It had used a well-known polling company to conduct a survey asking college bookstores why they would stock certain teaching aids. The first page of the survey results showed a pie chart with answers to "Why would you not want to carry this product?" The answers came back in two major categories: about 25 percent of respondents cited non-price factors, including convenience, product, and shelf space. About 75 percent of respondents said price. The audience looked forward in anticipation of seeing a breakout of the 75 percent answer of price.

But no, the next slide gave a further breakout of the product and convenience response slices of the main pie chart. No mention of *why* price was not acceptable was ever presented. Was it the price/performance ratio? Was it price relative to a substitute teaching aid? Was it the absolute price level? Was it lack of understanding by potential buyers? Was it the cost of stocking relative to the margin on the teaching aid (i.e., was the price too low?) The answer to *why* was not to be found in the professionally administered survey of buyers. A wasted opportunity, indeed.

> Contextual pricing does not mean your
> company needs to learn a new set of tools,
> but it may mean you need to provide more
> guidance to your market research suppliers.

Worse yet, established survey companies sometimes fail to adjust for three important factors in gathering evidence on pricing:

1. Respondents lie.
2. Often the trend is more important than the static situation.
3. Respondents are not inclined to work hard to really distinguish among options, so what will be big differences *when they are actually asked to spend* do not appear so large in surveys.

More reprehensible than respondent failings, surveyer use of boilerplate (stock) survey questions rarely match the market. For an educational-testing provider, the survey house substituted its stock affordability questions for the internally developed ones. Not surprisingly, in an industry under severe funding shortages, all the respondents checked the "severe budget squeeze" box, although many went on to buy the service.

Sadly, pricing is not a popularity contest nor is it often a win-win situation. Most buyers understand that, and so they game their responses when they see a likely benefit. Therefore, questions regarding price must be developed so that gaming is minimized. (It's tough to adjust for gaming—better to get it right from the start.) Some techniques for getting at the right answer include:

-   Ask questions about relative, not absolute, price preferences. Everyone can figure out that answering "What would you pay for this?" calls for checking a lower number. However, "Would you pay twice as much for multigaming capacity as for single game capacity?" is harder to game, plus the answers give the pricers some structural cues. Finally, it gives the respondent the relevant context for the pricing judgment.

- Test customer and potential-customer actions in addition to their responses. For instance, in a survey of multidwelling residential units and their telephone service buying preferences, using surveys and buyer interviews, the surveys produced a roughly even split between price and service being their top priorities (service was slightly ahead) among large property-management firms. When we timed the interviewee comments on price terms and service, however, it was a clean sweep: 100 percent of the large-entity respondents spent far more time talking about price and terms. This was then confirmed by looking at actual win/loss data, service records, and price differences. (Interestingly, smaller property management companies faithfully reflected their survey service/price answers.)

Market surveys also need to reflect market trends, while many surveys and other vehicles tend to be static—it's easier for people to answer what they are doing now. This is important to the research company because survey duration matters to their costs, and they can be detached from whether it actually reflects actions.

For a leading cable company, the static analysis of existing customers showed that there was no discernable difference in pricing for bundles that violated bundling rules (contained in Chapter 7) and bundles built in accordance with market bundling rules. For new sales, however, offers which reflected bundling rules experienced a lower discount and higher penetration. Since management was focused on new sales, this also was the more important pricing focus.[4]

We find that in many markets, it is *changes* in them that are the avenue for revenue improvement. Most surveys tend to resist incorporating both questions about the present and the future because that doubles the length of the survey. To avoid this, management might want to use other analytic tools before the survey stage, to rapidly home in on whether the current situation or trend is more relevant to pricing.

Again, the point is that market research firms applying standard questions and survey techniques to pricing questions often come up short or with mistaken conclusions. Worse than being useless, this supposed lack of conclusive data support for pricing actions empowers those who prefer doing nothing and those who prefer to guess.

As you think about your company's research into context, make sure that management actually investigates context.[5] A test of whether researchers are actually investigating context is whether the questions ask about *differences* in context. Here are some examples of differences in relevant context:

- Aftermarket price of the same car radio for a luxury car shows 0.82 price elasticity; for an economy car, elasticity measures 1.30.
- Telephony VoIP service shows 0.32 price elasticity when sold with a broadband access package, but elasticity of 1.25 if sold alone.
- WIMAX wireless broadband access is viewed as a complement to cable or telco (DSL) wire-line broadband access to people who travel on business, but seen as a substitute by those who work at fixed locations.
- Price sensitivity for direct-mail and e-mail-blast services varies along with the lifetime value of the product being promoted. In one market, a credit card solicitation had seven times the lifetime NPV (net present value) of a phone-service solicitation, and this translated into higher direct-mailer willingness to pay.

The point of this short list of examples is that to test pricing hypotheses, there needs to be a good understanding of underlying economics, uses, business processes, decision processes, and the consumer's mind. Doing so requires a sophisticated, multistep inquiry. If compressed into one-step research, much will be missed.

Very much in the tradition of great consumer management, we find that tools can and should be used sequentially. Often they are not used sequentially, because pricing is a hurried afterthought, and so time is limited. That is not the best practice! The best practice is to define the scope of potential contexts and then develop a list of contextual pricing candidates. At that point, you have the basic information required to test and make contextual pricing operational. In this second phase, modeling, surveying, and other examination of market behaviors and references are possible.

So, the best practice is to first create a wide funnel for potential market drivers, then narrow it by looking at the evidence, and meld it into a coherent contextually based set of decision rules. This should induce more confidence in pricing programs.

Implementation

To address context fully requires cutting across many organizational silos, in addition to building understanding of what goes on in the market.

To make product development, marketing, sales, finance, customer service, and other departments fully cognizant of context would require a shift in culture and focus at most companies. The good news is, however, that with your next market initiative or product, you can begin to move toward contextual pricing.

If possible, begin the next initiative with a symbol of why this is important. For instance, one year the former chairman of BellSouth (now AT&T) publically designated his top priority for the year as pricing and put his heir-apparent in charge of the initiative. Doing so was a clear symbol and sent a powerful message.

This is highly appropriate. Pricing is the embodiment of your company's mission—it transcends any given department and dominates your financial top line. Yet in many companies the pricing function underperforms and is nowhere near to living up to its potential. Unless your company has a CEO/COO-led revenue management culture, it is likely that pricing is frequently neglected, underresourced, and ad hoc. Yet it could grow to be the most powerful driver of revenue improvement. A classic example of top-level influence was when Lee Iacocca, head of Ford, set the price target range for the Ford Mustang, apparently to the disappointment of his development team.

> It is good to have a top management symbol of company determination to improve pricing.

Process Improvement

Today, a typical corporate pricing process is to start with a target list price and then tear it down. The pattern looks somewhat like Figure 13-1.

We suggest that the companies whose pricing flows follow this pattern can do better. Better pricing can result from beginning with a consideration of pricing context, not list price.

Culture and Acceptance

In any company there are likely to be some functional audiences who are still list price advocates. List price is a useful simplification for product designers. In many cases, product designers consider adding or subtracting features and offer components; sanity requires them to have a single

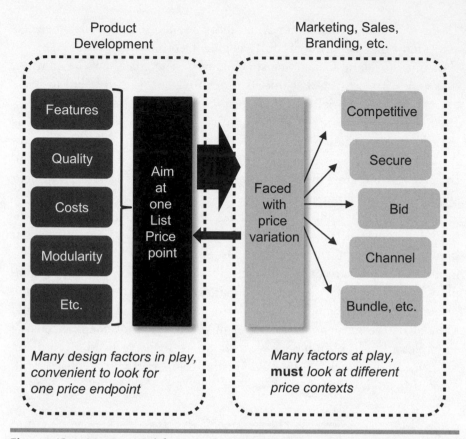

Figure 13-1 Managerial focus—the Great Divide: differences between "upstream" product development focus and "downstream" market facing pricing issues

scorecard: Has value increased as a result of a specific product improvement? Did it increase by more than the cost of the addition? From the point of view of the product (or service) developer, a single price target linked to one context is a very convenient—perhaps even necessary—benchmark. But as the functional focus moves from product creation to revenues and sales, the utility of list price diminishes. Consider the increasing degree of market contextual detail required by each step in the product development—marketing—sales evolution:

While convenience and isolation from markets allows product development to make do with a single list price, from the point of view of a P&L manager or a product manager or a sales rep, there are a *lot* of drawbacks to a list price. Influences on price not captured in list price for product managers include advertising and channel reach, which affect only parts of the market. For sales representatives, important influences not captured in list price include client loyalty and specific competitor offers. These are important factors, but not addressable by product development or R&D.

Perhaps the chief danger of creating a list price is that it often marks the end of a well-resourced pricing inquiry. With a list price established, product development signs off and hands the problem to marketing. Marketing hands the problem to sales and operations, etc. These functions must then unravel the consolidated list price and turn it into contextual prices. Often they must do this with fewer resources than went into developing a list price to begin with.

Even with inadequate resources for price study, line management will understand the pricing obtainable from different segments in different circumstances (contexts), but that takes time. Sadly, time is not your friend in setting prices. With the passage of time, more money is left on the table as customers become accustomed to a too-low price. Equally suboptimum is a too-high price, which may leave customers dissatisfied and ready to defect. Recovering from a bad initial price is expensive and difficult, sometimes so difficult that it requires a product relaunch.[6]

Sometimes more time is spent on "deal" pricing or adjusting discounts rather than initial price setting. This is actually good news. It is a sign your company is moving away from list pricing to contextual pricing, albeit in a roundabout way. The only trouble is that deal pricing is usually focused on one deal at a time, not an overall contextual approach. Hence the wheel must be reinvented with every negotiation. Wouldn't it be simpler if price were already adapted to contexts such as initial deals, add-on sales, competitive fights, and all the 20 or so common pricing situations?

To be sure, sometimes a list price does have market uses. One of them is that in mass markets the list price communicates a broad value. Often, pricing is the key message on product or service value. This message must be simple, or it cannot be readily conveyed. The actual price paid will often be compared with the public list price. This comparison has its own utility. For instance, the seller of large data archives set the list price 30 percent above the target price because internally buyers were evaluated based on the "discount" obtained. A generous differential makes all buyers look good—they got the discount the seller was more than ready to give them. Sort of like the children of Lake Woebegone, all buyers were made to be above average. But this is the messaging part of pricing, not the price-setting part of pricing.[7]

List price may have a symbolic or messaging role and is valuable for that reason.

Summary

Inculcating a contextual pricing approach cannot simply rely on the assumption that managers will recognize the market needs it and that the company will do better with contextual pricing. Resistance or indifference will be a powerful force. Resistance may take the form of endless meetings. As Verizon VP of business sales Deb Harris once urged: "Don't hold meetings about how to get up from your desks!" Develop a strategy employing energetic champions to facilitate implementation. Do not fall prey to hazards in acquiring the right market information. With proven internal success, the program will experience less resistance.

WHAT TO MAKE OF THE DATA?
CHOICE OF DATA ANALYSIS TECHNIQUES

Warren Buffett has a famous preference for making investment decisions based on first-hand experience. Some would call that "grandmother research." Others might complain about sample size. Perhaps, but it works. Another notable individual, Leonardo da Vinci, once said, "All our knowledge has its origins in our perceptions." And "Although nature commences with reason and ends in experience it is necessary for us to do the opposite, that is to commence with experience and from this to proceed to investigate the reason."

This means that management must choose the right scope of inquiry, as described below. Planners and managers must then get their hands dirty by conducting many industry interviews. These will be helpful in establishing some patterns. For example, those interviewed might say, "We used to be centralized and tried to approach the market through a highly disciplined process, but then we met a lot of resistance and the department was split up among several other departments. Everyone does it their own way now." Or they might say the opposite or some variation in between. The point is to conduct enough interviews to have a large enough inventory of case histories and how change is driving decision-maker frames of reference.

"Large enough" is often a smaller sample than many managers expect. Don't forget that confidence level is built not only by sample size but also that it is based on how much sample points vary from the predicted pattern. Thus, if sample points are tightly in line with prediction, a very small sample may be adequate.

Also, don't forget that this is not criminal law, where before someone is sentenced on the basis of fingerprints or other evidence that requires a statistical showing, the confidence level required is 98 percent or higher. That is because defendants are innocent until proven guilty. That is not true of business propositions—here, the best evidence wins. Even more important, intuition is given some weight.

Tools that can help illuminate the data include, of course, our old friends correlation and regression analysis. However, there are other useful tools worth mentioning:

- Discriminate function analysis, also known as disjunctive mapping, can help reach conclusions on relationships based on outcomes rather than on a predictive formula or "central tendency." In other words, it associates events with outcomes without worrying why there is a link.

- Min-max analysis, which could fairly be considered a survey technique rather than an analytic technique (it is both), can help sharpen respondent results by asking them which features they like best and which they like least, for instance. Over rounds of questions, this approach then isolates the most or least important, even if respondents initially say everything is similar in importance.

■ Freeing the data of respondent wishy-washiness and deceit can also be achieved via conjoint analysis.

■ Kriging can help interpolate from extreme points. This is useful because often the extreme points (zero value, high value, according to the contextual situation) can be established, and the argument lies in the midpoints.

■ Another tool is simulating markets. Harnessing the wisdom of crowds has proven useful to companies such as Google, Intel, Microsoft, and Best Buy. We like this tool because when these companies have created "prediction markets" that allow employees to forecast a range of prices (e.g., stock prices) and take-up volumes (e.g., for Gmail). Interestingly, often the internal market forecast beats marketing and other forecasts.

So there are some tools that take the pricing exercise from raw data to some degree of coherence. No tool, however, brings data to actionable pricing strategies or other conclusions. There is never perfect information for pricing. The final step still lies with humans, who may then build tools to extrapolate from their judgment.

Once the data is in hand, simple smarts will be the engine for selecting what is relevant and extrapolating it to the pricing tools. There will never be perfect information for pricing, but inference is possible. In *The Black Swan*, a book on statistics and highly infrequent events, the author cautions us that many real life events cannot be predicted on the basis of certainty but rather on "reasoned probability."[8] Note that he does not say mathematical probability: judgment still frames the question. Arthur Conan Doyle, doctor and author of the Sherlock Holmes books, and (incidentally) inventor of the life jacket, once wrote: "From a drop of water . . . a logician could infer the possibility of an Atlantic or a Niagara without having seen or heard of one or the other. So all life is a great chain, the nature of which is known whenever we are shown a single link of it."

Notes

1. Don't underrate philosophical opposition. While communism may have collapsed in the Soviet Union, it appears to be alive and well in various parts of the Fortune 500. Many managers are offended by the idea of material increases in price and killing off competitors. In one Belgian firm, management also complained that if they instituted a major price increase there would be social repercussions to the management team (e.g., fewer party invites, etc.).

2. Over many years some functions (e.g., sales or customer service) are told that it's their mission to overcome a flawed pricing structure or inappropriate price points. Because of this, the groups feeling the pain of bad pricing will see it as their mission to deny there is any problem—after all, they are there to fix it. Sometimes the motivation is even simpler, for instance, when the market wants variable ("pay by the drink") pricing, but the sales force believes that will reduce its sales commissions.

3. That would be either a channel issue or a product issue, depending on how you look at it. In either case, icebergs are not a pricing issue, although we often find that pricing is tied to channel, promotion, or product drivers.

4. Why did the embedded base not reflect compliance with sound bundling principles? We are not sure, but we suspect that the embedded base contained many bundles that were sold when there was still a huge unfulfilled demand for bundles. At that time bundles were bought by bundle enthusiasts, regardless of whether the bundle taxonomy was sound or contained flaws. Perhaps these early bundle buyers would have paid even more for their bundles then, and the lack of discount pattern simply shows that for early buyers there was no price pressure.

5. There are more disconnects than you might expect. After one pricing study, the CEO asked one of the authors of this book to stay to observe the initial implementation. Sitting in on the CMO's kickoff of the program, I was surprised when she walked up to the podium, blew the dust off of last year's marketing program document and rallied the troops. Afterward I said, "Lourdes, that is *not* what you agreed to at last week's meeting. Her response was,

"Yes, but that would have been a lot of work, it's much easier to just reuse last year's plan." True story.

6. Examples include AOL in 2010, Nike in 2009, and the classic 1982 Grey Poupon mustard relaunch. A relaunch is expensive and should be avoided, but it does show that management is decisive about pricing and understands that history is context.

7. The timing and pattern of price moves is highly communicative of your objectives and requirements of business partners. This can be very effective when direct communication is blocked or impractical. For examples, please see Rob Docters, "Price Is a Language," *Journal of Business Strategy*, May/June 2003.

8. Nassim Taleb, *The Black Swan*, Random House, 2007, pp. 50–52. This author echoes Albert Einstein who once commented, "Not everything that counts can be counted, and not everything that can be counted counts."

Chapter 14

Cheap and Cheerful Pricing Tools

Answer: . . .we put that question to the National Association of Insurance Salespersons Heavily Armed with Graphs.
Question: What was their answer?
Answer: They are surrounding your house right now.

—DAVE BARRY, *MONEY SECRETS*

Implementing a pricing tool into a company requires more than a smart algorithm. It must link to the market being addressed and to the specific price drivers relevant to the company. In short, some degree of customization is inevitably required for a tool to produce a useful pricing output. The customization requires that the tool be able to:

- Match the workflow and expectations of the internal users.
- Adapt to the market context.

Frequently, these goals can be accomplished more rapidly with a small stand-alone tool than with an enterprise-wide system. The simple tool won't do all the same things as the complicated one, but it may well pay for itself thousands of times over.

205

Some small, relatively narrow-focus tools—running on a spreadsheet, highly customized, provide you with guidance on price level, discounting, value message, or bundle components. Such tools cost from low to mid six digits when you include initial analysis. Another choice is a highly sophisticated program, such as PROS and Vendavo, with refined and automated interfaces, deeper integration into the work flow, and industrial-strength security features. In some cases such tools offer algorithms that would be very difficult to reproduce in-house. They also provide other benefits, such as programs to help management audit and control sales pricing and to do detailed analytics on costs, margins, and discounting. Their breadth of features and seven-digit pricing tend to facilitate user acceptance, but they are relatively expensive.[1]

The two choices are typically seen as alternatives but need not be. The nice thing about cheap tools is that they are cheap! Cheap tools are disposable. The timeframe for implementation is also a fraction of the timeframe for larger systems. Your company can rapidly build an inexpensive tool and then move to the big system with more understanding and in less of a rush.

Even if less expensive tools are not in your company's budget, there are even cheaper pricing tools now available on the Web that can serve some pricing purposes quite well—providing either a second opinion, an easy way to simulate what competitors might do, or an opportunity for training. One free site is called pricewitch.com. It uses a sophisticated algorithm to recommend product level pricing and bundle price points.[2]

Whether stopgap or permanent solutions, such tools can help your company reflect how context and price vary by market and by product. Where there is an appetite for better pricing by product or sales management, a simple spreadsheet-based tool can serve as an invaluable pricing engine. Best of all, they can be customized to the exact price context applicable to your products. Here are six popular and emerging categories of price tools and programs that serve often-unsupported pricing needs:

- **Product pricing**, which helps product management set prices for specific products, taking into account different purchase contexts.
- **Product value**, which turns a general value proposition into specific quantified benefits for a particular customer segment and context.

- **Discount scorecard**, which tells sales, sales management, and product management what should be the right discount for a product given a particular set of circumstances.
- **Bundling model**, which can take the various products and components in your company's offer set and rigorously calculate a baseline price for the bundle (i.e., the right "bundle discount").
- **Demand curve**, which links segmentation and price targets.
- **Patent program**, which can make it possible to defend price innovative pricing from imitation.

If any tool fills a void in your company's pricing needs, it will tend to be a high-return addition to the managerial capability suite.

The high-return price tools are: (1) a discount management tool, (2) a product pricing tool, (3) a product-value calculator for quantifying customer benefit, (4) a bundle-price calculator, (5) a demand curve linked to segmentation, and (6) an improved patent process for protecting intellectual property.

Product Price Tool

A product price tool provides product management with a starting point for offer price and helps facilitate the transition to contextual pricing.

Typically, the first step in building a tool is to investigate what drives price, isolating those drivers and testing them against history. These may pertain to the product, to the buyer or the segment, to the competition, and to potential usage. Frequently half the drivers are contextual in nature, rather than absolute measures of the product. Finally, it's important to get the results in usable form. Normally, there are no more than four or five drivers of product price.

In the case of a leading marketing information provider, for example, a four-part pricing mechanism captured more than 80 percent of the observed price variations. A disguised, but not simplified, example of such a tool is diagrammed in Figure 14-1:

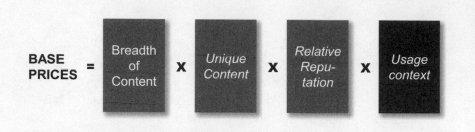

Figure 14-1 Contextual baseline prices: illustration of how, in one case, contextual baseline prices were calculated.

Notice how only one of the four components referred to the product itself and the other three were all relative to the competition's product? This simple structure, combined with weighting and coefficients, was much more sophisticated than the judgmental logic used previously for such decisions. The previous pricing practice focused on breadth but did not explicitly address the other factors—even though they were known to matter on some occasions.

The algorithm also made it easy for product management to adapt offers to different circumstances. For instance, for the "usage context" factor, the tool offered users three simple choices, so it was easy for product management to plug in one of three coefficients.

Since the tool quantified the net impact of these different contexts, it also proved it was worthwhile to bother pricing differentially for various contexts. Similarly, a contextual product pricing tool will frequently also quantify the benefits of branding and market communications, and what improvements in these areas would do to support pricing. In this case, the impact of reputation on price could be read directly from the tool. This was a useful input to the budgeting process.

A Product Value Tool

Frequently absent from value propositions is a quantification of product benefits, and the differential benefit compared with the competition's product. But when it is provided, such a value tool can be powerful. Take, for example, a video promoting Mobil 1 motor oil, which describes in detail the benefits of lower wear and reduced deposits, and offers to share with automobile-fleet owners a financial estimate of what this means in terms of better reliability and engine life for their cars.[3] Quantification of benefits has worked well to preserve the price of this superior-performing lube, especially in challenging price environments (contexts). Life insurance is another industry that takes showing value seriously. Hence, life insurance agents often have charts and models to show the consequences of purchase or nonpurchase of their policies.[4]

Yet many products are sold with no effort to actually quantify their benefits. Services, in particular, tend to be sold without adequate quantitative proof of differential value, when the facts may be much more cogent. The purchase decision consequences of a lack of support is described by a financial decision maker at the leading online automobile financing company: "I was asked to evaluate the two offers, and everyone agreed that [one vendor] had the better reputation, and was the class outfit. But while they said they were more reliable, they could not give me any numbers. So when it came to presenting a recommendation to management I had no choice but to choose [the lower priced vendor]."[5]

This should never happen! Every company must be able to construct an argument or a tool to give to the back-office staff, who can then rely on it if they choose. With no tool or argument in place, they would have to work very hard to justify a decision in your company's favor—and if they don't choose to do this, you may lose.

The heart of this sort of problem usually lies in either complexity or difficult analysis. Both can be addressed with a template or a tool-based calculation.

Comprehensive Services

For complex or comprehensive services, a spreadsheet template listing all the aspects of the service, and their value to the customer, will play a major role in achieving price goals.

The spreadsheet should include an estimate of the benefit for each element or attribute of the service. They may not be easy to estimate, but typically it's worth more of the seller's time to develop those estimates than of the buyer's time. Don't forget context here: choose circumstances that favor your product. If the potential buyer does not agree, they may modify your estimates or assumptions, but at least the burden of doing so is on them—lazy buyers can be your best friends.

For instance, a leading beverage company has a 12 single-spaced page document that lists product and service elements, and benefits offered to its largest customers. Such a comprehensive in-one-place list is already above-average practice, but when the company added a benefits calculator on a spreadsheet (which quantifies benefits proportioned to soda outlets and other scaling factors), the spreadsheet provided a powerful baseline for negotiation.

Difficult Analysis

When outcomes from the purchase are hard to predict and the differential between your offer and the competition's offer (or nonuse) has not been quantified, there is a big payoff for developing a tool to convert those benefits into specific dollars.

Frequently, the purpose of customer tours and education is both to convince customers of capabilities and show that people should take the need for the services seriously. An example is SunGard Availability Services, which gives tours of its impressive disaster backup facilities. The tours do convince potential customers that in the event of disaster, SunGard is fully capable of rapidly doing all that is possible to keep call centers or computer support in operation. It's a great sales procedure, but this company and its competitors do not supplement that impression by specifically quantifying the chances of such failure and what the differentials among different supplier choices mean in total dollars of impact. This is why often the driver of purchase here is regulation and legal pressures. However, that is a luxury that is not always available to sellers in other industries.

With statistical examination of history or modeling, or both, any difference can be modeled. Perhaps not to an academic level of confidence, but the modeling will certainly work better than guesswork and customer skepticism. For instance, extrapolating from infrequent events by using mathematical processes such as discriminate function analysis or Black-Scholes option pricing (not part of every buyer's evaluative toolchests) can often provide a number when simple math cannot. And sometimes any number is better than no number when it comes to supporting prices. "In the land of the blind, a single number can be king," to paraphrase an old expression.[6] This is particularly valuable when selling high-uncertainty services (e.g., insurance, backup systems, new hires, new distribution methods, warranties, etc.).

All these approaches help cement your value. With the addition of context, each tool can be made powerfully applicable to a segment or customer. While this requires effort, the rewards can be substantial and repeatable. Note that there are usually multiple approaches for estimating benefits, and the first vendor to educate buyers in a market on the best approach to estimate or calculate benefits has an advantage. In some cases, you may even be able to patent that approach.

Additionally, the incidence of an event and its magnitude (failure patterns) should suggest different business models: Severe consequences occurring infrequently suggest that you include "insurance" with your offer. Severe consequences with high frequency generally means risk-sharing with the customer. Minor consequences in low frequency suggest a warranty, and minor consequences with high frequency suggest tiering of service and repair.[7]

The Discount Scorecard

Customer buying behavior can be incorporated into a relatively simple model. The model must calculate risk and reflect shifts in context, and examine what this means for pricing.

The logic can be expressed as a simple "if-then" table. The "if" asks questions about the account, and the "then" says what must happen to the offer. The "then" is usually about what level of discount is appropriate and necessary, but it may also include carve-outs. For instance, if a deep discount is required because it appears that the buyer is looking exclusively at the price tag, it would be appropriate to limit the warranty or spare-parts inventory, or eliminate free shipping.

The if-then table, otherwise known as the discount scorecard, may reflect up to a half-dozen factors that have an impact on discounting and risk of customer loss. Sound complicated? Not really: a good discount scorecard asks four to six questions of the sales rep (or other decision maker), and those should relate directly to the salesperson's market experience. The rest of the calculation happens "behind the curtain."

Whereas the product-pricing tool addresses factors that affect the product as a whole across all target customers, the discount scorecard addresses differences and factors that apply specifically at the *account level*. For instance, a product-pricing tool will consider overall product usage levels but cannot distinguish between accounts that makes purchase decisions though a committee and those that have a single decision maker.

The technique for building a discount tool has three steps. First: identify potential price drivers through sales force and customer interviews. Second: assign weights "points" to each price driver (factor) that has been identified, through statistical analysis. Third: test the weights so that when applied retroactively to history, the model predicts outcomes. This requires some iteration, but that is useful also because it makes the company more comfortable with changing the point allocations as the market evolves. Testing against history also gives you a "predictivity" number—how well your company would have identified past losses due to pricing—and it also allows an estimate of revenues lost for lack of the tool.

Rollout of the tool requires some thought. It will be helpful if the sales force is familiar with the logic behind it, and is looking for ways to improve pricing. That suggests you might tie the use of the scorecard to compensation. Too often account teams believe they know all there is needed to know about pricing and resent the imposition of pricing guidance. This is why pricing organizations are often treated as enemies of sales. Yet we find that this tool can outperform the sales force on questions such as whether an account is likely to defect.[8]

A Bundle Modeling Tool

For product development teams looking to create a suite of bundles and adapt them for use in the battle with competitors, a model-based tool has proven useful. This model needs a full underpinning of bundle pricing logic; however, once it is set up, it is simple to use.

In a nutshell, the goal here is to identify the core of the bundle and develop the correlations to the core. A spreadsheet model simply multiplies the stand-alone values of the components by the correlation to get the expected in-bundle value. Then the spreadsheet just adds up the core value plus the in-bundle component values. Simple enough?

However, if you have different segments with different cores (e.g., the video-centric core subscribers, and the telephony-centric subscribers) and the list of potential bundle components is long, a spreadsheet is the best way to evaluate a long menu of options rapidly. Plus, it ensures that managers who are afraid of correlation have some comfort.

While the model itself is simple and very cheap, the results can be material. Almost all bundles proposed by management will contain some low-correlation or negative-correlation (substitutes, not complements) bundle candidates. This model makes the consequences of that plain. Furthermore, if you have run through the full list of potential bundle elements, it allows managers to test potential bundles rapidly—and so save precious market research dollars for the most desirable tests.

A Demand Curve

When a demand curve is matched with a supply curve, the result predicts both the price and quantity of goods sold in a competitive market—two of the most important questions any company manager might ask on behalf of his company. Yet market analysis based on supply-and-demand curves is relatively infrequent.

Price and quantity sold. Basic question, right? Some of the most famous instances of marketing success have stemmed from the use of supply-and-demand (S&D) analysis. Recently McDonald's appears to have used supply-and-demand analysis in moving to offer a suite of less expensive meals. This was a best-practice adaption to a change in the demand curve due to lower customer income. Other examples of successful S&D use come from electricity markets,[9] and the use of demand curves by computer and cell phone manufacturers[10]—that combined this analysis with clever buying strategies where suppliers bid below cost to participate in eventual higher volumes.

Companies spend millions on consumer research, market scans, and cost accounting—functional bases for supply-and-demand analysis—but rarely are these combined together into a demand curve for the market. It is not because the concept is novel. Supply and demand is the oldest tool in pricing and demand forecast: the interaction was noted by Adam Smith in *The Wealth of Nations* in 1776 and described by David Ricardo in *Principles of Political Economy and Taxation* in 1817.

The Missing Strategy Tool

While supply and demand is not context itself, it certainly summarizes important contextual information about contextual pricing forces, i.e., relative abundance of buyers and sellers. However, many companies have never performed such analysis or even think it is possible. Some managers say obtaining any information outside the company is difficult, and putting them together for an integrated supply-and-demand view is not something they can do in their spare time.

In some cases these managers rely on elasticity curves for promotional and incremental pricing. Elasticity shows the short-term response of customers to price changes in highly communicative, near-commodity markets. Elasticity is good for tactical pricing (e.g., optimizing inventory turns). Some pricing systems augment their elasticity analysis with inference engines that are helpful in separating out prices for individual products in multiple-product selling situations (e.g., advertising bundles and retail). That is a good use for computers, but it does not produce demand curves.

Why bother with supply-and-demand curves when software systems conveniently offer elasticity-based analysis? If all you ever want is tactical advice focused on promotions and inventory turns, there's no reason to bother. But if you are a senior manager asking how to grow revenues, enter new markets, and beat competition, you want a demand curve. Demand curves answer the big questions. Why don't senior managers focus on demand curves more often? Perhaps the old adage that "Fish are unaware of the water in which they live" explains this lack of focus. Every company is subject to supply-and-demand curves, and demand is every manager's concern. Every time someone says the word *market*, they really mean supply and demand—so to care about customers and markets is to care about your demand curve. Maybe it's time to make that focus explicit.

> Do not confuse elasticity figures with demand curves. Elasticity is deceptive in many ways, and the demand curve is much more strategic.

New-Product Development Tool

Two universally applicable examples of what a demand curve can do for your company relate to product development and competitive analysis. Starting with the former, product development often follows a process of relying on customer research to determine the point where most survey respondents indicate a willingness to buy. This simple yes-no inquiry leaves a lot to be desired. Typically it leaves money on the table, and does poorly at assessing how new products will *change* consumer price perceptions. This is why so many products are launched, only to be greeted with indifference, disappointing demand, or surprisingly overwhelming demand—or anything but the predicted demand.

With a demand curve, product developers can aim at multiple price points along the demand curve and clearly understand the likely uptake. Doing so beats building the product and then making guesses about how much to up-tier or down-tier the product to meet missed segments. A very typical example of a demand curve was in a mature equipment market where an elite segment was willing to pay more than 1,000 euros per year, and a huge, untapped, segment which was willing to buy if prices were pushed to less than 70 euros per year. This curve makes it clear that all segments cannot be addressed by one product targeted at the middle ground of 400 euros per year. Even more important, this curve prompted management to ask whether the low-priced segment might shift upward if enticed by introductory pricing and greater familiarity with the benefits.[11]

Demand Curves Address Sweeping Market Changes

Supply-and-demand curves often show critical interactions. Changes in supply curves seem to provoke changes in demand curves, and vice versa. For instance, when offered a new credible product or service at a new low price level, many buyers will take the time to learn about the value of such a product and buy despite no previous interest. This shift in demand is accelerated once there have been some sales and the concept has been proven. Examples include electronic navigation. As prices of GPS mapping devices have fallen, many consumers who formerly contented themselves with paper maps have now bought a GPS. In 2007, GPS volumes grew to 180 million, with an average selling price of $189 per unit. Such volumes—growing at 237 percent a year—would have been unthinkable in 2004, when the average price of a GPS was over $400. Elasticity analysis could not begin to suggest such results: short-term responses to price promotions for a $400 GPS would have fallen well short of today's market volume.

Competitive Pricing Strategy

A second, equally important use of the demand curve, is harnessing its utility in thinking through strategic responses to competition. Here's an example from the legal-publishing market. A premium publication called *Moore's Federal Practice* was under attack by a lower-priced publication called *Wright & Miller Federal Practice and Procedure*. A typical management response might have been to cut the price for *Moore's*, although this would either have run the risk of disappointing subscribers if it were accompanied by cutting content, or run the risk of alienating subscribers by attempting price discrimination across too large a gap. Instead, examination of the demand curve suggested to management that it ought to launch a lower-priced offer at a price where it attacked *Wright & Miller* from below. This version could be trimmed sufficiently so that there was little risk for defections from the principal *Moore's* subscriber base.

This strategy proved a marketplace success. The new publication, *Moore's Abridged*, attained the volume predicted by the demand curve (not immediately, but over time), and kept *Wright & Miller* from moving upmarket to attack the principal *Moore's* version.

Do-It-Yourself Building of Demand Curves

How does one construct a demand curve? The key task is to identify proxies for market sensitivity. Proxies could include a good segmentation,[12] or existing product tiers or different competitors that have staked out distinguishable market tiers. Begin with a chart showing prices and volumes as they are today. As an illustration: if there are 50 major brands of perfume, ranging from over $1,000 to $15 per ounce, and you can make rough estimates of volume, then a demand curve can be estimated based on this information. We would start with the highest priced perfume volume on the left, and then adding on additional, successively lower priced brands moving right. The fiftieth and least expensive perfume brand (or group of brands) should push the line to a market total. This will result in a very detailed "as is" demand curve from which management can apply judgment and market insights to estimate the maximum ("reserve") prices potentially obtainable from each part of the curve.

Lifecycles

We find that demand curves change as industries mature. When a market is young and growing, the demand curve tends to be convex: many segments pay a high price as customers embrace a new product. We suspect this comes from lack of comparison points for sellers, and because in young markets there are often relatively fewer sellers. Visually, the demand line is pretty flat until it falls abruptly, as you get to segments who have not yet understood the need for the product. An example is coffeehouses, where the entry of a Starbucks into a neighborhood actually raised the demand for coffee and benefited existing coffeehouses—that, in addition, could charge higher prices. Frequently, new products galvanize markets.

As industries mature, the demand curve becomes concave. Alternatives have eaten into the middle section of the curve. For instance, as the idea of premium-priced coffee and "cool" surroundings matured, Starbucks trimmed its number of locations; Starbucks and its alternatives found themselves in an increasingly less complementary relationship. For demand curves, a mnemonic is to think of people's faces: round when younger, gaunt when older.[13]

Knowing how your industry will evolve can be very useful. If you have, as we suggest, linked segments to different parts of the demand curve, you know which segments will likely show increasing price resistance—the middle of the curve. That will tell you which segment you need to begin to tier offers and launch new product architectures that can gracefully accommodate increasing price pressures. Given limited resources, better to be proactive in the right spot. For instance, in many markets we find it's the segments with the highest reserve prices early in the lifecycle that remain the most price-indifferent customers.

Product Portfolios

Finally, demand curves are useful for defensive strategy. Estée Lauder is a good example of a smart incumbent with highly strategic responses to actual and potential competition. Lauder regularly launches or purchases brands that combat newer, less expensive entrants. To reinforce this focus, Lauder splits management of high-end cosmetics and those aimed at discount (e.g., Target) shoppers. This has resulted in effective management of traditional Lauder brands, such as Youth Dew, and launches of new products, such as Flirt, aimed at younger buyers. Lauder has used an understanding of demand curves to build a formidable thicket of brands with nonoverlapping demographics and price points.[14]

When it comes to demand curves, the real mystery is why they are not more widely employed. Decision makers within both companies and government have been exposed to the power of this tool in school, yet fail to *ask* for robust answers on price and quantity. Perhaps managers should begin to consciously request a direct analysis of supply, demand, and price. Top managers and policy makers should be made aware if they are missing fundamental documentation of demand curves and not be distracted by secondary tools such as elasticities.

A Patent Program

Suppose your pricing dreams come true? You have developed a price structure or a tool that stymies competition, delights customers, and raises margins—what would you do then?

Despite ignorant advice that nothing can be defended via patent, and equally ignorant claims that everything can be defended via patent, there is a good record of patents helping to fend off or delay imitators in pricing. One of the most famous examples is Priceline.com, a popular website where a reverse auction begins with a buyer bid, for example, on a hotel room or an airplane flight. Priceline patented this approach, sued an early imitator, and won. This helped preserve its distinctive (and, implicitly, contextual) pricing approach.

The defense of price structures, and indeed all aspects of products, is likely to become much more patent-intensive. Evidence of this is that former Microsoft CTO Nathan Myhrvold raised $5 billion to amass several thousand patents and is now beginning the process of suing companies that infringe on them.[15] Many CEOs don't like this change in the business rules, but ignoring this trend can be dangerous. Acquiring patents and other intellectual property plays a defensive role, as well as an offensive one. For instance, a leading software firm was sued for infringing patents but obtained a no-cost settlement when it emerged that it had some patents that would form the basis for a counterclaim. Without those offsetting patents as a "tradeable," the results would have been much more expensive.

That's why you might need a patent program. In the same way that product teams today make sure that tax and other legal requirements are fulfilled, they should also have ready patent-identification and filing systems. The ease of use of such a system is key because within a short period after commercialization or being made public, a patent is not an option.

The patent program has two elements: One is a process element, which defines how patent opportunities are identified and selected, how managers are rewarded for good patents, how the application should be promptly written, the use of "patent pending," and how granted patents use should be pursued. The second element is more substantive: the patents are written initially for rapid approval, aggressively pursued, and even augmented through the purchase of licenses.[16]

What is contextual about pricing patents? Everything: by making your pricing patent specific to particular markets, segments, and situations, you are likely to arrive at a stronger patent and one which is more rapidly approved. The objective here is not to have patent applications gathering dust at the patent office (which many do) but to develop the portfolio of rights and then deploy them in your company's market. If they happen to have further uses you can always make some money by licensing them, as IBM now does, earning almost $1 billion per year from its intellectual properties.

Summary

Sometimes a small investment is better than none. Often a small investment can make a big difference. For instance, the White Star Line economized by not equipping the lookouts on the *Titanic* with binoculars. Who knows if doing so would have avoided the collision with an iceberg; at least in retrospect it seems they overlooked a worthwhile modest investment.

In the same way, rather than make product management rely on simple intuition in complex markets to set prices, a tool can pay its way. Your sales channels today may guess at the risk of customer defection or make up puffy hyperbole as to economic benefits (instead of providing cold hard facts), but some relatively inexpensive tools may produce much better revenue results. For market managers, a demand-curve roadmap of the market may offer important strategic insights.

Often, the obstacle to these basic investments in infrastructure is not a few hundred thousand dollars; rather, it's the fact that a pricing process which was long the province of intuition and experience is resistant to change.

Notes

1. Important to pricing, but not the focus of this book, is the role of incentives in instilling discipline. It can work wonders in getting sales to accept a new tool. See the excellent article by

Marc Hodac: "Pay for Performance: Besting Best Practices," ChiefExecutive.net, 2011.

2. There are many pricing engines on the Web oriented toward buyers; these compare prices, but few help product and sales management determine the best *selling* price. One Web site that helps sellers establish a price is www.pricewitch.com, which is free and fun to play with. The site can take your inputs and provide a suggested price target or a "second opinion" on internally developed prices. It also offers comments on price structure.

3. Mobill Las Vegas taxi field test video, at www.Mobill.com. It has a video of people discussing oil and engine wear, if that topic interests you.

4. Interestingly, these same insurance companies and health care insurers are relatively price-tool poor in the B2B marketing and sales efforts. While they have admirable statistics on when a group's policies will experience decaying economics because of adverse selection, they have not built tools that say at which point, and under what context, the company purchasing the policy is at risk to defect to another carrier because of price.

5. Senior director, www.carsdirect.com.

6. As adapted by O. Scott Rogers and Pat Clark, authorities on oil and gas law at Vinson & Elkins. Statistical wisdom is by Nassim Nicholas Taleb, *The Black Swan*, Ibid., pp. 88–92 and 138–139.

7. More on the structure implication of consequence and frequency can be found in *Winning the Profit Game*, Ibid., pp, 129–134. See also B. Shapiro, "What the Hell Is Market Oriented?" in J. Sviokla and B. Shapiro, *Keeping Customers*, Harvard Business Review Books, Cambridge, Mass., 1993.

8. For instance, one company which commissioned construction of a scorecard also had reps rate the "risk of loss" of different accounts. Midlevel sales management was not pleased with the study and was outraged when the draft model suggested that pharmaceutical client Novartis was in acute danger. Right before the meeting in which sales was going to protest, saying that the model was flawed, Novartis cancelled.

9. See A. Faruqui, et al., *Pricing in Competitive Electricity Markets*, Kluwer Academic Publishers, Boston, 2000.

10. Examples include Dell and Motorola. See "Winning the Profit Game. Smarter Pricing, Smarter Branding," Rob Docters et. al. McGraw-Hill, 2004, Chapter 5.
11. Sources: ABI Research and NPD Group, December 2007 "Black Friday" Report.
12. Unfortunately, some segmentations do not distinguish among different price sensitivities, as they are geared to channel differences or product categories that can blend different price sensitivities. However, most segmentations do reflect price differences as this is primary requirement of segmentation. See R. Frank, W. Massey and Y. Wind, *Economic Principles of Market Segmentation*, Prentice-Hall, 1972.
13. See "At Starbucks, Too Many, Too Quick," *The Wall Street Journal*, November 15, 2007, p. B1. Only five years earlier, the story was quite different. See "Despite the Jitters, Most Coffee Houses Survive Starbucks," *The Wall Street Journal*, September 29, 2002, p. 1.
14. "Estée Lauder's Dynasty: the Sweet Smell of Succession," D. Roth, danielroth.net, September 19, 2005. See also *Winning the Profit Game*, Ibid., pp. 218–219.
15. "New Salvo in Tech Patent Wars," *The Wall Street Journal*, December 9, 2010, p. B1. Another benefit of making patenting a program is that it makes taking out a patent cheaper and faster.
16. Taken from a March 16, 2011, address by Mark Nowotarski, president of Markets, Patent and Alliances, LLC, and patent agent.

Chapter 15

Key Contextual Data Is *Not* in Your Company's Databases

Oil is finite, but information is infinite.

—ERIC SCHMIDT, FORMER CEO OF GOOGLE

Life is infinitely stranger than anything the mind could invent.

—SIR ARTHUR CONAN DOYLE

A typical road to failure comes from a strategy that says, "Let's build a really big data warehouse, then build our pricing capability and strategy from that base." This plan simply does not work.

Why? Because no matter how large the database is, it will rarely capture the essential data required for pricing. The reasons for this are twofold:

- The data in the data warehouse is captured for other purposes.
- The likelihood that this data will also happen to support pricing strategy or pricing maintenance is quite *low*.

The former point doesn't mean that information cannot serve multiple purposes. Rather, it reveals that if it is not gathered for pricing, the applicability will be coincidental.

Consider the purposes of different databases that are the typical building blocks of a data warehouse:

- The bulk of data available in corporate systems is captured for accounting purposes, leading to corporate profitability reporting and dividends. Yet customers do not care about your profitability.
- Some data is captured for administrative and human resources, which again is of little interest to buyers and potential buyers.
- Customer support purposes seems like the right idea, but much of this data is centered on customers *after* the purchase and does not focus much on "Why did customers pay this price?"
- Data may include market price information, but until recently pricing has been the poor relative at the marketing family reunion. Most of marketing is focused on product, promotion, and channel—not pricing.
- Lately, some data has been gathered in systems for sales operations and sometimes for customer prospecting. Often this can be good, but rarely is it complete or compelling insight into customer-decision processes—that is generally left to the individual sales representative.

Companies cannot depend on coincidental overlap between pricing needs and other demands to ensure managers have necessary pricing inputs.

Pricing depends on understanding the customer and the customer's decision process and decision context. That information, unlike, for example, cost information, is not usually systematically gathered (although it should be known to managers). One reason is that internal priorities like accounting take precedence over pricing requirements. Also, managers often do not develop specific requirements for essential pricing data because specificity is challenging, without prior investigation.

The Impact of Competition

Contextual pricing factors were discussed in Chapter 3, and you may have noticed that much of this data was not in your company's database. As a reminder, however: one of the most important contexts is competition. What data does your company have systematically about its competitors? Can it be arranged or parsed by specific market? By product overlap? By channel? In most cases the answer is no. Even very large, smart, and well-resourced companies have limited competitive data.

> Contextual pricing, unlike cost information (for example), is based on data of which management is aware, but it is usually not systematically gathered. Managers need to develop concrete requirements for essential pricing data rather than random "grabs" of data in hopes that it will suffice.

The impact of competition on pricing is quite pervasive. Having robust information on context means you have available extensive and systematic information on competitors. For instance, frequently even the *number of competitors* that operate in each geography is not tracked. That is unfortunate because often the number of competitors can be a good approximation of "supply" to a market, and hence one half of the supply-and-demand equation.

Sadly, most companies tend to not keep systematic records of competitor price initiatives, price levels, product coverage, or geographic or competitive segmentation. In fact, one large consumer goods company specifically prohibits its competitive intelligence unit to keep on file anything that is not public—which of course is a small subset of the total information available.

The key point here is that the mere fact that your company "has a lot of data" is rarely adequate for pricing purposes. The amount of data in the world is literally infinite. That means that on a coincidental level, no matter what you have in your data warehouse, the chances of you having what is needed is virtually zero. To put it graphically, many managers believe the image below represents their likelihood of having the pricing data they need. This assumption is *wrong*. If drawn to scale, each of the circles would be invisibly small, and the chance of the data in each coincidentally overlapping with required pricing is literally zero. Thus, do *not* visualize your data as represented in Figure 15-1.

WRONG

Universe of market data

Figure 15-1 Mistaken conception of information: Venn diagram of how many managers view information as finite, and how they wrongly think building a big database will address contextual data needs. Planning is necessary.

A company database can have many terabytes of data but still not inform any of the key market-price drivers. Big divided by infinity is zero.

A Balanced View of the Information Needed

Of course, there is more than mere coincidence driving availability of data. Yet while management is no doubt working to see that the best information is captured, specifying the right pricing information is sometimes fiendishly difficult, and that difficulty is often dismissed when resources are being allocated. Market forces are often obscured without careful study. The trouble is that pricing information is different from that organically supplied by a company's operations.

What adds to the imperative for gathering of the right categories of data is that the same data can be viewed in different ways. For instance, college test results can be viewed in absolute terms (A, B, C, etc.) or they can be viewed as comparisons (top 5 percent, top 25 percent, etc.). Very different analysis results from these different views of the same data: one is subject to "grade inflation"; the other is immune. In the same way, pricing is often based not only on product effectiveness but also on the relative effectiveness of the product compared with some baseline, such as competitors or a previous generation of product.

Knowing what are the likely contextual comparison points helps. This reinforces the need for a focused gathering of price data. Hypothesizing the likely contextual needs is necessary because *information can be examined in many ways, possibly an infinite number of ways*.[1] Let's take a look at another nonpricing example: recent presidential election results are susceptible to different analysis, depending on whether they are viewed at a voter, state, ethnic group, or national level.

At a state level, linkages between results and demographics (e.g., education, income) are clear, but at another level those relationships may not be clear or not show reasonable confidence levels. For instance, a recent Republican candidate may have systematically captured the votes of wealthy age groups (ages 40 to 50), yet systematically lost the vote in wealthy states (Connecticut, California, etc.). So is wealth a good determinant of voter trends? That depends on your intended use.

Collecting contextual data is subject to the twin requirements that it cannot rely on coincidental collection and that it cannot be specified *too narrowly*. This is because necessary information cannot easily be anticipated a priori. As Sir Arthur Conan Doyle commented, "Life is stranger than anything the mind could invent." In a similar vein, advertising creative guru Patrick Thiede once commented, "If the photo exists, it cannot be a great idea."[2] Similarly, architect Dan Jansenson said that there must always be a site visit, and you must be open to what you see at the building site. No building can ever be designed from topological maps.

Thus the recommendation in gathering data to support contextual price is one of balance. If you accept any old source of data, you are likely to find you have no usable data. If you specify too narrowly, you may find you have missed the right way of looking at the market. In line with Jansenson's architectural requirement of a site visit, learn something about the likely pricing dynamics of the market *before* building a data warehouse. Being open to the dynamics of their market led accounts payable processor Tymetrics to discover its pricing did not just depend on payable through-put rates but also on the size of its network of electronic payees and how rapidly that network evolved. Again, this moves the information required for pricing from the internal and familiar, to the external and less familiar.

Build In a Systematic Look at Competition

Directly addressing the need for the right market data is not standard practice in building pricing data warehouses, but it can be. GE Patient Care recently integrated its competitive information sourcing with its pricing function sourcing. This was in recognition that competitive information was a key foundation for pricing. Internal information, however plentiful, would not suffice. Many companies would agree that competitors have an impact on their pricing, but few companies undertake the work of integrating this known factor into their pricing.[3]

Yet the rewards of finding what the right data are and then making sure that this data is part of the data warehouse are great. Many companies have employed talented statistical analysts to use the vast trove of internal company data to discover what drives customer defections and what drives price levels. The results have been modest. Typically such efforts yield relationships that explain about 25 to 35 percent of the results. In statistical terms, the R^2 is typically from 0.25 to 0.35. In other words, not very complete.[4]

When the inquiry begins with a query of management and customers, asking what matters to price and loyalty, the resulting list of candidate drivers is generally quite complete. When such a list is tested against market demand proxies and specially gathered data, the results generally explain 80 percent or more of the results. This level of explanation ($R^2 = 0.82$, in one case) leaves little to guesswork and simplifies price management. Further, when deployed in the field, the sales force rapidly gains confidence in the results.

In financial terms we have found this added degree of precision (explaining 80 percent of the price results, rather than 35 percent of the price outcomes) is worth an increase of 7 to 12 percent in revenues. For instance, typically there is a lot of unnecessary discounting, and understanding discount drivers might well cut the level of discounting in half—a major boost. This kind of gain will often justify the nontrivial investment in research programs and systems efforts to gather and deploy the needed pricing data. It also compounds the return from CRM and pricing engines.

Here's a test, in case you can't help but believe that the information needed for strong contextual pricing must be lurking somewhere in a company database. Suppose all your company's managers and sales reps were replaced with new managers and sales reps tomorrow. Would they get what they needed from the existing databases? Probably not. They would have a starting point, but they would sorely miss the insights of today's marketing and sales team. Without those insights, you suspect the company's performance would sag. This tells you that adequate contextual information is not in your company's databases.

Summary

Cold internal statistics will rarely suggest the contexts. Context requires more outwardly focused data: an understanding of how the customer will judge and compare your price offer. Thus, extensive interviews are required—both of one's own customers and those of competitors. We find that focus groups often help in this process. No more information should be required to initially develop contextual pricing scenarios than to create a good segmentation, but also no less.

Routinizing the process means asking sales to capture new data in their sales-information system or asking market research to ask the right questions. To fully capture the benefit of an evolutionary segmentation approach, sales management should dynamically adjust its account strategies to capture the value of favorable sales contexts and opportunities. One digital device manufacturer adopted an approach of scouting for signals of an impending contextual change at potential customers, such as changes in operating and pricing authority. If the manufacturer found such signs of impending migration, it dramatically increased account resources—aimed at likely *future* decision makers.

Successful institutionalization of contextual pricing will generate a unique store of knowledge of customer trends that won't be easily duplicated by competitors. In contrast to SIC codes, for example, contextual understanding can be redefined and refined over time. In a few years, the company will have a unique, proprietary insight into the history, transformation, and future of the market while competitors will have to constantly start anew with yet another snapshot to be discarded just as the market changes again.

Notes

1. John Matson, "Strange but True: Infinities Come in Different Sizes," *Scientific American*, July 19, 2007, p. 21 ff. The article notes that even finite sets of natural numbers, such as those between zero and one, have infinite decimal natural numbers packed in between.
2. From a speech when accepting the "Euro-best" award for creative advertising, in 1990.
3. Galileo Galilei, in his struggle to find acceptance for his astronomical findings, found a flat refusal by his contemporaries to even consider the facts. In a letter he wrote, "In spite of my oft-repeated efforts and invitations, they have refused, with the obstinacy of a glutted addict, to look at the planets or the moon through my glass [telescope]."
4. To be clear: the factors that constitute the 25 to 35 percent explanation are not in doubt—often confidence levels top more than 80 percent. However, this is like getting a cooking recipe and finding that it lists only 35 percent of the ingredients. While there may be no doubt as to the ingredients actually listed, this leaves a lot to guesswork.

Chapter 16

An Enabling Systems Architecture

It would appear that we have reached the limits of
what it is possible to achieve with computer technology,
although one should be careful with such statements,
as they tend to sound pretty silly in five years.

—JOHN VON NEUMANN

Throughout the past 10 years, strategic pricing has been a top priority for many companies. During this time, companies have made significant investments in their enabling processes and systems architecture to ensure that the bottom-line benefits of their pricing strategy are truly sustainable and have become deeply embedded in business operations.

High-performance companies have adopted sophisticated pricing solutions not only as a means to achieve significant and quantifiable bottom-line benefits but also as a source of competitive advantage. By eliminating Excel spreadsheets, ad hoc business intelligence reports, and e-mail as the primary ways to communicate pricing guidelines and approve pricing, such companies have increased total operating income from 1 percent to 3+ percent. Furthermore, the capabilities provided by pricing solutions allow companies to adapt quickly to changing market conditions and competitive threats. Without institutionalizing pricing strategy by implementing the appropriate supporting technology, companies will find the half-life of pure pricing strategy efforts to be shorter than they need to be.

Capturing, interpreting, and applying contextual information within your company's sales and pricing process and technology is the next evolution in high-performance pricing capabilities. In order to achieve this level of sophistication, there are two key systems architecture considerations above all others that must be incorporated:

1. **Collecting context.** By integration of the sales and pricing processes and applications.
2. **Applying context.** By flexibly adjusting the pricing strategies and algorithms to set and negotiate prices.

The holistic integration of sales and pricing provides a mechanism to leverage the sales force in collecting contextual information and ensures that it is considered when setting and negotiating price. Given that context is diverse, however, a system with flexibility in applying contextual information is important to address the diversity and keep up with a changing market and competitive environment.

Requirements of Pricing Solutions

Although the landscape of pricing solutions is broad and varied, virtually all of them typically include three core capabilities:

1. **Pricing analytics.** The ability to mine and explore transactional data to understand areas of opportunity for pricing and profitability improvements.
2. **Price setting.** The application of pricing strategies and algorithms to determine and optimize list and customer prices.
3. **Price administration and execution.** The management of pricing as it relates communicating target prices and allowable discounts so that sales resources can create quotes or contracts, and the transfer of pricing into order execution systems.

If combined with a solid strategy, governance, and data infrastructure, these solutions create a "closed-loop pricing" capability that sustains the value that pricing strategy can deliver. Closed-loop pricing is the incorporation of insights gathered from transaction pricing execution to refine and adjust pricing strategy on an ongoing basis, thus enabling an enterprise to adjust to changing market conditions to maximize returns.

Implementing an industrial-strength system, such as PROS or Vendavo, is a great way to ensure these key pricing capabilities are available to your business in support of your pricing initiative. While the resources to purchase, integrate, and operationalize these systems are not trivial, the returns can be material. We find that for a larger company, the costs amount to perhaps 0.01 to 0.05 percent of sales, while the returns from the price analytics alone have yielded millions within even 30 days. That said, the best technology for your company will vary with your industry, business objectives and pricing challenges.

Dimensions of the Pricing Decision

Companies generally use leading-practice pricing solutions to help evaluate and manage three main dimensions that are used to determine the right pricing decisions: customer, product, and market. Attributes such as the customer's size or importance to the company determine price or guidelines for discounting and other adjustments to the price.

Today's leading solutions have been instrumental in helping companies enact more effective pricing strategies, considering these three dimensions of pricing—and in the process, the strategies have had a substantial impact on the profitability of companies that use them. However, the benefits generated by such solutions will be fleeting—and the technologies themselves will become obsolete—if a business fails to accommodate the crucial fourth dimension of pricing: context, which defines the buying situation and provides a full picture of the micromarket for the sale. Applying context is the final puzzle piece that enables a company to tailor its value proposition in a way that will increase the likelihood of a purchase by customers.

Incorporating Context into Pricing Decisions through Technology

Incorporating context into pricing decisions through technology involves five major enhancements to pricing processes and their supporting systems. Each addresses the need for more relevant information, better decisions, management control, and operational alignment.

1. Altering the pricing waterfall
2. Enabling price setting with context
3. Refining deal constructs through the holistic integration of sales and pricing
4. Facilitating context-specific pricing approvals
5. Aligning contextual pricing with business operations

1. Altering the Pricing Waterfall

Fundamental to any pricing system is the pricing waterfall, a representation of all the revenue and cost elements contributing to the achieved net and pocket price and profitability of a particular transaction. The pricing waterfall drives not only the design of analytics in a pricing solution but also the algorithm to determine how a specific deal should be priced and how the net and pocket contribution will be modeled. This component affects all three of the core capability areas within a pricing solution. Most companies' pricing waterfalls today cannot account for the critical dimension of context, however; thus, two key enhancements to the pricing waterfall are required.

The First Enhancement. This involves the moving from list price to context-specific opening price. The classic pricing waterfall—the cornerstone of price analytics and price management—starts with list price as the highest benchmark for pricing and profitability and from that point forward "trickles down" to pocket price and pocket margin. As stated earlier, however, list price is irrelevant without context. Therefore, a company's waterfall should reflect the influence of context in setting an opening price. This is, in essence, a buildup to the price from which deal-specific negotiations begin.

As an example, in the banking industry, the base interest rate for a loan is entirely dependent upon larger, market-based indices. Contextual refinements to this interest rate are then applied based on inherent risk in the type of loan (e.g., mortgage, car, cash advance), the customer's risk assessment (e.g., credit score), and perhaps the business relationship. The net result is the context-specific interest rate.

The Second Enhancement. The second enhancement concerns the factors that determine the context of a specific deal. Because no company can anticipate all the possible drivers of context when designing and implementing a pricing solution, it should look to incorporate some "catchall buckets" in the pricing waterfall that will allow for the capturing of additional drivers as they are known. Through pricing analytics, the company should monitor new drivers added to the catchall buckets to determine if any is emerging and should be tracked independently. For example, an avionics-equipment manufacturer included standard discounting waterfall buckets such as volume discount but also added a placeholder for "other discount," for which the sales force was required to specify the reason for the discount. Over time, a trend emerged correlating heavier competitive match discount following major industry trade shows or exhibits where competitors offered temporary price promotions. This catchall bucket helped identify the need to consider proximity to trade show season as additional context in setting price and driving sales.

> Creating "catchall buckets" helps companies
> capture important contextual data.

2. Enabling Price Setting with Context

One difference between context and older value approaches lies in the scope of what information is gathered and applied in the pricing process. When setting prices, a systems architecture and design should allow for the incorporation of context to inform that price. Key to this ability are both descriptive and predictive analytics that generate a solid understanding of which factors have influenced and will influence a customer's buying behavior. With this insight, a company can design pricing solutions with the flexibility to apply various pricing strategies and algorithms based on context that, in turn, will set the appropriate price for maximizing value while maintaining or improving win probability.

A pricing system's architecture should include analytical capabilities to determine customers' price sensitivity and willingness to pay *not* at the average level, but at the detailed level of the contextual conditions of the buying situation. This can be done by implementing pricing power and pricing risk designations to a combination of factors used in the price setting algorithms within the pricing solution. Furthermore, by coupling the analytics and transactional history in a pricing solution with the optimization capabilities to detect factors that are driving a difference in pricing and/or profitability, pricing professionals have the inputs necessary to model response to price changes. For example, at one pet products company, statistical analysis was performed to determine which pricing levers had the most impact on yielding a successful markdown result.

Although it is valuable to analyze history to understand contextual drivers that have yielded different price sensitivities and willingness to pay, more valuable still is the ability to forecast changes in context, in one month's or one year's time, and construct robust what-if models of how this could affect business results. Implementing predictive analytics as a part of a pricing system's architecture can help companies further increase profitability. Predictive analytics are enabled by sophisticated statistical, forecasting, and modeling capabilities, and can be implemented as the next layer above descriptive pricing analytics or in combination with other functional data (from such areas as the supply chain and R&D) to set context-specific prices.

At one international aerospace and high-tech manufacturer, predictive analytics are being used to model potential variability in key factors such as raw materials prices, consumer demand fluctuations, and manufacturing-defect rates. These analyses are incorporated into future bids and programs in the form of additional risk-mitigation items or justifiable cost contingencies.

Oftentimes, different contexts defining the micromarket of a transaction require different pricing strategies to be applied—for the same product or service. In the oil and gas industry, for example, pricing can be associated with several market indices, such as Platts Global Petrochemical Index or Oil Price Information Service (OPIS). The difference between these two is that the former is associated with the refinery and tends to favor a cost-plus approach, while the latter is based on prices at the terminals and therefore is more market/value-based. For one global oil and gas company, depending on the level of risk that is expected in the market and/or the level of favorable (or unfavorable) pricing volatility projected, the application of one index versus another for pricing of longer-term contracts will drive very different bottom-line results.

Seagate, a manufacturer of data storage solutions, typically takes a premium approach to pricing. However, during the highly competitive "back to school" season, the company applied competitor-based pricing to capture market share.

We emphasize that while the concept of varying prices according to context is intuitive—everyone knows a street vendor's umbrella costs more when it is raining—the challenge to a large enterprise is to execute this concept accurately, at scale, across thousands of deals involving billions of dollars. As the above two examples illustrate, having flexibility within a pricing system to set prices via different strategies, depending on the context expected for that transaction can be a potent competitive weapon.

Not only should the pricing strategy applied vary based on context, but the actual pricing logic implemented in the pricing solution also must be extended to consider all key drivers of context. The way in which pricing systems derive and set prices can be compared, in the simplest form, to a formula in Excel. For a simple cost-plus pricing strategy, the algorithm to set price can be thought of as follows:

$$Where\ Customer\ segment = A$$

$$Product\ family = B$$

$$Market = M$$

$$Price\ f(x) = Cost + Markup$$

When considering context in the way in which it prices, a company must consider context not only in defining the micromarket or micro-segment for pricing but also in the variables for the pricing algorithm as follows:

$$Where\ Customer\ segment = A$$

$$Product\ family = B$$

$$Market = M$$

$$Product\ lifecycle = L$$

$$Season = S$$

$$Competitive\ environment = E$$

$$Need/Want = W \ldots etc.$$

$$Price\ f(x) = Cost + Base\ markup + Adjustment\ for\ L +$$
$$Adjustment\ for\ S + Adjustment\ for\ E +$$
$$Adjust\ for\ W \ldots etc.$$

In the meatpacking industry, there are a number of factors that are considered to optimize prices and profitability such as size, marbling, certification, commodities market indices, current supply, yield from an animal, seasonal concerns, amount of processing, and other customer requests. To support this type of capability in a pricing system's architecture, a company must have a foundational layer of data that provides the inputs for each contextual element in the formula. As discussed in the previous chapter, much of this key contextual data may not yet be in a company's databases or systems and therefore will have to be captured to be used in price-setting logic.

A company must have a foundational layer
of data that provides the inputs for each
contextual element in the formula.

The combination of descriptive and predictive analytics, price-setting capabilities and a solid understanding of context-driving pricing, and profitability differentiation can yield powerful business results—as one global alcoholic beverage manufacturer has proved. A holistic systems architecture provided "what-if" style, bottom-up sales-and-pricing planning and executive roll-ups of modeled business results. The enabling systems architecture increased profitability as a result of optimized prices and accurate forecasts, and it yielded higher operational efficiency and lower overall cost to produce.

3. Refining Deal Constructs through the Holistic Integration of Sales and Pricing

The price-setting function within a pricing solution is just the starting point for integrating context into the pricing process. A company also must gather additional context and interpret and apply that context to a specific deal to extract the optimal value and provide a winning value proposition to a customer. This is particularly important in business models that include quoting or contracting processes with negotiations leading up to the actual sale execution. At a high level, the sales and pricing process is represented in Figure 16-1.

The process begins with customer relationship and opportunity management. Leads are generated and qualified, and pricing iterations are executed to model the deal. Much of the contextual information about customers, their value drivers, their buying preferences, and the competitive situation are gathered on the front lines by the sales force. Oftentimes, this context exists only as institutional knowledge and is not captured in a company's system or database. Therefore, a company should see that it has a robust customer-relationship and sales-management process embedded into its systems architecture via CRM tools to ensure that context is captured and can be passed to other business processes and applications. More specifically, structured data about customers captured in account management modules can be integrated with sales leads and opportunity tracking. This can be further integrated into

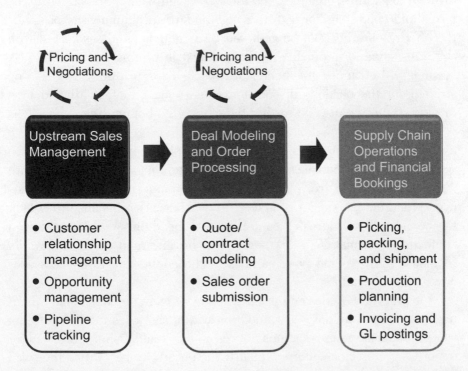

Figure 16-1 Holistic sales and pricing process.

the pricing engine to deliver all the customer and buying situation context to systematically determine the right pricing structure. For example, a global services company incorporates information about customer operations, up-front investments needed to mobilize a project, and availability of resources with given skill sets to inform how it will structure the pricing of a job for an individual customer.

During the upstream opportunity-management process, the terms and conditions of the deal are negotiated; this is additional context that must be considered in order to have a complete picture of the pricing structure. Capturing this data for a company's system can be challenging because such data is generally a mix of tangible and intangible items: payment terms, freight terms, fulfillment commitments, delivery times, issue resolution, design services, engineering support, length and depth of customer/vendor relationship, warranty, cost escalators, and pass-through expenses. Additionally, much of this data is unstructured—stored in documents instead of database fields—which further makes it difficult to capture, organize, and analyze. The first step in collecting the terms and conditions for a deal is to standardize, as much as possible, the offerings so they can be gathered in a database and associated with the transaction(s) to provide the full context in pricing and analytics. A secondary, but important, benefit is that it helps to inform the service strategy for the portfolio or segment of customers that, if aligned with pricing strategy, can yield further benefits to the bottom line.

Incorporating contextual information into a company's pricing architecture also provides very valuable tools in pricing negotiations: information and increased confidence. Oftentimes, when faced with "You are too expensive" or "The competition can do it for less" tactics from procurement, sales teams tend to concede price because they lack the confidence to address these allegations head-on. With the captured contextual information, sales teams can be informed as to achievable (demonstrated) pricing power and have the confidence to address procurement's allegations.

Integrating the sales and pricing applications in the systems architecture also helps facilitate user adoption within the sales force. Upstream sales-management applications for customer relationship and lead or opportunity management are typically the portal through which the sales force enters and views data. By making this portal a one-stop shop for relationship management, opportunity tracking, and pricing—and enabling mobile technology to deliver this in a convenient way—a company can significantly increase the likelihood of capturing higher amounts of quality contextual data. Finally, automated data sharing across the applications reduces time spent by the sales force and ensures consistency in the contextual data used to drive pricing and operations decisions.

4. Facilitating Context-Specific Pricing Approvals

Pricing decisions and actions are typically initiated long before the final sale is booked or the order is processed and filled. In a negotiated B2B transaction, the initial quote is crucial, but there will often be multiple subsequent refinements of pricing. The key question is: at what point in the sales process does an organization have the full context to make a decision on price? The answer: at almost any point, but with variable degrees of confidence.

> The sales process usually has adequate contextual information for better pricing, but confidence in that information may be uneven.

With each step in the process, more context is gathered that will further inform the right pricing approach and price level required to meet the buying situation—driving up the confidence level that the price is right. The pricing systems architecture must be designed and implemented with tight integration between the pricing solution or engine and the upstream sales-management application to ensure that context is collected and delivered, and can be applied at the time of pricing determination and negotiation.

With context being captured with deals upstream in the sales process, a company can monitor and correct bad pricing and negotiation practices before it's too late. This third type of pricing analytics should be incorporated into a company's overall enabling systems architecture to ensure that pricing guidance and policies are being implemented throughout the sales progression. Because the opportunities or deals are in progress, audit and corrections can ensure a company doesn't get locked into a deal or contract with unfavorable pricing structures. In recent years, for example, a printing company bid to secure the contract for a state board of education. Enticed by the idea of becoming the sole source provider for printing services, it submitted a heavily discounted list of prices, secure in the belief that volume would make up the difference. The printer won the contract, but its pricing did not incorporate the extra delivery costs associated with the fact that the schools to which it would ship its materials to had no loading docks and often required walk-up delivery. Had there been a more comprehensive opportunity management process to identify this critical issue, the printer would not have made such a costly mistake.

5. Aligning Contextual Pricing with Business Operations

One critical but often overlooked process and systems link is the one between the deal construct shaped by the sales and pricing organizations and the operations and execution capabilities of the finance, supply chain, and R&D functions. Simply put, while there is little value in a pricing architecture that does not support a company's ability to set and execute context-specific pricing, there is no value—and much harm—in investing in a pricing architecture so complex that it cannot be effectively used by the organization.

As mentioned previously, there are tangible and intangible components of a deal's pricing construct, and when these are included, a company must be sure that it can deliver on those commitments. Additionally, in order to have visibility into the full life cycle of a deal from an analytics perspective, the systems architecture must be designed and implemented to ensure all relevant data is captured. Finally, contextual information is valuable in the R&D process as new products and services are being developed.

A well-designed pricing architecture will feed crucial information on market response and willingness to pay back upstream to enable constant improvements to the features—or costs—of the products and services being sold. In all these cases, integration of downstream processes and systems is critical to ensuring that information on the context-specific *outcomes* of pricing strategy is transferred from the sales and pricing system into the ERP system and can be extracted for continuous improvement of pricing and profitability.

Ensuring that the pricing procedure in the ERP system is aligned with the pricing waterfall (and therefore with the quote/contract modeling algorithm and pricing-analytics data structure) guarantees consistent execution of a company's pricing strategy. It follows, therefore, that if the pricing waterfall is altered to include contextual items, the order processing and fulfillment ERP functions also must reflect these contextual pricing elements. By following this leading practice approach, one global glass manufacturer saved hundreds of man-hours in designing and implementing its integrated, enabling systems architecture between pricing and ERP execution.

Furthermore, supply-chain operations and the execution of these processes in the ERP system must also be aligned—you must be able to deliver on the service levels incorporated into your pricing structure. For instance, if a company charges a premium for a product because it commits to filling every order within a certain timeframe, the company must be able to prioritize that customer and ensure that expedited delivery services can be invoked for that customer or order. One global industrial equipment manufacturer aligned its operations to deliver replacement parts in 24 hours or less and priced accordingly for that service. It understood its customers' value driver for uptime/production efficiency and incorporated that context into not only the way it priced but also the way it executed. The inverse is also true: an industry-leading technology equipment provider was able to link its pricing tools directly to its supply-chain tools so that the pricing team could have near-real-time information on current and impending inventory levels. This allows them to dynamically change prices and up-sell or down-sell recommendations to the front-line sales reps and ensure optimal supply-demand balancing.

End-to-End Systems Architecture for Contextual Pricing

The capstone to an enabling contextual pricing systems architecture is the holistic integration of sales and pricing processes and technology—from upstream opportunity and negotiation management to pricing and further order execution and financial accounting. Figure 16-2 illustrates such an integrated architecture:

If we step through the architecture from a data-flow perspective, we begin with a sales management application (e.g., CRM or SalesForce. com) that provides the backbone to compile and integrate the institutional knowledge and other contextual details that will inform the price-setting function. Should your company not have a robust sales management

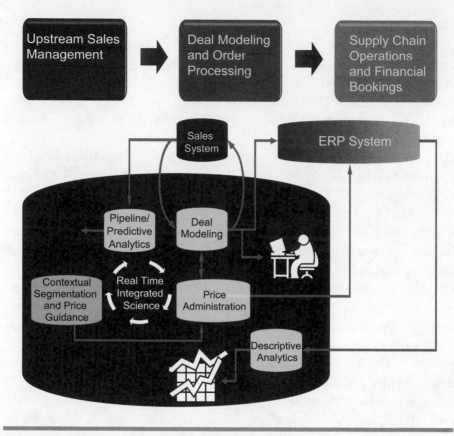

Figure 16-2 End-to-end systems architecture

system, incorporating some of this functionality into the pricing system itself could be a first step. This is the key interface point with the sales force, so mobile update capabilities are important in this architecture to ensure ease of use and adoption by this key user group. Additionally, reporting on this pipeline of information is crucial to proactively drive the best deal and pricing constructs. Finally, implementing an approval process and workflow that optimizes efficiency in negotiations and cycle time to respond to customers within this system ensures that the right deal context is available to make an informed, profitable business decision.

The pricing application should be tightly integrated to this sales-management application. From an architectural perspective, real-time or high-frequency batched interfaces should be used to synchronize data between the applications. As key customer, product, market, and contextual information are captured, it should be passed to the pricing application so as to avoid additional effort for data entry and maintenance. This lessens the burden on the sales force, thereby improving the likelihood of adoption. Furthermore, by having bidirectional integration and synchronization, data quality and consistency across these applications are ensured and build credibility in the data across the board. In one large implementation integrating sales and pricing applications, for example, the architecture was designed and supported approximately 50,000 messages for data integration daily and 30,000 messages for security integration based on yearly 60,000 deal transaction volumes.

Within the pricing application, there are three main considerations that drive contextual pricing in the enabling systems architecture. First, the waterfall design should drive the deal modeling logic by incorporating the contextual information. Second, the design should allow flexibility to apply different pricing strategies based on the context or buying situation. Each pricing strategy implemented should also consider contextual elements in the algorithm to set context-specific opening prices versus list prices. And finally, time-phase pricing in the deal modeling should allow a better representation of the financial implications of the transaction, especially with business models that are highly asset-intense or use rebate or incentive programs over the life of the arrangement.

The pricing application should be integrated with the ERP systems in order to maintain process efficiency and data consistency. Not only should the price setting engine interface with ERP to send approved prices to be applied to sales orders, but it should also be integrated to pass approved contracts and quotes with the full deal structure. By doing this, orders can be created with reference to "umbrella" agreements and a full life cycle analysis of the deal is possible—better allowing for value realization from plan to actuality.

> The key to enabling a system's architecture for contextual pricing is the holistic integration of sales and pricing processes and technology—from upstream opportunity and negotiation management to pricing and further order execution and financial accounting.

Finally, a robust analytics engine completes the closed-loop pricing cycle by providing insight, both descriptive (historic) and predictive. By associating the contextual elements to the transaction, the business is better able to analyze factors contributing to higher realized price. Advanced analytics and statistical interpretations based on this data can be used to generate predictive forecasts of how different context will translate into the price or volume responses.

Summary

The holistic integration of sales and pricing provides a mechanism to leverage the sales force in collecting contextual information and ensuring that it is considered when setting and negotiating price. Doing so entails:

1. **Collecting context.** By integration of the sales and pricing processes and applications.
2. **Applying context.** By flexibly adjusting the pricing strategies and algorithms to set and negotiate prices.

Given that context is very diverse, a system with flexibility in applying contextual information is important in keeping up with multiple changing markets and competitive environments.

Chapter 17

Creative Pricing

Avoid bold strokes in foreign policy. Focus on steady progress.

—PRESIDENT DWIGHT D. EISENHOWER,
FAREWELL ADDRESS (1961)

This book began with a perspective of how competition made context the most important element of pricing. Subsequent chapters showed how different competitors had gained advantages through smarter and creative contextual pricing.

How can you leverage the insights contained in this book for your business, beginning today? Given the diverse pricing lessons described throughout, the question may arise: how to convert essential knowledge into enduring understanding?

The answer is practice. Practice understanding how customers think. Practice trying out new structures and strategies. Practice implementing new pricing ideas. Practice is how athletes build up their skills; they try out new techniques and refine them until they become proficient. This is also how musicians develop their songs.

Building upon the musical analogy: listening to different takes of familiar Beatles' songs, one is struck at how much the works evolved. For instance, George Harrison started with a version of "Greensleeves" (hardly radical, that song having been composed around 1580) and ended up with the masterpiece "While My Guitar Gently Weeps" in about 15 takes. Similarly, "A Day in the Life" builds from two separate developing songs in different keys to a unified magnum opus mastered by George Martin.

In the same way that marketing tries new advertising campaigns and sales tries new sales strategies, pricing must actively experiment with and test new pricing approaches. This is more than testing new price levels. It should also extend to new bundles, price structures, and strategies.

Pricing has, somewhat unfairly, gained the reputation for being an arcane and academic discipline. Not so. If you can understand how your customers think, you can identify the elements of context that will most shape price. The more practice and feedback you have in this, the easier pricing strategy will become. Practice makes perfect. Intelligent preparation makes practice less painful. In this regard, pricing is just like physical exercise, social interactions, communication, or any other aspect of life.

Another analogy to general pricing is Wall Street and its pricing, where context is king. Rarely can any one player in financial markets set the price of a stock or bond for long periods of time. At best, participants in financial markets set an initial price, or shape the price for a particular transaction. Most transaction prices are shaped by supply and demand, which in turn are driven by events and fundamental changes in context, such as the economy.

How does one succeed in such an environment? An impartial observer of Wall Street notes: "The world is a messy, complex, and contingent place . . . which our brains are not equipped to evaluate. We deceive ourselves into thinking that experts can foresee the next 'big thing.' High scorers [on Wall Street] were 'thinkers who know many small things (tricks of the trade) . . . and see [outcomes] as flexible 'ad hocery' that requires stitching together diverse sources of information."[1]

Our recommendation regarding pricing strategy and practice echoes that statement. Learn the "tricks of the trade" as well as the rules, focus on steady progress, be creative and flexible, ad hoc, and you will be a superior pricer. We note that the industries with frequent price changes (both level and structure) are more adept at pricing. Airlines deal with price changes, multiplicity of price points, bundles, and add-ons that would leave most other industries dumbstruck.

Incidentally, earlier you may have noticed that we did not, violating convention, provide you with a definition of pricing. Instead we place that definition here, as a means for integrating the entire book's perspective on pricing.

A Definition of Pricing

Pricing is best defined as an "outcome." Pricing is the outcome of four contextual factors:

- Situation
- Objectives
- Perception
- Capabilities

Before we provide the longer definition of pricing, note that situation, objectives, perception, and capabilities are not shaped exclusively by your company's actions. Rather, pricers must accept that there are many influences that they do not control, just as on Wall Street. One major result is that unless you have a lot of market power, you won't be able to fight buyer preferences in price structure. A Broadway show title put it nicely: *Your Arms Too Short to Box With God*.

Fighting is bad, influence is good. As a roadmap in considering what to influence, here is some detail regarding the four components of price:

Situation

This is the factual basis containing the comparison points buyers use to determine whether they want to buy, and at what price they want to buy. The situation includes the nature of your product, the number of and effectiveness of competition, and customer economics. While your company can change some elements of context, you cannot control all of them.

Objectives

Objectives are *what* and *how* buyers want to purchase. A key point emphasized in this book is that objectives change over time as potential buyers learn more about their needs and options. As context changes, so do objectives. Purchase and price objectives are typically linked to broader corporate objectives—rarely do purchase criteria stand alone.

Buyers are often quite diverse in their objectives, hence the need for segmentation and contextual pricing. The diversity of objectives is manifested only if buyers actually have the opportunity to express their differences. If all vendors offer the same product under the same price structure, then there is little room for differing objectives to develop or be realized in market transactions. The result will be a homogenous focus on price level. If your company sells into a market where all vendors offer the same price structure, take advantage of that situation and offer the buyers the missing price structure they want.

Perception

Perception comprises the filters that distill essential understanding within the dark recesses of the buyers' minds. It is likely that your buyers' perceptions are influenced by cumulative experience in similar purchases. For this reason, perception is probably rooted in many things you cannot influence easily (e.g., a focus on convenience versus quality of product, on likely span of ownership, etc.) Some influence is possible, given branding programs, but as we observed earlier in this book, it is actually difficult to change long-standing perceptions—and in any case it is really the customers who "own the brand," not the seller.[2]

Capabilities

Capabilities are management's ability to shape effective pricing: to do the thinking required and to execute the required strategy. Budget constraints have an impact on capabilities, and this is why creativity is important. Mechanistic blocking and tackling requires resources and can be countered by mechanistic blocking and tackling by opponents of equal resources. Only with creativity can you have greater competitive power with fewer resources.

The Importance of Creativity

With creativity, your company can have an impact beyond reasonable expectations. It will require leveraging all the "tricks of the trade." Below are some instances of how creative pricing overcame the usual obstacles impeding pricing:

IT Limitations

The need for IT work to support new pricing initiatives can result in long delays in implementing the pricing your company needs (e.g., moving billing from fixed-price sales to pay-by-use). Here's an example of a solution:

At a large developer of billing system software located in Phoenix, Arizona, every significant change to its billing system product was vetted and costed in detail by the six functional departments that were affected. This took over a month and consumed several hundred person-hours. Often the process had to be iterated in whole or in part because some obstacle would be identified by one function, the fix for which required reappraisal by the other departments. The solution was to have the six best and most knowledgeable senior staff do a high-level assessment of the project and its costs. This approach was quick (one or two meetings) and worked out most of the issues—often in a more creative way than solutions from detailed analysts. Lesson: avoid the armies of programmers until you have solved the potential obstacles.

Sales Force Issues

The sales force can be quite conservative in accepting changes. This is why trial should be part of the repertoire: trial results are evidence that sales forces tend to accept. To obtain the best trial results, find champions for the new pricing. Note that some members of your sales team may be best able to identify relevant context. Often we find that some sales reps enjoy selling products *above* list price. Those reps have mastered contextual pricing. Lesson: if convincing the sales force (or others) is vital, develop the kind of evidence they will accept.

Legal Issues

The degree to which corporate legal staff intervenes in pricing seems to vary by company. Sometimes a company is very conservative for good reasons; for example, a Department of Justice consent decree can burden a company more than others. However, often it is a function of how business-oriented the legal staff is in its ability to balance perceived legal risk versus opportunity. If you can, lead the legal counsel to be more aggressive in their search for permissible ways to affect pricing.

As described earlier in the book, intellectual property rights are becoming more important in pricing and in business in general. In that regard, it's important to get specialized patent and trademark counsel involved as soon as possible. Counsel who is not expert in this area will be cognizant of his or her lack of expertise and may delay the patent or trademark process while trying to come up to speed. Lesson: try to set an aggressive application date for patents or trade secrets, so as to reduce the time a general counsel can delay the process before going to specialized counsel.

Marketing Issues

While marketing can be the home base for pricing, often these departments are more oriented toward product development and branding. Pricing is viewed as an orphan or even an alien intruder. Two litmus tests that signal hostility to serious pricing efforts are:

- Overreliance on surveys as the basis for pricing
- Unwillingness to supplement limited pricing data with judgment, and when data *is* available, it is attacked as inadequate (this shows a lack of maturity in dealing with pricing data)

Lesson: the solution to these issues is to build a set of pricing tools and to insist that they be used. This forces the use of data and, once used, resistors find that the results are not so bad.[3]

Will these solutions apply to your business? Possibly. However, the knowledge that there *are* creative solutions to roadblocks will certainly help you overcome such limitations.[4]

Closing this book with a final musical analogy, recall how the Beatles got new sounds from old instruments. The final tones on "A Day in the Life" come from hitting the piano frame (a cast iron pan) with a hammer, an alarm clock is featured in "Strawberry Fields," and four tracks (four-track recorders were then standard equipment) were mercilessly overdubbed to create the dizzying array of effects for their albums.

Pricing can benefit from creative new uses of existing pricing instruments. For instance, while the "coupon" is standard practice in consumer marketing, it has only recently been employed in B2B marketing. Yet many B2B companies are finding the coupon is an ideal tool for many B2B applications. The coupon may not require any systems work (if in the form of a mail-in rebate), it can be targeted in a very precise fashion (a specific person or title within a specific company), it is often invisible to competitors, and we have found it useful in bypassing some gatekeepers.

Just as a consumer pricing tool (a coupon) can serve a useful purpose in a new setting, we regularly see new applications for proven pricing strategies. With insights into context, timing, and customer-decision processes, pricing innovation can be low risk and high return.

Notes

1. "Financial Flimflam," Michael Shermer, *Scientific American*, March 2011, p. 77.
2. Also see Chapter 3 of *Winning the Profit Game. Smarter Pricing and Smarter Branding*, Ibid.
3. There is a Dutch expression, loosely translated: "What foods the farmer does not know, he does not want to taste." This applies to many managers, and one objective is to give them a taste of effective pricing tools.
4. Edward Teller, the coinventor of the H-bomb, was once asked what was the biggest obstacle to developing the first nuclear weapon. His response was, "The biggest obstacle was not knowing that it was possible." Stanford University, 1978.

Index

About the Authors

Rob Docters is managing partner of Abbey Road, LLP, a consultancy specializing in pricing strategy. He has helped over three hundred clients in software, communications, consumer goods, information services, financial services, transportation, and entertainment to increase revenues and defend or capture new markets.

Before Abbey Road, Rob was a senior vice president of Strategy, Business Development, and Pricing at LexisNexis, a leading information services firm. At LexisNexis he was part of the management team credited by *The Wall Street Journal* with a "turn-around" of LexisNexis.

Prior to LexisNexis, Rob was a senior vice president at Ernst & Young, helping lead the Toronto strategy and marketing practice. Before that, he was a principal at Booz, Allen & Hamilton, Inc., in New York. He has assisted clients in North America, Europe, and Australia.

Rob was the lead author of *Winning the Profit Game: Smarter Pricing and Smarter Branding*, published by McGraw-Hill. He has taught at Columbia University School of Business, the GE Welch Center for Management Training, the Royal Institute of Management, and other schools.

Rob holds degrees from Stanford (A.B. Economics), The College of William and Mary (J.D.), and Columbia University (M.B.A.). He is a member of the New York Bar.

He holds several patents on new price structures, and is a frequent contributor to the *Journal of Business Strategy* and other publications. Readers are invited to send comments and questions to rdocters@abbeyllp.com.

John Hanson is a partner at Accenture, where he leads the North American Pricing and Profit Optimization strategy practice. He previously served as an executive at a leading pricing software solutions provider and was a partner at Oliver Wyman.

John has been involved in pricing strategy, primarily in the communications and high technology industries, for 15 years. He is a frequent writer and speaker on pricing issues.

John holds an A.B. from Harvard College and an M.B.A. from Georgetown University, McDonough School of Business.

Cecilia Nguyen is a senior manager with Accenture's Pricing and Profit Optimization strategy practice. During her career, she has focused on pricing strategy and solutions in industries ranging from industrial manufacturing to professional services.

Cecilia has been involved in numerous pricing solution implementations which have successfully delivered leading-practice business processes and analytics. Furthermore, she has been a featured speaker at several pricing technology vendor conferences and works closely with leading vendors in the space through directing Accenture's alliances.

Cecilia holds a B.A. in Chemistry from the University of Delaware.

Michael Barzelay currently holds the London School of Economics' (LSE's) first professorial chair in public management. He codirects the Department of Management's new MSc. Public Management and Governance program.

Michael is known for his work in organizational decision making, particularly large organizations such as governmental agencies, large companies, and other institutions. This work includes bidding procedures and the study of how large institutions develop buying criteria and priorities, which includes decisions on price level and structure.

Michael serves as the founding executive director of the Center for Transformation and Strategic Initiatives, a Washington, D.C.–based nonprofit organization. In addition, he coedits *Governance: An International Journal of Policy, Institutions, and Administration*, published by Blackwell.

His publications include *Preparing for the Future: Strategic Planning in the U.S. Air Force* (Brookings, 2003), which received the Brownlow Book Award.

Before joining LSE in 1995, Michael was associate professor of public policy at Harvard's John F. Kennedy School of Government.

Michael holds degrees from Stanford University (A.B.), the Yale School of Organization and Management (M.P.P.M.), and Yale University (Ph.D. in Political Science).